OTHER VOLUMES IN THE CONCORD LIBRARY
Series Editor: John Elder

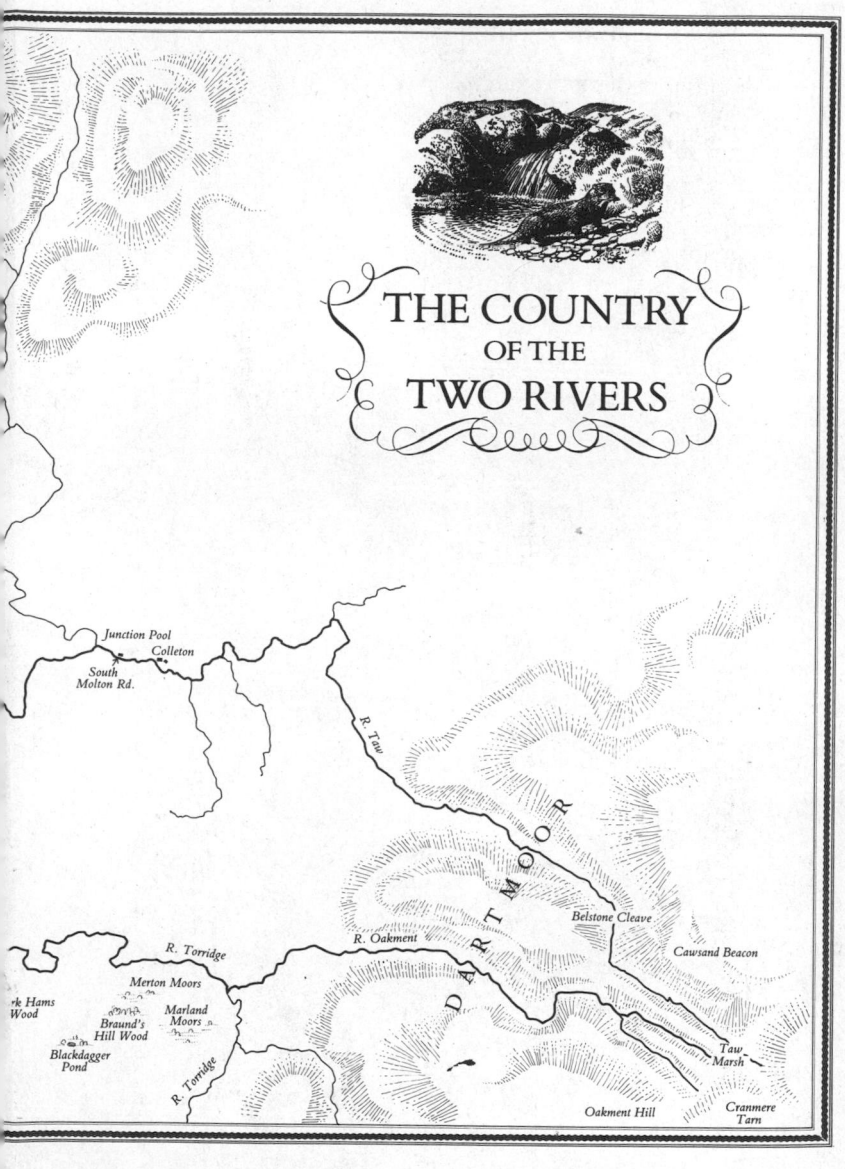

THE COUNTRY
OF THE
TWO RIVERS

Junction Pool
Colleton
South
Molton Rd.

R. Taw

D A R T M O O R

Belstone Cleave

Cawsand Beacon

R. Torridge

R. Oakment

Merton Moors

rk Hams
Wood

Braund's
Hill Wood

Marland
Moors

Blackdagger
Pond

R. Torridge

Taw
Marsh

Oakment Hill

Cranmere
Tarn

by

HENRY WILLIAMSON

TARKA THE OTTER

Tarka the Otter

His Joyful Water-Life and Death in the Country of the Two Rivers

HENRY WILLIAMSON

WITH AN INTRODUCTION BY ROBERT FINCH

ILLUSTRATED BY C. F. TUNNICLIFFE

BEACON PRESS · BOSTON

To
WILLIAM HENRY ROGERS

Beacon Press
25 Beacon Street
Boston, Massachusetts 02108

Beacon Press books
are published under the auspices of
the Unitarian Universalist Association of Congregations.

First published in 1927
Introduction © 1990 by Beacon Press
First Beacon Paperback edition published in 1990
All rights reserved
Printed in the United States of America

99 98 97 96 95   2 3 4 5 6 7 8

Map courtesy of Webb & Bower (Publishers) Ltd.,
from *The Illustrated Tarka the Otter*, first
published in 1985.

Library of Congress Cataloging-in-Publication Data
Williamson, Henry, 1985-1977.
Tarka the otter: his joyful water-life and death in the country
of the two rivers / by Henry Williamson : with an introduction by
Robert Finch : illustrations by C. F. Tunnicliffe.
p. cm.
Reprint. Originally published: London : Dutton. 1927.
Summary: Tarka the otter pursues an active life, sometimes playful
and sometimes dangerous, in the Devonshire countryside.
1. Otters–Fiction. [1. Otters–Fiction.] I. Tunnicliffe, C.F.
(Charles Frederick), 1901-1979, ill. II. Title.
PR6045.I55T37   1990
823'.912-dc20   90-55169
[Fic]   AC
ISBN 0-8070-8507-3

INTRODUCTION

The Strange, Familiar World of Tarka

IF FOR NOTHING ELSE (AND THERE IS MUCH, MUCH else), *Tarka the Otter* would be distinguished by being, as far as I know, the only book in the English language to begin with the word *dimmity*. *Dimmity?* It stops us—at least American readers—in our tracks before we even start. *Dimmity?* Is it a name? Or perhaps a nonsense nursery rhyme word, like Pooh's "Rum-tum-tiddle-um-tum"? American dictionaries don't recognize it. I had to go to my compact *Oxford English Dictionary* to find even a close variant. *Dimmit*, in the dialect of southwestern England, means dusk or twilight—a meaning which a less impatient reader will find made clear from context by the end of the first paragraph. And so, having deciphered the first word of this "children's nature classic," we're off.

The word, as it turns out, is no stylistic anomaly. Far from it. On almost every page one encounters words like *leat, holt, gins, vair, fitch, cockchafers, ammil, oolypuggers, tilth, ackymal, crackey, ruddock, potwalloper, scriddick, vuz-peg, uvver, spurring, quatting, glidders, linhays, scrikkits, turves, clitter, goyal,* and *belving*—words which are foreign to American, and, I suspect, most British readers not from the West Country of England (and many of which have no doubt passed from active use even in Devon, the county of the book's setting, since its first publication in 1927). They form, among other things, almost a lexicon of Devonshire country dialect.

The characteristic use of Devon words is only one, and a fairly obvious, method that Williamson uses to create such a strong sense of place. Another are the different place names that appear on the headings of each page. They are almost never mentioned in the narrative itself, but they suggest what is, in fact, the truth: that every action is rooted in and drawn from an actual location in the wild moor and fen country of Devon. Even today, according to Eleanor Graham, "the whole movement of the story can be followed minutely, up and down the Two Rivers, round the coast of the Severn Sea from Lynton to the Estuary." Even if they are not literally real, they suggest a land—to use one of Williamson's favorite phrases—"of true imagination," like the Forest of Arden or Yoknapatawpha County.

Every marvel of this many-marveled book resides in the rootedness of its language, from its dialect vocabulary to its stunning imagery to its unsurpassed precision of description. The prose is unabashedly lush (Williamson once admitted that "what the critics say about [*Tarka's*] being too tightly packed is right"), but it is never simply for effect. Always the aim is not stylistic brilliance but sensory or poetic accuracy:

Water covered the pond ice, deep enough to sail a feather.

[Tarka] had seen the hair of faintest light where the ream
of a backfin had cut the surface and glimmered with the
moon-frosted slide.

When a badger kills a vuz-peg, or hedgehog, it "bit
through the spines as though they were marram-
grasses"—a simile any nature writer could be proud
of. But it is the unexpected extension of the image
in the following sentence that has the touch of
genius: "Iggiwick squealed, like marram grass in
flame." One despairs, in fact, of explaining the wonder of the book's language short of quoting it in full.

Such superb imagery is always in service of the
book's primary intent: to create a fully imagined,
particular world of nature. Williamson's metaphors,
for example, are not human-nature or nature-hu-
man, but almost exclusively nature-nature:

the young moon was like a luminous grub spinning a
cocoon around itself in the sky.

Even the passing of time is described not in human-
made hours, but in terms of biological processes:

Tarka awakened, saw the egg, dived, brought it to the
couch, and ate it before the shadow of a grass-stalk had
moved its own width on the bank.

When artificial objects are described, natural
similes are often used to bring the human world
down to size. The wheels and rods of a power station
"gleamed behind glass windows like the wings of
dragonflies." A wrecked destroyer on the coast "lay

broken and sea-scattered . . . in bits like beetle fragments in a gorse-spider's grey web-tunnel."

Williamson knows this otter-country in his bones,
and he is determined to make us feel it as well.
Nothing is carelessly or perfunctorily drawn. In
fact, what finally impresses even more than the
poetic imagery is his incredible passion for texture
and detail, a passion as universal and as indiscrimi-
nate as nature's own. Like Tarka, who will stop to
take a trout while being pursued by hounds, Williamson cannot seem to resist the interesting detail.
He will, for instance, deliberately interrupt a heart-
stopping chase scene with a brilliantly precise
image:

> His heart beat as fast as water-drops drip without dribbling.

In the middle of the mortal hunt in chapter 18, he
goes so far as to insert an entire paragraph describ-
ing fern growth in an ancient water wheel, in which
he pauses to give us not only the fern species' names,
but their *sex* as well!

This passion for concrete identity, for finished
creation, not only reflects nature's abundance of
vitality. It also suggests a sense of natural contingency—or what a modern ecologist might term
"the connectedness of everything." In addition to
being remarkably textured, objects in Williamson's
landscapes are also connected to everything else, in
time as well as space.

This temporal contingency appears in the very
beginning of the narrative—in the extended natural

history of the fallen oak that forms the holt, or den, *Intro-*
where Tarka is born; but there is an implied natural *duction*
history, or ecological sequence, in nearly every line.
Sometimes it is an ecological set piece, as in the
capsule history of a dead trout:

> The sickly trout . . . had been a cannibal trout and had
> eaten more than fifty times its own weight of smaller
> trout. . . . A rat ate the body the next day, and Old Nog
> speared and swallowed the rat three nights later.

More often it is a casual sense of continuity that
infuses nearly every scene:

> [Tarka] ran up into the sandhills, where his passing sowed
> round orange-red seeds from the split dry pods of the
> stinking iris.

Nor is human activity excluded from this net of
contingency, as on the marsh of Horsey Island,

> where grew Russian thistles, sprung from a single seed
> blown from the estuary off a Baltic timber ship years
> before. . . .

If *Tarka* conveys an "ecological message," it is
through such subtle, pervasive details that seep
into our sensibilities in the manner of the soft ferns
on Canal Bridge in the narrative that fill up the
cracks created by the stress of too many automobiles.
This ingrained sense of ecological and evolutionary
drama was something relatively new in popular nature writing of the time, something which would
not appear full-blown in this country for another

xiii

two decades, with the appearance of Aldo Leopold's
A Sand County Almanac in 1948.

One of the fresh pleasures of this book for an American audience is the rediscovery of the very different sense of landscape conveyed by most English nature writing. American literary landscapes tend to be either pristine wilderness or bucolic countryside, or else such settings threatened and despoiled by the twin devils of technology and capitalism. Tarka's world, on the other hand, is no cordoned-off wildlife preserve, but a working landscape with both people and animals going about their businesses of breaking up shipwrecks for wood, digging out holts, trapping otters, stalking poultry, etc. In doing so they lead separate lives that nonetheless often intersect, both deliberately and accidentally.

Though there are magical qualities and mythic elements in Williamson's evocation of the Devonshire landscape, it is not a romanticized landscape, and it is indelibly modern. In Tarka's travels he encounters spillways and concrete dams of electric power stations, pursues trout poisoned by tar road runoff, and plays with discarded cocoa tins.

Still, the wildlife of this area of coastal Britain seems, in many respects, wilder than we might expect. This is no remote corner of the British Isles—not the Outer Hebrides or the Shetlands—but Devonshire, a county less than 200 miles from London and thickly settled for centuries, with several hundred people per square mile. Yet it is—or was—also

a place that contains otters, salmon, seals, conger *Intro-*
eels, skuas, puffins, badgers, and an occasional *duction*
Greenland falcon.

There is something else characteristically English
about Tarka's world that is harder to put a finger
on. One can only call it a heaviness, a penchant for
dark, dense landscape descriptions that remind one
of the landscapes of Williamson's literary predeces-
sors—Richard Jefferies (one of Williamson's favorite writers), W. H. Hudson, and Edward Thomas.
There is undeniably a kind of enthusiastic, if not
joyful, melancholy in much English nature writing.
Perhaps it comes from a sense of living on land literally fashioned from the compost of previous lives
and cultures:

> the fragments of [vanished species'] bones lie on the rock
> of the original creation, under the lichens and grasses
> and mosses, or in the museums of towns.

Human culture itself seems as dense and as deep as
natural history in a place like England, where otters
have slid on remnants of Roman walls for a thousand generations.

English nature writing is also imbued with a deep
sense of mortality, which can seem morbid to American sensibilities which have always recoiled from
any sense of limits—death being the ultimate limit.
There are strains of this element in our own literature. One can find it, say, in Loren Eiseley, or Rob-
inson Jeffers. But it is a minority strain, a protest
against the blind and destructive optimism of Amer-

ican progress, whereas in the English it seems the
dominant note.

The English sense of landscape as being composted
of former lives accounts, in part, for the prevalence
of death-in-life and life-in-death images in *Tarka*. In
one scene an eel takes refuge in the skull of a bullock; in another, Tarka sleeps one night in a cromlech, "the burying place of an ancient man, whose
bones were grass and heather and dust in the sun."
This element again is something that tends to
strike American readers as a bit morbid—like the
gravedigger's scene in *Hamlet*—since we prefer, for
whatever cultural reasons, to keep the categories
of life and death as separate as possible. But in
Tarka, and in Williamson's other nature books, it is
a literally natural element, growing directly out of
his ecological perspective. After a grisly description
of the hanging corpses of trapped hawks and owls,
Williamson adds:

> The hues and sheens of plumage were gone, and their eyes'
> light; soon they would drop to the earth, and flowers dream
> out of their dust.

Such juxtapositions are often used to create effects
of dramatic irony and reversal reminiscent of Eliza-
bethan drama. A lobster ends up eating an otter cub
that had crawled into its trap to get at the crusta-
cean and drowned. A shag, or cormorant, which has
been pursuing a pollack underwater, is killed by
an eel, which is subsequently chased off by a seal:

The pollack escaped and soon afterwards was feeding with *Intro-* other fish on the crab-nibbled corpse of the shag. *duction*

The book is full of such reversals of roles, of predator becoming prey, and prey becoming predator. But the purpose of such images is not simply dramatic irony. In nature, roles are a tenuous and mutable thing. Such a viewpoint represents a concept of character which in its own way is more complex than that in most human dramas, for in this natural drama each plant and animal "plays many parts" in its time. In such a world, even a bone can become a love-token, as in this marvelous moment:

Tarka played with a shoulder-blade because White-tip had touched it in passing. He ran at it and bit the cold bone as though it were White-tip.

The most powerful of the book's death-in-life images occur in the magnificent winter chapters. Williamson rewrote this particular section dozens of times, and the language in it frequently assumes a formal, ritualistic tone:

Like a spirit freed by the sun's ruin and levelling all things before a new creation the wind drove grains of sand against the legs and ruffled feathers of the little birds, as though it would breathe annihilation upon them, strip their frail bones of skin and flesh, and grind them until they became again that which was before the earth's old travail.

The stark tableaus that solidify before our eyes in these chapters are unsurpassed, I think, in the literature of winter. The effects are more remarkable in that they are achieved largely by restraint—by indirect or implied action, and the use of selective details:

> [Old Nog] called to his mate, who was standing in the ebb to her knees, fifty yards beyond the tide. She did not move; nor did the tide.

The many death scenes in *Tarka* are notable for their empathetic matter-of-factness, as if to remind us not only that death is common and unexceptional in nature, but that a good death—one that is swift, clean, and vigorous—can also be part of a joyful life. In doing so they embody the central paradox of the book (and, I think, the key to its peculiar power), which is stated in its subtitle: *His joyful Water-Life* <u>and</u> *Death in the Country of the Two Rivers.* Not only does this deliberately remove any superficial suspense about the fate of its protagonist —we know that Tarka will die within the pages of the book, and we are meant to know—but it makes the intriguing suggestion, right at the start, that death, as well as life, can be a joyful thing.

But wherefore "joyful"? Violence, fear, and death are everywhere in *Tarka*. The book revels in their imagery, ironies, and paradoxes. Yet its ultimate effect is one of joy, though not for what usually constitutes joy in novels about human beings—attainment or recovery of love, redemption from evil, discovery of one's true identity, achievement of a quest or ambition, restoration of order and values. *Tarka's* joy does not reside in the outcome of its plot, but in the very texture of the existence it depicts, in the joyful intensity of life lived fully in the freedom and the fate of the wild:

> The noise of the great waters filled Tarka with joy.

> the sun took the water, breaking brilliant and hot in every plash; the otter galloped with instant joy and sank in bog to his belly.

> The rat had a jolly and murderous life, and died before it could fear.

This joy is not contingent upon such human requirements as security, physical comforts, and the satisfaction of animal appetites. Rather, the capacity for joy seems a very essence of these animals' being. During the long winter ice lock-up, when the walls of their stomachs press against one another and their tongues are blistered from licking ice in an attempt to obtain even some fresh water, the otters still spend time—and precious energy—sliding down snowy hills in play. Such inherent playfulness, in fact, has the power to transform their world. As Williamson describes the magically lovely Ammil, or morning frost,

> The brimming light gladdened Tarka, and he rolled for several minutes, playing with a shining ball found in the grass—the old dropping of a wild pony.

Such scenes suggest not unthinking or mere animal pleasure, but rather the ancient Greek ideal of the

full exercise of one's faculties, of life completing and
fulfilling itself, not in the success or failure of plans,
ambitions, and desires, but in every moment of existence, in the sense of one's life flowing as clean
and unfettered, as true to itself, as the line of an
otter's ream widening down a leat to the sea.

This is the paradox and challenge of the book—
that a life at once so harsh and unforgiving seems
also undeniably joyful. In this respect, *Tarka* offers
something more than substantial literary pleasure.
It may, in the unassuming telling of its tale, offer a
paradigm of how our lives might—perhaps must—
be changed if we are to survive the growing on-
slaught of self-created ecological crises. Though
Tarka's life may be, in our terms, an utterly amoral
one, it may also embody a relevant ethical code, a
pattern for living. In the strength of its story it conveys more convincingly than any environmental
tract the sense that a life in nature, in all its guises,
rooted in an acceptance of the terms of existence,
can be as rewarding as any of human devising. By
convincing us of Tarka's joy, it may prepare us to
change our sympathies, that is, our notion of what
constitutes joy, and "a joyful life." For these creatures, whose bodies are deeply scarred and worn by
an uninsulated natural existence, harbor neither
blame, nor self-pity, nor envy, nor corrosive resent-
ment, nor despair, but rather draw sustenance and
joy in being a part of something larger than themselves.

Much of the book's effectiveness depends, no doubt,
on the choice of otters as the protagonists. Though
much of their life seems unrelated to ours, we are
nonetheless irresistibly drawn to otters. There is
something in us that identifies with their inveterate
curiosity, playfulness, and optimism. Like otters we
recognize and react to the familiar, but we too seem
in essence water-wanderers, following our water-
wills, forever turning to new interests and new loves.

The book is written literally from the otter's perspective—usually from the surface of a stream, or
low to the ground. Even the metaphors seem drawn
from an otter's imagination: a cloud crosses the
moon "like the seal [footprint] of an otter"; Tarka
drifts past "a narrow island, shaped like an otter,
with a rudder [tail] of mud carved at its lower end
by the swift waters." To paraphrase Emerson, in
Tarka's world all the thoughts of an otter are otter.

Williamson conveys the sense of Tarka's life almost wholly through action, sense impressions, and
emotional reactions that seem wholly justifiable
from observation. He does not burden Tarka with
human thought, but he grants him a range of response to life equal in stature to our own—and in
some ways surpassing it, as in the otters' extraordinary response to smells.

More impressively, he often manages to make
purely physical experiences resonate with emotional
overtones in the reader. One superb example of this
occurs when Tarka is driven away from White-tip

by an older and more powerful dog-otter. Defeated in love, Tarka allows himself to be carried passively downstream under bridges, over falls, through harbors and out with the tide. And in this long "slide to salt water," he seems to enact the longing that any of us, suffering such keen anguish of loss, might feel for the solace of such a letting go into antiseptic waters.

There is no question of the author's deep admiration for these animals. Yet it is not a sentimental admiration; there is no false nobility in his creatures. Tarka's life in a state of nature is solitary, short, and brutish (though hardly poor and nasty), and he is as ready to kill as to be killed. Moreover, the otter's playfulness extends to mortal games, for, like his human pursuers, Tarka is also capable of killing for the fun of it.

If the otter's life is strongly familiar in many ways, and even seductive, it is also undeniably strange—and that, too, is an intentional part of its compelling power. Williamson creates a peculiar tension of sympathy in this book, one that continually catches us up short in our anthropomorphic expectations. These animals obviously feel affection and concern toward one another. They suffer not only physical pain, but feelings of loss and grief, and yet there is a disturbing ephemerality to these familiar emotions. Their joys and griefs are intense but short-lived. Tarka's mother fights fiercely, and at great personal risk, in a futile attempt to free her daughter, who is pathetically caught in a foot trap.

But she leaves her when a man and dog approach, *Intro-*
and though subsequently she whistles for her in *duction*
longing,

> at the end of the night, when they reached the big river,
> the lost cub was forgotten.

What we come to realize, with a certain uneasiness,
is that for all their attractiveness, there is a biological imperative underlying all of the otters' behavior;
one that, I think, is intended to keep us at a distance.
Moreover, we also come to realize, with some self-
embarrassment, that our anxiety and concern for
these creatures are not only futile but irrelevant.
These animals will never be safe, nor do they want
to be.

Nonetheless, the book persuades us—in ways
entirely different from the arguments of evolution,
though it is aware of these—that the difference between human beings and otters (and, by extension,
all of life) is not one of kind but of degree. Our
memories, enthusiasms and loyalties, for example,
are only relatively longer and more enduring than
those of Tarka and White-tip.

The otters' lives in this book are not reflective ones,
and yet they prompt us to reflection, to ask, What
is this world, at once so familiar and compelling,
and yet so alien? For Tarka and his companions are
not just ourselves charmingly displaced into fur and
webbed feet; they are not even animal figures imbued with identifiably human desires and feelings.
They are something else. There is, finally, some-

thing unbridgeably strange and alien about Tarka and his world. But it is not, as in science fiction and fantasy, the strangeness of the unknown or the unknowable; it is the strangeness of the *previously* known. It is a familiar alienness, something we connect with in spite of ourselves, an acknowledgment of sensibilities whose source we once shared, and which we can still recognize, but which have diverged and evolved along paths and into forms we cannot follow, except in sympathetic imagination. We feel their tug, like phantom limbs.

At the end of the first half of the book, the author himself makes a sudden, startling appearance in the first person. It is startling because it is totally unexpected; the narrator, to this point, has been an exceptionally unintrusive one. Williamson does not subsequently reappear in the narrative, but his image remains, mysterious and undefined. Who was this man, this Henry Williamson? Or rather, what do we know of him that has bearing upon the creation of this remarkable book?

Born on December 1, 1895, in Bedfordshire, on the outskirts of London, Williamson served as an infantryman and officer in France during World War I. His war experience was used directly in later novels like *The Wet Flanders Plain* and *The Patriot's Progress* (which, he said, were written "to deglamorize war"); nonetheless, it also seems to inform the hunt scenes in *Tarka*, with their sense of ubiquitous danger and unrelenting pursuit.

After the war Williamson became a journalist in *Intro-*
London, but he soon left on a motorcycle for the *duction*
West Country. In a village in North Devon he
rented a small ancient cottage built of clay and straw
(the model, we are told, for "Skirr Cottage" in the
book) and there began to write prolifically and to
explore intensely the surrounding countryside for
which his imagination seems to have been made.

Williamson was not only an intense but also a
remarkably perceptive observer of wildlife. He
claimed to have seen only two otters before coming
to Devon, one in a German field-gun emplacement
during the war. The prototype and inspiration for
Tarka is said to have been an orphaned cub otter,
which Williamson took home and raised. As it grew,
a bond developed between man and animal, and
they took many walks in the Devon countryside together. One day Williamson found the otter caught
in a rabbit gin, or trap. As with Tarka, three of its
toes had been severed. Williamson released it, but
the maimed otter escaped and he never saw it again.
Much of the topography in *Tarka* Williamson dis-
covered in long, fruitless searches for his otter up
and down the river courses of the Taw and the
Torridge.

Williamson worked on *Tarka* for nearly four
years, from 1923 to 1927, during which time he published several other nature and animal books. But
Tarka was a labor of love, and Williamson com-
pletely rewrote it seventeen times, each time "cutting out untruths and inaccuracies, facile descrip-

tions, inventions not of true imagination." In his fabricated drama he was determined not only to be geographically and ecologically accurate, but to be true to the known and knowable facts of animal behavior. When the book was published, many of the incidents of behavior were questioned, but today, over sixty years after its publication, *Tarka* is still generally regarded as a remarkably reliable chronicle of otter natural history.

In 1925, while still at work on *Tarka*, Henry Williamson married and soon was a father. His wife, Loetitia, became ill, and Williamson, always short of money, cared for house, mother, and baby son while pursuing the always-quixotic quest of making a living from writing. Near the end of the book, on the night before the last hunt, a weary Tarka sleeps in a holt by a weir-pool, where "he dreamed of a journey with Tarquol [his son] down to a strange sea, where they were never hungry, and never hunted." This passage, though dramatically effective, strikes the reader as somewhat unotterly, and uncharacteristically anthropomorphic. One is tempted to hear, between its lines, the author's own weariness, his yearning for release from the economic woes and domestic pressures that continually beset him during the completion of his masterpiece.

One of the strongest elements in *Tarka* is its vivid depictions of the hunt scenes. Williamson's son, Richard, has said that his father was both attracted to and repelled by the Hunt. Part of his ambivalence surely came from the fact that his wife was the daughter of one of the landed gentry who regularly *Intro-* rode to hounds. He seemed fascinated by the ritual *duction* and skill of the hunt, yet could refer to the hunters themselves as "barbarians."

In his curious discourse on hunting and the imagination that begins chapter 14, he gives the advocates of hunting their due, crediting them with the protection of many species that might otherwise be exterminated by farmers and other land-workers. He also admired and sought the deep country knowledge of the ways of animals possessed by many of the men who persecuted them. Yet without any editorializing, his description of the final hunt is one of the most damning indictments of "blood sport" ever written.

For Williamson, I think, there was a fundamental difference between the indisputable violence, unconscious cruelty, and lack of interspecies compassion that characterizes, on one hand, natural predation, and, on the other, sport hunting as depicted in *Tarka*. The difference cannot be the "sporting" element per se. Tarka, after all, kills for sport. Nor can we really say it is the unfair odds. What chance, after all, do trout in a locked pool have against a hungry otter? The difference, rather, seems to be one of time. All natural hunts are swift and dispassionate, whether they are successful or not. The cheetah seizes the gazelle or it does not. The frog stabs the fly with its tongue, or catches air. An otter rips out the belly of a salmon, or misses it by a whisker's breadth. But in *Tarka*, the otter

xxvii

hunts go on unconscionably (in one instance for over ten hours), driving both hounds and otters to the limits of exhaustion, and beyond the limits either would naturally endure in pursuit or escape. The violence which nature never commits, and which Williamson does not forgive, is the pushing of the participants in the hunt beyond their natures, their capacities, their abilities. Williamson once called war the human activity most removed from "the natural." In the same way, the relentless compulsiveness of the book's final hunt—the sacrificing of its participants to achieve what seems, in the end, a paltry and inconclusive victory—is in the deepest sense unnatural. A man who later wrote of men dying in muddy trenches at the orders of vain and ignorant generals expressed, in his notebooks of these years, his contempt for "fat, cigarette smokers in cars, lounging back, while the animal gasps for breath somewhere below the river."

Yet Williamson does not let this underlying sentiment thwart the drama of the hunt. From the stately, formal introduction of the hounds at the beginning of chapter 18 to Tarka's final going out to sea, the pursuit of the otter is presented in epic fashion. The dimension and narrative force of Williamson's depiction of the final hunt contain an obsessive majesty, reminiscent of the final chase scenes in *Moby Dick,* and the last few pages pulse with the necessity characteristic of high tragedy, where all the elements come together in a manner at once inevitable and unpredictable.

After submitting the finished manuscript of *Tarka*,
Williamson had to fight to retain some sections that
his publisher, who saw a market for the book as
school prizes, thought that schoolchildren would not
understand. The book, as it turned out, was recognized immediately as adult literature, winning the
Hawthornden Prize for imaginative literature in
1927, and the praise of such imposing literary figures as Thomas Hardy, Arnold Bennett, Walter De
la Mare, and Edward Garnett. Still. *Tarka*'s reputa-
tion, in this country at least, has survived mainly as
that of a "children's classic."

I find this strange, and misleading, for *Tarka* does
not seem, in many respects, a children's book at all.
Its harrowingly objective descriptions of death and
casual violence do not belong on the same shelf with
Beatrix Potter, Kenneth Grahame, A. A. Milne,
or even Rudyard Kipling. Its depictions of animal
sexuality are also not characteristic of most juvenile
literature. There is no false monogamy or faithful-
ness in these creatures; they are faithful only to their
own natures. In fact, in its accurate description and
implied acceptance of natural sexuality, it is still
quite modern.

What, finally, is it then? What does this singular
book pretend to be? Williamson called it a "novel."
It is surely that, not merely because its specific
events are fictional, but because the sequence and
structure of those events is rooted in an interior
logic of their own. Perhaps, though in a less con-
ventional sense, it also really is a children's book.

These animals' short-lived griefs and joys are not shallow, but childlike; they pass quickly, like a child's, because they are so keenly and freely expressed, rather than harbored and nursed. The narrative also contains a childlike confusion of emotions, where violence and play often go hand in hand, in juxtapositions that may strike adult sensibilities as unseemly, but which are innocent and acceptable in a world that has not yet sorted spontaneous emotions into proper and improper categories. In the world of a child or an animal, nothing that is natural is ugly or inappropriate. Instead of morality, *Tarka* offers its readers an extraordinary responsiveness to life, a world where death and even decomposition are handled with both remarkable directness and grace.

In the end, one is tempted to say that *Tarka* is a book sui generis. It seems one of those curious works that attain a level of imagination reached only once in an author's career, and which both invent and exhaust the possibilities of a particular mode of writing. In our own literature, *Moby Dick* and *Walden* are two such examples. Perhaps W. H. Hudson's *Green Mansions* is an English instance, though that novel lacks, for me at least, the sense of exploring new imaginative ground that characterizes *Tarka*.

With all such books there seems to be some element of serendipity, some fortuitous juxtaposition of subject matter with a ripeness of the author's abil-

ities. Though *Tarka* achieved great success for Williamson, and though he was to write over forty more
books before his death in 1977 (including the highly
popular *Salar the Salmon* in 1935), *Tarka* represents
a high-water mark in his career, the work in which
he seemed willingly to expend the best of himself
as a writer.

Whatever the book finally is, it is surely an excep-
tional act of the imagination, a world so thoroughly
invented and deeply devised that we come to believe
in it without reservation, not because we identify it
with ourselves and our knowledge of the world—any
more than we "identify" with the world of *Macbeth*
or *The Odyssey*—but because it identifies so com-
pletely with itself, and we are swept along.

But for all the author's careful attention to fact
and detail, *Tarka* ultimately convinces us on a level
other than factual accuracy, even—perhaps espe-
cially—when it enters areas unsusceptible to verifica-
tion, where, as Williamson puts it, "imagination
arises from the world of things."

One of the finest instances of this kind of "literary
truth" occurs in chapter 13 when, after a long sepa-
ration, Tarka and White-tip happen upon one another. It is hardly a romantic setting:

> In the meadow near the lime-washed mill was a dump of
> house rubbish, tipped there by dust-carts, and spread
> about. A sow and her growing litter were routing in a mess
> of rotten flesh and vegetable food.

Intro-
duction Here, amid garbage and pigs, the two otters en-
gage in a strange game, which consists of going back
and forth through a fence made of upended iron
bedsteads, coming near but not looking at one another, then suddenly going off to romp together in a
nearby pool. The game is repeated over and over:

> Each was pretending not to see the other; so happy were
> they to be together, that they were trying to recover the
> keen joy of meeting.

Such wonderful evocations of playful love disarm
us of any resistance, and make considerations of an-
thropomorphism as irrelevant as the "artificiality"
of Romeo and Juliet's love-sparring in rhymed
iambic pentameters. In the face of passages like this
—and the book is mortared with them—commen-
tary must stop and simply acknowledge the scope of
achievement.

ROBERT FINCH
BREWSTER, MASSACHUSETTS

ILLUSTRATIONS

Nearly all these were made from authentic scenes in the actual country described, and some details, such as the style of caps worn by huntsmen and whips, therefore vary from the original text.

THE FIRST YEAR

CHAPTER ONE

DIMMITY OVER MEADOW AND WATER, THE EVE-STAR shining above the hill, and Old Nog the heron crying *kra-a-ark!* as his slow dark wings carried him down to the estuary. A whiteness drifting above the sere reeds of the riverside, for the owl had flown from under the middle arch of the stone bridge that once had carried the canal across the river.

Below Canal Bridge, on the right bank, grew twelve great trees, with roots awash. Thirteen had stood there—eleven oaks and two ash trees—but the oak nearest the North Star had never thriven, since first a pale green hook had pushed out of a swelled black acorn left by floods on the bank more than three centuries before. In its second year a bullock's hoof had crushed the seedling, breaking its two ruddy leaves, and the sapling grew up crooked. The cleft of its fork held the rains of two hundred years, until frost made a wedge of ice that split the trunk; another century's weather wore it hollow, while every flood took more earth and stones from under it. And one rainy night, when salmon and peal from the sea were swimming against the brown rushing water, the tree had suddenly groaned. Every root carried the groans of the moving trunk, and the voles ran in fear from their tunnels. It rocked until dawn; and when the wind left the land it gave a loud cry, scaring the white owl from its roost, and fell into the river as the sun was rising.

Now the water had dropped back, and dry sticks

Weare lodged on the branches marked the top of the flood.
Giffard The river flowed slowly through the pool, a-glimmer
Water with the clear green western sky. At the tail of the
pool it quickened smoothly into paws of water, with
star-streaming claws. The water murmured against
the stones. Jets and rills ran fast and shallow to an
island, on which grew a leaning willow tree. Down
from here the river moved swift and polished. Alder
and sallow grew on its banks. Round a bend it hastened, musical over many stretches of shillet; at the
end of the bend it merged into a dull silence of deep
saltwater, and its bright spirit was lost. The banks
below were mud, channered by the sluices of guts
draining the marsh. Every twelve hours the sea
passed an arm under Halfpenny Bridge, a minute's
heron-flight below, and the spring tides felt the banks
as far as the bend. The water moved down again
immediately, for the tide's-head had no rest.

The tree lay black in the glimmering salmon pool.
Over the meadow a mist was moving, white and
silent as the fringe of down on the owl's feathers.
Since the fading of shadows it had been straying from
the wood beyond the mill-leat, bearing in its breath
the scents of the day, when bees had bended bluebell
and primrose. Now the bees slept, and mice were
running through the flowers. Over the old year's
leaves the vapour moved, silent and wan, the wraith
of waters once filling the ancient wide river-bed
—men say that the sea's tides covered all this land,
when the Roman galleys drifted up under the hills.

Earth trickled by the gap in the bank to the broken

4

roots below. Voles were at work, clearing their *Owlery* tunnels, scraping new shafts and galleries, biting the *Holt* rootlets which hindered them. An otter curled in the dry upper hollow of the fallen oak heard them, and uncurling, shook herself on four short legs. Through a woodpecker's hole above her she saw the star-cluster of the Hunting Dogs as faint points of light. She was hungry. Since noon the otter had lain there, sometimes twitching in sleep.

The white owl alighted on the upright branch of the tree, and the otter heard the scratch of its talons as they gripped the bark. She looked from the opening, and the brush of her whiskers on the wood was heard by the bird, whose ear-holes, hidden by feathers, were as large as those of a cat. The owl was hearkening, however, for the prick of the claws of mice on leaves, and when it heard these tiny noises, it stared until it saw movement, and with a skirling screech that made the mouse crouch in a fixity of terror sailed to the ground and clutched it in a foot. The otter gave but a glance to the bird; she was using all her senses to find enemies. She stood rigid. The hair on her back was raised. Her long tail was held straight. Only her nose moved as it worked at the scents brought by the mist from the wood. Mingled with the flower odours, which were unpleasant to her, was the taint that had given her a sudden shock; causing her heart to beat quickly, for power of running and fighting if cornered: the taint most dreaded by the otters who wandered and hunted and played in the country of the Two Rivers —the scent of Deadlock, the great pied hound with

The Owlery Holt, with Canal Bridge upstream.

the belving tongue, leader of the pack whose kills *The* were notched on many hunting poles. *Kelt*

The otter had been hunted that morning. Deadlock *Pool* had chopped at her pate, and his teeth had grooved a mark in her fur, as she ran over a stony shallow. The pack had been whipped off when the Master had seen that she was heavy with young, and she had swum away down the river, and hidden in the hollow of the water-lapped trunk.

The mist moved down with the river; her heart slowed; she forgot quickly. She put her head and shoulders under water, holding her breath, and steadying herself by pressing her tail, which was thick and strong and tapered from where her backbone ended, against the rough bark. She was listening and watching for fish. Not even the voles peeping from their holes again heard the otter as she slid into the water.

Her dark form came within the inverted cone of water-light wherein movement above was visible to a trout waving fins and tail behind a sunken bough. While the otter was swimming down to the rocky bed, she saw the glint of scales as the fish sped in zigzag course to its cave. The otter was six feet under the surface, and at this depth her eyes, set level with the short fur of the head, could detect any movement above her in the water lit by star-rays. She could see about four times her own length in front, but beyond all was obscure, for the surface reflected the dark bed of the river. Swimming above the weeds of the pool, she followed the way of the trout, searching every big boulder. She was way-wise in the salmon pool. In

The underwater pursuit her acute sense of smell was use-
Kelt less, for she could not breathe.

Pool She peered around the rocks, and in every cave in
the bank. She swam without haste, in a slow and easy
motion, with kicks of her thick webbed hindfeet, and
strokes of her tail which she used as a rudder to
swing herself up or down or sideways. She found the
fish under an ash-tree root, and as it tried to dart
away over her head, she threw herself sideways and
backwards and seized it in her teeth. By a bay in the
bank, broken and beaten by the hooves of cattle
going to drink, she ate her prey, holding it in her forepaws and cranching with her head on one side. She
ate to the tail, which was left on a wad of drying mud
cast from a hoof; and she was drinking a draught of
water when a whistling cry came from under Canal
Bridge. It had a thin, hard, musical quality, and
carried far down the river. She answered gladly, for it
was the call of the dog-otter with whom she had mated
nearly nine weeks before. He had followed her down
from the weir by the scent lying in her seals, or foot-
prints, left on many scours, and on the otter-path across
the meadowland of the river's bend. He swam in the
deep water, hidden except for his nose, which pushed
a ream on the surface placid in the windless night.

As she watched, the ream became a swirl. The
otter on land heard the instant hiss of breath in the
nostrils before they sank. Immediately she slipped into
the river with the least ripple tracing where she had
entered. The dog-otter had sniffed the scent of a fish.

Bubbles began to rise in the pool, making two

8

chains with silver-pointed links, which moved steadily *The*
upstream. Twenty yards above the swirl, which *Kelt*
lingered as the sway of constellations between black *Pool*
branches, a flat wide head fierce with whiskers looked
up and went under again, the top of a back following
in the down-going curve so smooth that the bubbles
rising after it were just rocked. Time of breathing-in
was less than half a second.

The bubbles, eking out of nostrils, ran over pate and
neck and shook off between the shoulders, to rise in
clusters the size of hawthorn peggles; the dog-otter
was swimming with his forelegs tucked against his
chest. Near the bridge the bubbles rose large as oak-
apples; he was kicking four webs together, having
sighted the fish. The bubbles ended in another swirl
by a weed-fringed sterling, and a delicate swift water-
arrow shot away between the two piers of the middle
arch—the peal, or sea-trout, had gone down, passing
three inches off the snapt jaws.

The river became silent again, save where it murmured by root and rock. Old Nog the heron alighted
by a drain behind the sea-wall of the marsh two
miles below Halfpenny Bridge, whither he had
straightly flown. The white owl had just caught by
an old straw rick its second mouse, which, like the
first, caught five minutes before, was swallowed whole.

Where water clawed the stones at the tail of the pool
the peal leapt to save itself from the bigger enemy
ever trudging and peering behind it. It fell on the
shillets, on its side, and flapped, once, then lay still,
moving only its gills. Then the dog-otter was standing

The by it, holding up his nose to sniff the air when a thin,
Island wavy, snarling cry rose out of the river. It was the
Run bitch's yinny-yikker, or threat. She ran upon the fish,
pulled it away from the dog, who was not hungry,
and started to eat it.

While she was chawing the bones and flesh of the
head the dog played with a stone, and only when she
had turned away from the broken fish did he approach
and lick her face in greeting. Her narrow lower jaw
dropped in a wide yawn which showed the long canine
teeth, curved backwards for holding fish, and kept
white by the strength of bites. The yawn marked
the end of a mood of anxiety. The dog had caught and
eaten a peal on his journey, and was ready for sport
and play, but the bitch did not follow him into the
river. She felt the stir of her young, snarled at the
dog in sudden fear, and turned away from the water.

She ran over the bullocks' drinking place and passed
through willows to the meadow, seeking old dry
grasses and mosses under the hawthorns growing by
the mill-leat, and gathering them in her mouth with
wool pulled from the over-arching blackberry brambles whose prickles had caught in the fleeces of sheep.
She returned to the river bank and swam with her
webbed hindfeet to the oak tree, climbed to the
barky lip of the holt, and crawled within. Two yards
inside she strewed her burden on the wood-dust, and
departed by water for the dry, sand-coloured reeds
of the old summer's growth which she bit off, frequently pausing to listen. After several journeys she
sought trout by cruising under water along the bank,

and loach which she found by stirring up the sand *Owlery* and stones of the shallow whereon they lurked. The *Holt* whistles of the dog were sometimes answered, but so anxious was she to finish making the couch in the hollow tree that she left off feeding while still hungry, and ran over the water-meadow to an inland pond for the floss of reed-maces which grew there. On the way she surprised a young rabbit, killing it with two bites behind the ear, and tearing the skin in her haste to feed. Later in the night a badger found the head and feet and skin as he lumbered after slugs and worms, and chewed them up.

The moon rose up two hours before the dawn, and the shaken light on the waters gladdened her, for she was young, and whistling to her mate, she swam to the high arched bridge up-river and hid among the sticks and branches posited by the flood on the bow of the stone cutwater. Here he found her, and as he scrambled up she slipped into the river and swam under the arch to the lower end of the cutwater, meeting him nose-to-nose in a maze of bubbles, and swimming back under the arch. They played for half an hour, turning on their backs with sideway sweeps of rudders, and never touching, although their noses at each swirling encounter were but a few inches apart. It was an old game they played, and it gave them delight and made them hungry, so they went hunting for frogs and eels in a ditch which drained the water-meadow.

Here they disturbed Old Nog, who was overlooking one of his many fishing places along the valley.

Yew "Krark!" He flapped away before them, his long, thin,
Tree green toes scratching the water. The otters hunted
Meadow the ditch until the moon paled of its gleam, when
they went back to the river. They played for awhile,
but jackdaws were beginning to talk in soft, deep,
raven-like croaks in the wood, as they wakened and
stretched wings and sought fleas. A lark was singing.
The dog turned east, and ran along the otter-path
used by otters long before the weir was made for the
grist-mill below Leaning Willow Island. His holt was
in the weir-pool. The bitch drifted lazily with spread
limbs, over shallow and through pit, to the rippled
water by the hollow tree, into which she crept. Cocks
crew in the distant village as she was licking herself
and when she was clean she turned in the couch and
made a snug sleeping place, and resting chin on
rudder, was asleep.

The rising sun silvered the mist lying low and dense
on the meadow, where cattle stood on unseen legs.
Over the mist the white owl was flying, on broad soft
wings. It wafted itself along, light as the mist; the sun
showed the snowy feathers on breast and underwings,
and lit the yellow-gold and grey of its back. It sailed
under the middle arch of the bridge, and pulled itself
by its talons into one of the spaces left in the stonework by masons. Throughout the daylight it stood
among the bones and skulls of mice, often blinking,
and sometimes yawning. At dimmity it flew down
the right bank of the river and perched on the same
branch of the fallen oak and skirred to its mate, who
roosted by day in a barn near the village.

It flew away; it fluttered down upon many mice in *Owlery* the fields; but the otter did not leave the holt. The in- *Holt* stincts which had served her life so far were consumed in a strange and remote feeling that smouldered in her eyes. She lay on her side, in pain, and a little scared. The song of the river, hastening around Leaning Willow Island, stole into the holt and soothed her; the whistles of her mate above the bridge were a comfort.

When the moon gleamed out of the clouds in the east, pale and wasted as a bird in snow, the occasional whistles of the dog ceased. She did not care, for now she needed no comfort. She listened for another cry, feeble and mewing, and whenever she heard it, she rounded her neck to caress with a gentle tongue a head smaller than one of her own paws. All the next day and night, and the day after, she lay curled for the warming of three blind cubs; and while the red of sunset was still over the hill, she slid into the water and roved along the left bank, looking in front and above her, now left, now right, now left again. A glint in the darkness! Her back looped as the hind legs were drawn under for the full thrust of webs, and bubbles wriggled off her back larger than oak-apples; she was only a little slower than when she had last chased a trout. Her rudder, about two-thirds as long as her body and two inches thick at the base, gave her such a power of swiftness in turning that she snatched the fish two feet above as it flashed over her head.

She ate it ravenously, half standing in shallow water, yinnying at shadows as she chawed and swallowed.

The After four hasty laps she went under again. She
Kelt caught an eel, ate the lower part of it and returned
Pool to the holt. But she was still hungry and left them a
second time, running up the bank to stand upright
with the breeze drawing across her nostrils. Blackbirds in the wood were shrilling at tawny owls which
had not yet hooted. The otter dropped on her forepads and ran to water again. The weight of her
rudder dragging on a sandy scour enabled her to
immerge noiselessly while running.

The eldest and biggest of the litter was a dog-cub,
and when he drew his first breath he was less than
five inches long from his nose to where his wee tail
joined his backbone. His fur was soft and grey as the
buds of the willow before they open at Eastertide. He
was called Tarka, which was the name given to otters
many years ago by men dwelling in hut-circles on the
moor. It means Little Water Wanderer, or, Wandering as Water.

With his two sisters he mewed when hungry, seeking
the warmth of his mother, who uncurled and held up
a paw whenever tiny pads would stray in her fur,
and tiny noses snuffle against her. She was careful
that they should be clean, and many times in the
nights and days of their blind helplessness she rolled
on her back, ceasing her kind of purr to twist her
head and lick them. And sometimes her short ears
would stiffen as she started up, her eyes fierce with a
tawny glow and the coarse hair of her neck bristling,
having heard some danger sound. By day the dog
was far away, sleeping in a holt by the weir-pool

which had its rocky entrance underwater, but in the *Owlery* darkness his whistle would move the fierceness from *Holt* her eyes, and she would lie down to sigh happily as her young struggled to draw life from her.

This was her first litter, and she was overjoyed when Tarka's lids ungummed, and his eyes peeped upon her, blue and wondering. He was then eleven days old. Before the coming of her cubs, her world had been a wilderness, but now her world was in the eyes of her firstborn. After a day of sight-seeing he began to play, tapping her nose with a paw and biting her whiskers. He kicked against the other cubs, growing lustily, and his eyes darkened, and he tried harder than ever to bite his mother's whiskers, which tickled him when he was being held between her paws and washed. Once, when he was milk-happy and had snarled his first snarl without frightening her into stopping the licking of his belly, he was so furious that he tried to bite off her head. She opened her mouth and panted, which is the way otters laugh among themselves, while he kicked and struggled, and she pretended to bite through his neck. Tarka was not afraid, and clawed her whiskers and struggled to be free. His mother released him very gently: on wobbly legs he returned to the assault of her head, but he snarled so much that he was sick; and when she had tidied him he fell asleep under her throat.

When his eyes had been opened a fortnight, Tarka knew so much that he could crawl as far as a yard from her, and stay away although in her anxiety she mewed to him to return. She was afraid of the day-

Owlery light by the opening of the holt, but Tarka had no
Holt fear. He liked to stare at the waterflies dancing their
sun-dance over the ripples. One morning as he was
blinking away the brightness a bird about the size of
a sparrow alighted on a twig over the hole. A sparrow
in size, but not in colour! It may have been that the
Quill Spirit had painted the bird with colours stolen
from rock and leaf and sky and fern, and enriched
them by its fervour, for the bird's feet were pinker
than the rock-veins in the cleaves of Dartmoor, his
wings were greener than opening buds of hawthorn,
his neck and head were bluer than the autumn noonday sky, his breast was browner than bracken. He
had a black beak nearly as long as his body. He was
Halcyon the kingfisher. His feathers were now at
their brightest, for his mate had just laid her seven
glossy white eggs at the end of a tunnel in the bank.

Halcyon peered with a bright brown eye at Tarka
who wanted the bird to play with. A wind ruffled one
of the emerald feathers, and Halcyon crouched to
peer into the water. Tarka mewed to him to come
and be played with, and at the sound the bird gave
a sudden piercing whistle and flew upriver, leaving
Tarka creasing his nose as he blinked at the perching
place, unable to understand why it was not there.

He went back to his mother and played the biting-
game with her, after which he slept. When he awoke
again, he saw one of his sisters playing with something and immediately wanted it. The cub was pat-
ting it with one paw, holding her head sideways; but
as it did not run, she patted it with the other paw

while holding her head to that side. Tarka was *Owlery*
slowly crawling towards it, meaning to take it for *Holt*
himself, when he noticed that it was looking at him.
The look frightened him and he tissed at it. The other
cub jumped back and tissed as well, and the noise
awakened the youngest cub, who spat at her mother.
The mother licked its face, yawned, and closed her eyes.

Again Tarka crawled towards the thing looking at
him. He sniffed at it and crept away. He crept back
to it, but the other cub tissed and so he returned to
his mother. When next he went towards it, the look
in its eyes had changed, and he boldly touched it
with his nose and shifted it with a paw. It looked at
him no longer, for it was only the skull of a field-vole,
and light coming down the woodpecker's hole from
above had put shadows into its empty eyes. Tarka
moved it between his paws; some of its teeth dropped
out and rattled inside the hollow. The sound pleased
him. He played with the skull until he heard one of
his sisters mewing in hunger, when he hurried back
to his mother.

One evening, while the cubs were alone, Tarka was
playing with his rattle when he saw a live vole, that
had come into the holt through an opening by the
roots. As the way was large enough for a rat to pass,
he crept easily along the tunnel, up which the vole
had fled in fright as soon as it smelled him. The tunnel ended at the broken roots, to which part of the
earth that had nourished them still clung. Little
green leaves were growing out of this earth, for the
oak's disaster had been as a blessing to many seeds of

Root charlock which had been lying buried in the cold
Walk earth long before the acorn had sprouted.

Voles, which are the red mice of the fields, were
squeaking among the roots as they hurried to their
holes; for the explorer ran among them, crying the
alarm that a great weasel was coming. Tarka did not
know that his scent had filled them with terror;
indeed, he did not know what a vole was. He had
seen movement and gone to it, for he was always ready
to play, and play was movement. The squeaks ceased.

All was quiet and he heard, for the first time, the
jets and rills on the stones which made the ancient
song of the river. He wanted to get nearer to the
sounds and crawled along a root. When he was half-
way along it, he saw that there was nothing on either
side of him. He was alone on the root. He tried to
turn back, but the claws of one hindfoot slipped and
there he clung, curved across the wood, unable to go
up or down. He mewed to his mother, but she did
not come. His cries grew more and more plaintive as
he became colder.

About five minutes afterwards a ream passed under
the stone bridge and moved into deeper and quieter
water where its raised lines were carried to the banks
before being smoothed away by the flow. The angular
wave pushed steadily down the river. The bitch was
returning. She had caught and eaten six small trout
and two eels during the uneasy half-hour she had
been away. When nearly opposite the holt she turned
across the current, and had almost reached it when
she flung head and shoulders out of the water. While
rising she was staring, sniffing the air, and listening;

and before all the drops running off her whiskers had *Root Pit* splashed, her head was underwater and her body doubling with the effort of thrusting four webs together. Then more drops splashed by the holt. A pebble rolled down the bank.

The bitch had heard Tarka's cries, and fear had shocked her into the swiftest movements. She was in the root-pit beside Tarka while the stars were still shaking in the undulation of the old ream. He trembled with cold. A score of hearts under browny-red coats beat faster at the otter's chiding yikker as she picked up her cub by the neck and carried him to the shore. She swam with her head held high and carefully, lest the water should touch him. Afterwards, lying on the warm couch, she forgot her fright and closed her eyes in enjoyment of her young.

The next night Tarka crept along the root again, and fell in the same way. He was crawling around, when a strange-smelling animal leaned over him, wetting him with drops from its jowl. He tissed at it and tissed again when he heard the yinny-yikker of his mother and the snap of her teeth as the animal was driven away. Then something bit the back of his neck and lifted him up. With the cub dangling from her mouth, the bitch threatened the dog, who had followed her in curiosity to the holt. The dog tried to look into the tree on the following night, but the bitch dragged him down by the rudder, as though she would drown him. The dog thought this was fun, and ragrowstered with her under and on the water all the way to Leaning Willow Island, where she left him, remembering Tarka.

CHAPTER TWO

IN MID-MAY THE BUDS OF THE FALLEN OAK BEGAN to open hopefully and to show their ruddy leaves. Seven small kingfishers perched on an alder branch outside the entrance of their tunnel, while the wind stirred the fledgling down between their feathers, and they waited for loach or beetle or shrimp or elver or troutling. At sunset seven beaks were laid on shoulders, sometimes to lift at a whistle shriller and louder than the whistle of their parents; but the night was to other hunters.

While the moon was full and bright the otters went to hunt the fish lying in the Tunnel Pool below Half-penny Bridge—bass, grey mullet, and flukes, or flat-fish. The cubs were two months old and they had learned to squeeze through the inner opening of the holt and run along the root, in order to play on the grassy bank. One night as they were playing rough-and-tumble round the base of an ash tree, they heard their mother's whistle. This cry was not as piercing as the dog's call to his mate, but like wet fingers drawn down a pane of glass. Immediately Tarka stopped biting the tail of his younger sister, and the third cub ceased to gnaw his neck. As fast as they could they ran across the root and into the holt. The bitch was waiting for them, with a trout in her mouth. Tarka sniffed at it as she was breaking it up, then turned away, for he did not like the smell of it. The cubs struggled for their own food, so the bitch lay down and fed them with her milk until she grew

tired of them. Shaking them off, she went away with *Owlery*
the dog, who had swum upriver with her.   *Holt*

When next she returned, she brought two skinned
frogs, which she had caught in the reed-grown,
marshy bed of the old canal. She dropped them in
the holt and slid back into the river, heedless of the
cubs' cries. Tarka licked a frog and liked the taste of
it; he bared his milk teeth at his sisters, but he did
not eat it. They rolled and snarled and played until
their mother's return, when they ran to her. She had
brought an eel, which she bit into pieces, beginning
near the tail, but leaving the head above the paired
fins. Tarka swallowed little pieces of the fish and
licked his small sister's head afterwards, because it
tasted nice. Then he licked his own paws. He was
cleaning himself for the first time.

The new food changed them almost at once. They
grew swift and fierce. Their frolics on the bank often
ceased at the cry of a night-bird, or the distant bark
of a cattle dog in the village. They started whenever
their mother started. They began to fear. Sometimes
at sunset, when their mother left the holt, they ran on
the bank and mewed to her as she hunted upstream.
She would leave the water and chase them back
again to the holt. Her smooth movements near them
on land were often broken; she would stand still and
uncertain, or run on, jerky with fear. Many times she
stood upright and listened, her nose towards the village. People occasionally walked over Canal Bridge,
which now carried a drive to a house near the weir;
and whenever she heard voices she ceased to hunt,

21

and swam down the river to be near the cubs. Human voices frightened her; but the thunderous noises of trains in the valley and the long, whisking lights of motor-cars on the road beyond the railway were ignored because she was used to them, and knew them to be harmless.

The buds of the ash, sullen for so long in their coverings shaped like the black hooves of cattle, broke into browny-green sprays. The cuckoo sang all night. Reed-buntings chattered among the rising green, water-holding stems of balsam; soon Antares would burn dull red in the low southern night sky.

One warm evening when the river was low, the mother swam down to the holt and called the cubs into the water, and although they were ravening, she did not climb up, but waited for them with a fish below the tree. They whimpered and peered, moving their heads sideways and telling her that below was fearful. She lay on her back in the water and let the fish go, in order to catch it, and rise with it gleaming again. The two youngest cubs ran back over the damp, trodden couch to get through the tunnel, but they were too fat to squeeze through. Perhaps Tarka would have gone with them, if he had not wanted the fish so much. His eyes were on it, he smelled it, his mouth filled with eat-water. He mewed, he yikkered, he tissed, but there was no fish. The otter swam on her back and called him into the water.

Tarka watched her. He wanted the fish, but he dared not let go with his feet. The fish came no nearer, so he dropped down into the black, star-shivery

water. He was clutched in a cold and terrible em- *Grassy*
brace, so that he could neither see nor breathe, and *Islet*
although he tried to walk, it smothered him, choked
him, roared in his ears, and stifled every mew for
help, until his mother swam under him. Pressing pads
and tail against her back, Tarka was carried to the
stony margin of an islet, where the closed flowers of
the water-crowsfoot were floating among their
leaves. He spluttered and sneezed and shook water
out of his eyes, and saw the stars above him, and felt
his mother's tongue on his head.

When he had eaten the fish, Tarka began to enjoy
the strangeness. He was playing with the fishtail
when he heard the whistle so often listened to from
the holt. When he saw the animal with the wide flat
head and great bristling whiskers that had loomed
over his head once before, Tarka tissed and snarled
at it and ran for his mother. He snapped at the nose
sniffing at him. The dog turned on his back and tried
to touch Tarka with his paws, in play. Tarka watched
him and wanted to roll as well, but he was awed by
the stranger's size.

An hour later, the three cubs had eaten their fish
happily on the stones. The bitch had grown tired of
coaxing the other cubs to enter the water and had
dragged them by their scruffs out of the holt and
dropped them into the river.

The first otter to go into deep water had felt the
same fear that Tarka felt that night; for his ancestors,
thousands of years ago, had been hunters in woods
and along the banks of rivers, running the scent of

TARKA THE OTTER

Grassy Islet blooded creatures on the earth, like all the members of the weasel race to which they belonged. This race had several tribes in the country of the Two Rivers. Biggest were the brocks, a tribe of badgers who lived in holts scratched among roots of trees and bushes, and rarely went to water except to drink. They were related to the fitches or stoats, who chased rabbits and jumped upon birds on the earth; and to the vairs or weasels, who sucked the blood of mice and dragged fledglings from the nest; and to the grey fitches or polecats, so rare in the forests; and to the pine-martens, a tribe so harried by man that one only remained, and he had found sanctuary in a wood where a gin was never tilled and a gun was never fired, where the red deer was never roused and the fox never chased. He was old; his canine teeth worn down. Otters knew the ponds in this wood and they played in them by day, while herons stalked in the shallows and nothing feared the old lady who sometimes sat on the bank, watching the wild creatures which she thought of as the small and persecuted kinsfolk of man.

Long ago, when moose roared in the forest at the mouth of the Two Rivers, otters had followed eels migrating in autumn from ponds and swamps to the sea. They had followed them into shallow water; and one fierce old dog had run through the water so often that he swam, and later, in his great hunger, had put under his head to seize them so often that he dived. Other otters had imitated him. There was a web of skin between the toes, as in the feet of wolves and

24

dogs, and generations of swimming otters had caused *The* the spread of the toes to increase and the web of skin *Kelt* to widen between them. Claws grew shorter. Tails *Pool* used as rudders became longer, thicker, and powerful with muscles. Otters became hunters under water.

The moose are gone, and their bones lie under the sand in the soft coal which was the forest by the estuary, thousands of years ago. Yet otters have not been hunters in water long enough for the habit to become an instinct. And so the original water-fear was born with Tarka, whose mind had to overlay a weak instinct with habit, just as his ancestor had done when he was hungry.

When he went into the water the next night and tried to walk towards his mother, he floated. He was so pleased that he set out across the river by himself, finding that he could turn easily towards his mother by swinging his hindquarters and rudder. He turned and turned many times in his happiness; east towards Willow Island and the water-song, west towards the kingfishers' nest, and Peal Rock below Canal Bridge, and the otter-path crossing the big bend. North again and then south-west, where the gales came from, up and down, backwards and forwards, sometimes swallowing water, at other times sniffling it up his nose, sneezing, spitting, coughing, but always swimming. He learned to hold his nose above the ream, or ripple, pushed in front of it.

While swimming in this happy way, he noticed the moon. It danced on the water just before his nose. Often he had seen the moon, just outside the hollow

Moon tree, and had tried to touch it with a paw. Now he
Field tried to bite it, but it swam away from him. He
chased it. It wriggled like a silver fish and he followed
to the sedges on the far bank of the river, but it no
longer wriggled. It was waiting to play with him.
Across the river Tarka could hear the mewing of his
sisters, but he set off after the moon over the meadow.
He ran among buttercups and cuckoo-flowers and
grasses bending with bright points. Farther and
farther from the river he ran, the moonlight gleaming
on his coat. Really it was brown like the dust in an
October puff-ball, but the water sleeked the hair.

As he stopped to listen to the bleat of lambs, a
moth whurred by his head and tickled him. While
he was scratching, a bird flying with irregular wing-
beats and sudden hawk-like glidings took the moth
in its wide gape and flew out of his sight. Tarka forgot
the moon-play. He crouched in the grasses, which
rose above his head like the trees of a forest, some
with tops like his rudder, others like his whiskers, and
all whispering as they swayed. The nightjar returned,
clapping its wings over its head with the noise of a
dry stick cracking. Tarka was glad to hear his mother
calling him. He mewed. He listened and her whistle
was nearer, so he ran away in the wet grasses. The
cub did not know how alarmed his mother was nor
did he know that less than fifty flaps away a bird
with great eyes and wings spanning a yard was flying
upon him. The nightjar had seen the bird, too, and
had clapped its wings as a danger signal to its mate
whose two eggs were laid among ferns in the wood.

26

The nightjar twirled and planed away; Tarka *Moon* scampered on. The great bird, who had raised two *Field* tufts of feathers on its head, dropped with taloned feet spread for a clutch. The otter saw it drop and ran forwards so swiftly that the sound of her going through the grasses was like the first wind which uncoils as it runs before the south-westerly gale. The bird, which was a short-eared owl, thought that Tarka was a small rabbit, and fanned above him while it considered whether or not he was small enough to be attacked. It did not hesitate longer than the time of six flaps, but stopped, while screaking to terrify and subdue its prey. But Tarka came of a family fiercer and quicker in movement than the owl. Tissing with rage, he jumped and bit his assailant as a foot grasped his back and four talons pierced his skin. The other foot of the bird grasped grasses and it had turned with clacking beak to peck the base of the cub's skull when the paw-stroke of the bitch tore half the feathers from its breast. She stood on it, bit once, twice, thrice, in a second of time, and so the owl died.

Tarka was nipped in the neck, shaken, picked up, bumped all the way back to the bank, scraped over the stones, and dropped into the water. Obediently he followed his mother across the river, to where the dog was lying on his back and gravely watching two cubs playing with the tip of his rudder.

Fish were brought alive to the cubs when they had been swimming about a fortnight, and dropped in the shallowest water. And when they were nearly three months old their mother took them downstream, past

The Leaning Willow Island, and across the bend, to where
Tunnel the banks were glidden into mud smoothed by the
Pool sea. The tide had lapsed from the mud, leaving fresh
water to tear the rocky bed below.

Tarka galloped through the tall green reeds to the
river, stopping by a gut to sniff at the tracks of a
curlew, which had been feeding there during the ebb-
tide. Near the water he found another track, of five
toes well spread, and the prick of five claws. The dog
had walked there. Just above Halfpenny Bridge they
saw him, half out of the water, and chewing a fish
which he did not trouble to hold in his paws. He
craunched it from the head downwards, gulping his
bites quickly, and as soon as the tail was swallowed,
he turned and went under water for more.

The bitch took her cubs to a pool below the bridge
and walked with them across a shallow tail of water.
She stared at the stones, brown and slippery with seaweed, and the cubs stared also. They watched the
glimmers in the claws of water, sometimes trying to
bite them. While they were watching the mother ran
along the bank to the top of the pool and slid into the
water. More often than usual her head looked up as
she swam from bank to bank, for she was not hunting,
but driving the fish down to the cubs. Tarka became
excited and, seeing a fish, he swam after it and went
underwater to get it. In order to travel faster, he
struck out with all four webs together, and lo! Tarka
was swimming like an otter near a fish. It was the
biggest fish he had seen, and although he kicked after
it at the rate of nearly two hundred kicks a minute,

28

he lost it after a yard. He yikkered in his anger, and *Leaning*
oh! Tarka was no longer swimming like an otter, but *Willow*
gasping and coughing on the surface, a poor little *Island*
sick-feeling cub mewing for his mother.

He felt better when he had eaten a mullet caught by
his mother. The fish had come up with the tide and
remained in the still pool. Late in the night Tarka
caught a pollywiggle, or tadpole, in a watery hoof-
hole and thought himself a real hunter as he played
with it, passing it from paw to paw and rolling on his
back in the mud. He was quite selfish over his prey
when his mother went to see what he was doing, and
cried, *Iss-iss-ic-yang!* an old weasel threat, which,
being interpreted, means, Go away, or I will drink
your blood!

Old Nog the heron, beating his great loose wings
over Leaning Willow Island as the sun was making
yellow the top of the tall tree, saw five brown heads in
the salmon pool. Three small heads and a larger head
turned to the left by the fallen tree, and the largest
head went on up-river alone. The cubs were tired
and did not like being washed when they were in the
holt. Afterwards Tarka pushed his sister from his
mother's neck, the most comfortable place in the holt,
and immediately fell asleep. Sometimes his hindlegs
kicked, gently. He was trying to catch a shining fish
that wriggled just before his nose, when he was
abruptly flung awake. He yawned, but his mother,
tissing through her teeth, frightened him into silence.
The day was bright outside the hole.

A kingfisher sped down the river, crying a short,

Owlery shrill *peet!* as it passed the holt. The otter got on her
Holt forelegs and stared towards the opening. Soon after
the kingfisher had gone, a turtle dove alighted on the
ash tree above the holt and looked about her; she
had just flown off her two eggs, nearly dropping
through a loose raft-like nest in a hawthorn by the
weir. The bird held out a wing and began to straighten
the filaments of a flight-quill which had struck a
twig during her sudden flight out of the bush-top.
She drew the feather through her beak thrice, shook
her wings, listened, and went on preening.

Tarka closed his eyes again, breathed deeply and
settled to sleep on the youngest cub's neck. He looked
up when his mother ran to the opening. The otter
was listening to a sound like the high, thin twang of
a mosquito. Hair bristled on her neck. From far away
there came a deep rolling sound, and a screaming
cheer. The otter instantly returned to her cubs and
stood over them in a protective attitude, for she knew
that hounds were hunting the water.

Tarka crouched down, listening to the cries. They
became more distinct. Always a deeper, gruffer note
was heard among them. The sounds, almost continuous, became louder and louder. Nearer came
another sound—the wings of the dove striking
against twigs as it flew away.

A minute later the pair of cole-tits that had a nest in
a hole of the ash tree began to make their small,
wheezy notes of alarm. The white owl had flown from
the bridge and was perched against the ivy of the
trunk, turning its head from side to side and blinking.

One cole-tit, about as long as a man's finger, flittered *Owlery* with rage on the twigs a few inches from the gold-grey *Holt* head. The owl blinked slowly; the baying swelled under the bridge; it swung its head round without moving its body and stared straight behind it. *Chizzy-chizzy-chizzy-te!* wheezed the cole-tit as the owl floated away. Tarka was used to this sound, for usually it greeted him whenever he looked out of the holt in daylight.

Chizzy-chizzy-chizzy-te! the bird wheezed again, and then Tarka saw the big head of the dog-otter by the opening, and his wet paws on the bark. The bitch tissed at him, her teeth snapped at his head, and the dog was gone.

The cries were now very loud. Tarka heard thuds in the wood all around him. The cubs crouched in the darkest corner. Nearer came the shouts of men, until the thuds of running feet ceased on the bank. The water began to wash against and lap the half-drowned trunk, claws scraped the wood, the opening grew dark and the tongue he had heard above the others boomed in the hollow. The otter crouched back, larger than usual, for her body was rigid and all the hair of her back stood straight. Swish, swish swept her rudder. She recognized another sound and tissed every time it cried the names of hounds, in a voice thin and high as though it were trying to become as the horn which so often took its rightful breath. The voice ceased. The horn sang its plain note. Whips cracked.

By their big feet hounds pulled themselves out of the

Owlery water, except the one who threw his deep tongue at
Holt the holt opening. He was all black and white, with
great flews, and the biggest stallion-hound in the
pack. He was black from nose to neck, except for the
pallid nicks of old quarrel scars on his muzzle and
head. No hound quarrelled with him now, for Deadlock was master of all. In his veins ran the blood of
the Talbots, and one of his bloodhound ancestors had
eaten man. He had mastiff in him. His dam and sire
had pulled down many a deer at bay in the waters of
the moor, and died fireside deaths after faithful service to red coats. A pink weal ran down his belly, for
in his second stag-hunting season the great pied
hound had been ripped open by the brow-point of a
stag; and his pace had gone from him afterwards.
The otter-hunters bought him for a guinea, liking his
long legs, and now Deadlock was the truest marking
hound in the country of the Two Rivers.

He held by his paws, and his teeth tore at the sodden
tinder-wood. He could thrust in only his head. While
he was kicking the water for a foothold, the otter ran
forward and bit him through the ear, piercing the
earmark where the blue initial letters of his original
pack were tattooed. Deadlock yarred through his
bared teeth. Three small mouths at the other end of
the holt opened and tissed in immense fright.

Then Tarka heard a cry which he was to hear often
in his wanderings; a cry which to many otters of the
Two Rivers had meant that the longest swimming,
the fastest land-looping, the quietest slipping from
drain or holt were unavailing.

Tally Ho!   *Owlery*
The cry came from down the river, just above *Holt*
Leaning Willow Island, from the throat of an old
man in a blue coat and white breeches, who had been
leaning his bearded chin on hands clasping a ground-
ash pole nearly as long and as old as himself. From
his look-out place he had seen something moving
down like brown thongweed just under the clear and
shallow water. Off came the hat, grey as lichen, to be
held aloft while he cried again,

Tally Ho!
The horn of the huntsman sang short and urgent
notes; the air by the holt was scored by the names of
hounds as he ran with them to where, amidst purple-
streaked stems of hemlock, the old man was standing
on the shillets.

Soon afterwards the horn sounded again near the
holt and the baying of hounds grew louder. Footfalls
banged the wood above Tarka's head, as a man
climbed along the trunk. The water began to lap:
hound-taint from a high-yelping throat came into
the holt: the bitch grew larger along her back when,
above her head, a man's voice cried snarlingly,
Go'rn leave it, Captain! Go'rn leave it! A thong swished,
a lash cracked. *Go'rn leave it, Captain!*

The high yelping lessened with the taint of breath.
The cries went up the river. The rudder of the bitch
twitched. The hair on her back fell slanting; but it
rose when something scratched above. Her nose
pointed, she breathed through her mouth. She
moved away uneasily. Tarka sneezed. Tobacco

33

Owlery smoke. A man was sitting in the branches over
Holt them.

After half an hour the cries came down to the holt
again. They passed, and then Tarka heard a new and
terrible noise—the noise as of mammoth iron-toed
centipedes crossing on the stones, or shillets, at the
tail of the pool.

Tally Ho! Look out, he's coming down!

Iron toes scraped the shillets faster. Here, across the
shallow, a dozen men and women stood almost leg-
to-leg in the water, stirring the stream with their iron-
shod poles to stop the dog-otter passing down to the
next pool.

Tarka and the cubs breathed fast again. Deadlock's
great bellow swam nearer, with the high yelping of
Captain. Many wavelets slapped against the tree. A
dozen hounds were giving tongue between Canal
Bridge and the stickle above Leaning Willow Island.
A shaggy face looked into the holt and a voice cried
just over Tarka's head, *Go'rn leave it, Dewdrop! Go'rn
leave it!* Boots knocked on the trunk. *Is-isss-iss! Go'rn
leave it!* And Dewdrop left it, bitten in the nose.

Unable to break the stickle, the dog-otter went back
under the bridge. Baying became fainter. The notes
of the cole-tits in the ash tree were heard again.

In the quiet hollow the otter unstiffened and
scratched for ticks as though the hunt had never come
there. Hounds and men were above the bridge, where
another stickle was standing. The water flowed with
small murmurs. She heard the rustling clicks of
dragon-flies' wings over the sun-plashy ripples.

34

Silence, the tranquil *chee-chee* of a cole-tit seeking a *Owlery* grub in an oak-apple, and the sunbeam through the *Holt* woodpecker hole roving over the damp wood dust on the floor. The otter lay down, she dozed, she jumped up when sudden cries of *Tally Ho!* and a confused clamour arose beyond the bridge. Now all the sounds of the past hours were increasing together, of tongues, and horns, and cheers; and very soon they were overborne by a deep new noise like the rumbling of the mill when the water-wheel was turning. Then with the deep rumbling came the prolonged thin rattle of the horn, and the triumphant whooping of whips and huntsman. The sounds slowed and ceased, except for the lone baying of a hound; they broke out again, and slowed away into silence, but long afterwards the strange blowing noises made by their mother frightened the huddled cubs.

Sometimes the slits of the owl's lids opened, and dark eyes would watch a drop of water falling from one of the thin horns of lime hanging from crevices between stones of the arch. Yellow ripple-light no longer passed across the stonework of Canal Bridge. The sun made shadows on the meadow slightly longer than the trees were tall. For more than an hour the water had been peaceful. A blackbird sang in the sycamore growing by the bridge. The otter looked out of the holt and listened. She feared sunlight on the field less than the taint of hounds still coming down on the water, and, calling her cubs, she slid into the river and ran out under the bank,

D

Beam and to the grass. *Iss-iss-ss!* The ground in patches was
Pool damp with the water run off hounds' flews, flanks,
and sterns. Only a carrion crow saw them hastening
across the meadow to the leat, and its croaks followed
them into the wood where bees were burring round
purple spires of foxgloves, and chiffchaffs flitted
through honeysuckle bines. Otter and cubs passed
low and swift among the green seed-heads of the
bluebells; and uphill over blackening leaves, until
they saw the river again below them, where the sun-
points glittered, and a young kingfisher drew a blue
line in the shade of oak trees.

CHAPTER THREE

THE SHOCK-HEADED FLOWERS OF THE YELLOW goat's beard, or John-go-to-bed-at-noon, had been closed six hours when a grey wagtail skipped airily over the sky-gleams of the brook, flitting from stone to stone whereon it perched with dancing tail and feet. In the light of the sun more gold than at noon the drakeflies were straying low over the clear water, and the bird fluttered above its perch on a mossy stone, and took one. The water reflected the colour of its breast, paler than kingcups. It did not fly, it skipped through the air, calling blithely *chissik chiss-ik*, until it came to the verge of a pool by a riven sycamore. On a sandy scour it ran, leaving tracks of fragile feet and dipping as it took in its beak the flies which were crawling there. It skipped to the ripple line and sipped a drop, holding up its head to drink. Two sips had been taken when it flew up in alarm, and from a branch of the sycamore peered below.

The brook swirled fast by the farther bank; under the sycamore it moved dark and deep. From the water a nose had appeared and the sight of it had alarmed the wagtail. Two dark eyes and a small brown head fierce with whiskers rose up and looked around. Seeing no enemy, the otter swam to the shore and walked out on the sand, her rudder dripping wet behind her. She stopped, sniffing and listening, before running forward and examining all entrances under the bared roots of the sycamore tree

Burnt in the steep bank. The otter knew the holt, for she *Sycamore* had slept there during her own cubhood, when her *Holt* mother had left the river and followed the brook to get to the White Clay Pits.

The wagtail was still watching when the otter came out of the holt again. It flew away as she whistled. Two heads moved across the pool and a third behind, slightly larger, for Tarka followed his sisters. The cubs crawled into the holt, leaving seals, or marks of five toes and running pad, in the sand with the prints of the wagtail.

The sycamore was riven and burnt by lightning, yet sap still gave it a few leaves for summer. Its old trunk was beloved by two mouse-like birds which crept up the whitest tinder and held themselves by their spread tails as they looked in the cracks for woodlice and spiders. Every spring this pair of treecreepers made a nest between the trunk and the loose bark, of twigs, tinderwood, dry grasses, and feathers. Here burred the bumblebees to their homes in the crannies, and when the first frosts stiffened the grasses they tucked their heads under their fore-legs and slept, if they did not die, until the primroses came again. Here, when the trees were nearly bare, waddled Iggiwick, the grunting vuz-peg, or hedgehog, with a coat of the tree's dry leaves, black-patched with autumn's falling-mark, and on the earth he curled and closed meek eyes and dozed into a long rest. The tree was the friend of all, and it had one human friend, who as a child had seen it first when trailing in summer after her father hunting the otters of the brook. She had imagined that the old charred sycamore was a *Burnt* giant with many legs, who had been burnt in a fire *Sycamore* and had rushed to the bank to cool himself, and that *Holt* its roots, bared by floods, were thin legs bent at wooden knees and fixed in the water. The brook was determined to drown the giant, who was burrowing his toes for a hold. The maid grew tall and beautiful, but still the old giant sat cooling his thirteen legs, and every June, when she passed by with her father, following the otter hounds, he wore a fresh green wig.

Many otters had slept in the cave behind the roots; some had died there, and the floods of the brook had taken their bones away.

Mother and cubs curled up together against the dry earth of the holt's end, five feet away from the water. The cubs fell into a deep sleep, torn with dreams wherein an immense black face showed its long fangs. Tarka slept with his small paws on the neck of his mother, and her paw held him there. They snuggled warm in the holt, but the bitch did not sleep.

At dimmity, when day and night hunters see each other between the two lights, she heard the blackbirds scolding the wood owls; and when the blackbirds were silent, roosting in thorn or ivy with puffed feathers, she heard a badger drinking and grunting as he swallowed. The owls' bubbling quaver settled into the regular hunting calls; then the otter yawned and slept.

She awoke when the wood owl had made a score of journeys with mice to its nestlings in the old eyrie of a trapped buzzard, when the badger had walked many

Corncrake miles from its earth in the oakwood. She was hungry.
Meadow Leaving her cubs asleep, she crept out of the holt. At
the water edge she listened nearly a minute. Then
she turned and climbed the bank, running into the
meadow where cows snuffled at her as she stood on
her hindlegs. Hearing no danger sound, she went
down to the river, entered quietly and swam across
to the shallows. She walked through a matted and
floating growth of water-crowsfoot, and came to summer plants growing out of stones—figwort, angelica,
water-hemlock. Returning through the jungle with
a crackling of sappy hollow stems and the breaking
of rank florets and umbels, she walked among nettles
which stung her nose and made her sneeze. Thence
she passed under branches of blackthorn, which
combed her back as she ran into the marshy field. As
in the meadow, she explored as far as the centre,
rising to her full height to listen. She heard the
munching of cattle, and the harsh *crake crake* of a
landrail throwing its voice about the uncropped
bunches of marsh grasses and the bitten clumps of
flowering rush. Then swiftly back to the brook by
another way, through tall balsam stalks to the water,
where she climbed on a boulder and lay across it, her
head near the stream. She clung by her rudder to the
reverse side of the stone, and whistled for the cubs.

Tarka had been peering from the holt and, at the
first whistle he moved forward into the water, making
hardly a ripple. He swam across the pool with his
forelegs tucked under him, kicking with the hindlegs
only. The toes were spread at the thrust, so that two

webs drove him forward with one kick. Behind him *Upalong* swam the cubs, the arrowy ripples pushed from their noses breaking against each other. They followed Tarka across the floating crowsfoot flowers and reached their mother who lay so still. They spoke to her, nuzzling her with their heads and mewing their hunger. When she would not speak to them they bit her rudder, they cajoled and wheedled, they made angry tissing noises, but she did not move. They left her; and suddenly she sprang up with an otter-laugh, which was not so much a sound as the expression of lips curled back from teeth, and the rolling of the head. She was boisterous with joy after the day's fright, and had been shamming death in fun. Calling the cubs to follow her, she sank into the water and swam upstream.

The cubs knew that she was looking for fish, and they followed her by scent in the line of bubbles that was breaking along on the surface. She looked up with a fish in her mouth and they raced for it, yikkering threats to each other. The otter led them out of the pool and to a shallow; she dropped the fish, a trout of three ounces, and went to the gravelly bank where the water was deeper. Tarka picked up the live trout and took it on a mossy boulder, where he ate it in less than a minute.

The otter caught small fish so quickly in the narrow water that Tarka was soon gorged; and the other cubs in their quick hunger were able to snatch a fish from him while he was rolling on his back in order to have the pleasure of clawing it over his head.

Bitch playing with cubs. Young Tarka is on the right.

The bitch cubs were smaller than Tarka, but quicker *Scratching* in movement. Sometimes they swam along the bank *Fox* under water, looking left and right; but their mother *Quarry* had scared the fish before them and they rarely saw the gleam which was a fish curving back over her head. Often they snapped at stones or roots, mistaking them for trout.

At the end of the night, Burnt Sycamore Holt lay a mile and a half behind them. It was time to hide when buzzards were seen soaring above the oak and larch woods. The bitch led them out of the water, through willows and ash trees and brambles, and across a narrow-gauge railway track to a fir plantation. Two years before her mother had taken her to a large rabbit bury near the edge of the quarry, and now she led her own cubs there. A scent strange to Tarka was on the dry soil before the tunnel, but his mother did not heed it. She ran down the tunnel and immediately a fox crept out of it by another way, not wanting to meet a bitch otter with cubs underground, or indeed anywhere.

While the otters were cleaning themselves, the fox was sitting down outside the hole, sometimes yawning; he had within him a fill of mice, beetles, and young rabbits. He was drowsy. He remembered his scratching post, the stump of a sapling larch, and walked there, to rub his flanks against it. Reddish hairs lay around it on the ground; one side was polished. When he had scratched enough he walked to a grey stone wall behind a cattle shippen and climbed upon it, waiting for the sun.

Badslake The disused rabbit bury was dry and echoed the
Farm greater noises of day—the screeching of whistles as
light engincs, drawing trucks of white clay from the
pits on the moor where the brook took its source,
slowly approached the crossing of the lane below;
the voice, up the valley, of a man chaunting *coo-coo-*
coo-coo-coo, and the barks of a dog running round a
field while cows swung in a file long a narrow, trodden way, to the milking shed; the buzz, like a blowfly
in a spider's web, of a motor-car passing slowly over
the little bridge and the rails beyond; the whee-
ooing of buzzards and the croaking of crows above
the larch wood. These noises did not disturb the
otters.

At dimmit light they went down to the brook again,
meeting the fox, who was quietly lapping to quench
his thirst made by swallowing the fur of so many
mice. He looked at the otter; the otter looked at him.
The fox went on lapping until the water was spoiled
by their musky scent, when he went up the hill to
sniff in his earth. For ten minutes he sniffed and
pondered, until his curiosity was satisfied, and then
he started his nightly prowl—after a little scratching
against his post.

The otter took her cubs up the brook and over a
field. Away from water her movements were uneasy.
Often she stopped in her low running to stare with
raised head and working nostrils. A galvanized iron
chicken coop in a field caused her to make a wide
loop—the scent of man was there. A pair of boots left
by a tramp in a hedge made Tarka tiss with fear,

turn about, and run away. The cubs were now as *Waymoor* active and alert as their mother.

At last they reached the ditch remembered by the otter. She leaned down to the brown-scummed water, clinging to the bank by her rudder. Bull frogs had been croaking a moment before she arrived there, but now they were silent and burrowing in the mud. With paw and nose she sought under the weed, nipping them and dropping them on the grass. The cubs seized them and turned away, yikkering; and when she had caught all she could find, the otter ran back to the cubs and began to flay the frogs, for the skins were tough.

They left some of the frogs uneaten, for there were eels in the ditch. Iggiwick, the vuz-peg—his coat was like furze and his face like a pig's—found the remains, and was gleefully chewing when a badger grunted near. With a squeak of terror the vuz-peg rolled himself in a ball, but the badger bit through the spines as though they were marram grasses. Iggiwick squealed like marram grass in flame. Later in the night nothing was left except the trotters, teeth, and spiny coat of poor Iggiwick.

They were too far off to hear the dying squeals of the vuz-peg, for during the half-hour before the badger caught him they had travelled a mile up the brook. The otter swam in front, the cubs scrambling behind her. Often a fish would dodge back by her whiskers, missing the snap of her teeth by the space of a fin, and the cubs would bump into one another in their eagerness to get it. When this happened, the

Willes- otter would turn again to her prowling from bank to
well bank, and leave the fish to be caught by them.

Moor The brook became smaller and narrower, and at
the end of the night it was less than a yard across. The
next evening they left the rushes in the wet ground
where they had been sleeping, and crossing a road,
came to a boggy tract where curlew and snipe lived.
Tarka ran over the line of a hare, and followed it in
curiosity until his mother called him back. Mosses
made the way soft and held many scents—of marsh
orchid, stinking iris, bog pimpernel; of wild duck,
stoat, short-eared owl, magpie, and, once, the rank-
smelling flight-quill of a raven.

They reached a thread of water and followed it
downward until it was joined by another thread.
The two made a stream, which hastened under
whitish banks of clay. The otter sought for fish, but
finding none, climbed out of the channel by a slanting otter-path and crossed the railway track near a
tall, dark chimney that rose out of buildings. It was
a brick factory. An otter had travelled before them,
and in a hollow behind birch trees about a quarter
of a mile on they heard a whistle; and running
towards the call, they came to a deep reed-fringed
pond, on the clay side of which a grown dog-otter was
playing with the wings of a drake. Tarka kept behind
his mother, being frightened of the stranger. He had
a split ear, done in a fight two years before. Mother
and cubs went into the pond, leaving him rolling on
the bank and tossing the wings with his paws.

The pond was an old pit from which white clay had

been dug. The water was deeper than any the cubs *Merton* had swum in. Round the edge grew reed-maces; it *Moors* was early June and the wind-shaken anthers were dropping the yellow pollen on the juicy heads which would pass, with autumn, into the drab hues of decay. Ten ducklings were hiding in the reeds, while their mother circled in the starry sky, telling them, with soft cries of *quaz-qua-a-a-az-quaz*, not to move. She had flown up when the dog-otter had caught and eaten the drake, swimming up underneath it. At the time of capture the drake had been trying to swallow a frog, by quapping with its bill, which held one of the legs. When the otter's teeth had gripped the drake, the frog had escaped; but it commenced to swell on the water and so it could not swim down to the pit's floor. Tarka saw it above him as he pushed about eagerly under water: the frog showed darkly in the dim surface mirror which reflected the grey sludge of the pond's bed. Tarka caught it, and ate it under a thorn bush planted by a thrush beside the pond.

Mother and cubs roved about in the water for a while, and the dog joined them. The frogs and eels, having seen them, were hiding, and so the bitch climbed out through grey-lichened whitethorn bushes and ran among rush-clumps to the next pit. They hunted through four ponds before they had caught enough to be ready for romping. The fourth pond was larger than the others, and so deep that Tarka had not breath enough to follow the grown otters down in the gloomy water, although he tried many

Marland times. He knew they were playing, and mewed to
Moor them to come up. Sometimes a string of luminous
bubbles shook up and past him, but that was all he
saw of the fun; he could see above him, but all was
obscure beneath, although he could sometimes hear
them.

The old dog-otter was happy, because he had
another otter to play with him. His wander years
were past; he had killed salmon in the Severn, eaten
pollack on the rocks of Portland Bill, and lampreys
in the Exe. Now he dwelled among the reeds and
rushes of the White Clay Pits, and whenever otters
journeyed to the ponds, which formed an irregular
chain in a wide flat valley drained by the stream, the
old dog, who was rather deaf, would join them; and
in the deep pond, he would lure one or another down
to a rusted, weed-grown engine that had lain for
years half-buried in the clayey ooze. A great joy it
was to him to hide in the funnel, and to swim out
upon the otter seeking him. Again and again after
taking in air he would swim down to his engine, but
if any otter except himself tried to hide in the funnel,
he would bite it furiously with the few worn teeth that
remained in his jaws.

For three years he had lived on the frogs and eels
and wildfowl of the ponds. The clay-diggers often
saw him as they went home in the trucks; they called
him Marland Jimmy.

The pollen-holding anthers of the reed-maces
withered and dropped into the water, but still the
bitch and cubs stayed in the land of ponds. Here

Tarka tasted his first pheasant, caught by the bitch *Black-* in the woods where game was preserved. It was a *dagger* cock-bird, and had only one wing, the other having *Pond* dropped off in the winter, after a shot-gun wound. The bird was a swift runner, and nearly pecked out the eye of the otter before it died.

By day they slept in the reeds. From his couch of bitten and pressed-down hollow stems, Tarka watched the dragonflies which flew glittering over the water. On a reed beside him was fixed the brittle greyish mask of a nymph which had crept out of the pond the day before, having done with the years of preying on pollywiggle, minnow, and water-flea. The sun looked upon it; it dried; it heaved at its mask, which split down the back. Legs and head of a colourless insect crept out with short and flaccid wings. It clung limply to the reed, while its wings uncreased and hardened in the heat. It took the dragonish breath of noon and changed it into gleams of scarlet; its eyes grew lustrous with summer fire. The pond glittered. Its wings, held low near its body, glittered a little, they spread wide and were tremulous for flight. It was gone among the whirring dragonflies, whose bodies were banded with yellow and black, and bright with emerald, and red, and blue.

Cuckoos were calling, and sedge-warblers chattering among the green pennons of the reeds. Sometimes one flew over the pond with a mild and hawklike flight, calling *wuck-oo*, *wuck-wuck-oo*, and the little agitated warblers flew after it. The hen cuckoos

49

Black- did not sing their name, but made a low gobbling
dagger cry as they answered their mates. They were noisy
Pond about the pond, as they sought warblers' nests
wherein to drop their small, thick-shelled, greyish-
brown eggs. Once a cuckoo was flying over with an
egg in its beak when a sparrowhawk dashed at the
bird and the egg dropped into the water. *Splap!*
Tarka awakened, saw the egg, dived, brought it to
the couch, and ate it before the shadow of a grass-
stalk had moved its own width on the bank.

CHAPTER FOUR

TARKA WAS ROLLING ON HIS BACK IN THE BEAMS of the sun one morning, when he heard the distant note of the hunting horn and soon afterwards the tongues of hounds. The bitch listened, and when the baying became louder, she pressed through the reeds with the cubs and took to the bramble undergrowth beyond the north bank of the pond. A south wind was blowing. She ran down the wind, the cubs following just behind her. When she stopped to listen, she also licked her neck; and a human observer might have thought that this act showed her to have no fear of being hunted.

The heart of the otter was beating quickly; and whenever she stopped to listen, her aroused nervous force was as a burden, only to be eased by movement.

Now the hounds were hunting Marland Jimmy, who was swimming about the pond and looking at them from among the reeds. When he was tired of swimming backwards and forwards under water, he crept out through brambles and ran across a few acres of boggy moorland to the stream. He was fat and, for an otter, slow on his broad pads. Hounds were after him when he was half-way across the rushy tract, where lichens and mosses held a distinct scent of him. The old otter reached the stream and went down with the water until he came to a drainpipe, where he had often sheltered. Soon the tongue of Deadlock boomed up the pipe, but he lodged there in safety. Then a terrier named Bite'm

Mere crept to within a foot of him and yapped in his face.
Brook His hearing having dulled with the years, the otter
was not disturbed by these noises; nor was he
alarmed by the thuds of an iron bar over his head.
Bite'm was called back and another terrier yapped
away at him until it, too, was recalled. Voices of men
quietened; and after a few minutes the sounds came
down the length of pipe behind him, followed by
a disgusting smell. Marland Jimmy endured the
smell and more thumpings above him; and when, an
hour later, he crept out into bright light, the water
passed away from him with a coloured smear on its
surface. The old otter licked the greyish-yellow fur
of his belly, and nibbled the smarting skin between
his toes, all the rest of the afternoon, but the smell of
paraffin stayed on him.

The bitch and cubs were safe, for although hounds
drew down the brook, finding and carrying their
line to a wood, the hunt was stopped by a keeper.
Young pheasants were in the wood, and gins were
tilled for their enemies. Hanging from the branch of
a tree in this preserve were the corpses of many vairs
and fitches, some green, others hairless and dry, some
with brown blood clotting broken paws and noses.
All showed their teeth in death, as in life. With
them were bundles of claws and beaks and feathers,
which once had been dwarf owls, kestrels, magpies,
sparrowhawks, and buzzards. The hues and sheens
of plumage were gone, and their eyes' light; soon
they would drop to the earth, and flowers dream
out of their dust.

52

The brook was a haunt of dippers, whose cries *Braund's* were sudden as the cries of water-and-stones; speedy *Hill* little brown birds, white-breasted, who in flight were *Wood* like drab kingfishers. A tawny owl perching against the trunk of a larch tree also saw the otters coming up the stream, and its eyes, soft with light as the dark blue sloe is soft with bloom, watched them until they crept into a rocky cleft below a fall, where royal ferns cast their great shadows and water-violets were cooled by dripping mosses.

After sunset a swarm of cockchafers whirred and flipped about the top of the larch, and the owl, hungry after huddling still for fifteen hours, flapped up through the maze of cone-knotted twigs and caught two in its feet. It ate them in the air, bending to take them in its beak; and when it had caught and swallowed a dozen, it let out a quavering hoot to its mate—for the tawny owls liked to be near each other in their hunting—and, perched on a low branch of another tree, listened and watched for a young rabbit. After a few moments, its head was tilted sharply downward: the otter and cubs were going through the wood.

At midnight the western sky was pale blue and hollow like a mussel-shell on the seashore. The light lingered on the hill-line, where trees were dark. Under the summer stars a hundred swifts were screaming as they played away the night, two miles above the earth; in fine weather they kept on the wing for many days and nights together, never roosting. Their puny screams were heard by Tarka

Braund's Hill Wood as he rubbed his neck against the grassy mound of an ants' nest.

While he was enjoying the feeling a loud chakkering noise came down from the wood. The otters swung round. Four heads pointed towards the trees. The bitch ceased to nibble her fur; the other cubs forgot their play with the head of a corncrake. The noise, distinct in the dewfall, was met by other cries as harsh and angry.

When the curious otters reached the wood, other noises were mingled with the chakkering. Green points of light glinted in the undergrowth about them, like moonlight in dewdrops, for many vairs were watching a fight of the two dog-fitches on the woodland path. Running along the bank of a ditch beside the path, the fitches had met at the mouth of a drainpipe, out of which strayed a hunger-making smell. The pipe, covered with grass sods, lay beside an oak-log felled for a path across the ditch. Both ways had been made by the keeper; one for himself, and the other for fitches and vairs, whose liking for pipes and covered ways he knew. There were many such ways in the wood, and to make them more attractive, the keeper had placed the flesh and entrails of dead rabbits inside the pipes.

Each dog-fitch was trying to break the other's neck by a bite behind the ear. They rolled and snapped and scratched with their long claws, their black-tipped tails twitching with rage.

Every stoat and weasel which heard them ran to watch the fight on the pathway made by the hob-

54

nailed boots of the keeper. Tawny and dwarf owls *Braund's* peered down from branches of oak trees, while from *Hill* afar a fox listened, and prowled on again. A crow *Wood* awoke in an ivy-thick holly, muttered *aa-aa!* and laid its beak among its neck-feathers once more. Tarka circled round the stoats with the other cubs, mewing and yikkering with excitement; and then he smelled the rabbit flesh inside the drainpipe. The youngest cub also smelled it. She was quicker than Tarka, and her head and shoulders were inside one end when he ran in at the other. He had bared his teeth to snatch the flesh when there was a hard snap, a knock of iron on the pipe, a blow on the side of his head, and a loud whimpering and tissing from the cub.

Immediately the bitch was by her, running round outside the pipe in her anguish. She panted and blew as she had in the hollow tree when her mate was being worried by hounds, she ran up the ditch and mewed to the cub to follow, she returned and licked its rudder. The green points of light flicked out together.

Disturbed by the clatter in the drainpipe, a pheasant crew in the covert, and a cock defied the pheasant from its roost among hens in an apple tree by the keeper's cottage below the wood. The bitch scraped at the sods covering the pipe, blowing and gasping anew when a retriever started to bark. She ran away, whistling the cubs to follow her, but returned to the cry of the cub, who had fallen out of the pipe and was dangling by its rudder.

The barking changed to an eager whine when a door of the cottage opened and a man's voice spoke. Sounds came up distinctly from the combe below. While the otter tore with her teeth at the chain, the spring, and the closed jaws of the gin, Tarka and the other cub ran among the oak-saplings, rustling the buff leaves of an old year and breaking the stalks of seeded bluebells whose caps dropped round black seeds on the earth. There were faggots of hazel wands just inside the wood, cut and drying for a thatcher, who would split them and make spears for binding the reed of cottage roofs. They burrowed under the faggot, driving out a vair that had been sucking the blood of an aerymouse or pipistrelle bat. The small weasel made a loud *kak-kak-kak* of rage at them and vanished with the limp aerymouse in its mouth. A loud barking was coming from the field, with the yikkering of the otter. Tarka heard the yelp of the retriever, but the sound that followed made him tiss, for it was the shout of a man.

When the keeper, hurrying up the field, was within twenty yards of the wood's edge, the otter left the chain she had been breaking her teeth on and ran away. The retriever rushed at the cub to worry it, but the ferocity of the unfamiliar beast made it hesitate. The otter remained standing by her cub even when the keeper was pushing through the undergrowth. Thinking that a fox or badger was in the gin, he went forward to kill it with a blow of the holly staff he carried. He was peering forward when the retriever, a young animal, ran to him snarling;

something flung itself violently against his legs—the *Braund's* otter weighed fifteen pounds—and nearly bit through *Hill* the leather of his boot at the ankle. He struck at it, *Wood* but hit only earth. He hurried back to the cottage for his gun, calling the retriever to heel, lest it be injured.

The struggles of the cub pulled the iron peg out of the ground, and it was able to drag itself out of the ditch and slowly away among the saplings. The bitch whistled to Tarka and the other cub, who ran out from under the faggot and followed her. The mother ran on with them a little way, then returned to the cub that followed so slowly with the gin ripping brambles and clanking against stones and roots. Pheasants in the covert crew from their roosting branches; blackbirds flew from the hollies with wild alarms; wrens and robins complained in the brambles. Hedgehogs rolled themselves into spiny balls, and voles crouched by the withered mosses under the oaks.

Behind the otters came the noise of the keeper crashing through undergrowth, and the retriever's feet pattering near them, *Wough-wough-wough!* to its master. Blood ran down the face of the otter where the wounded cub had bitten her as she was trying to free the gin which gripped its rudder. The cub threw itself up and down, writhing and blowing, and not knowing what had happened; it snapped at its mother's paws, at her ears, at her nose, at her neck. The otter left it to fight the pestering retriever, her eyes yellow and gem-like.

Torridge When the keeper came up the cub was gasping with the weight of the iron it had dragged over a hundred yards. He fired at the noise in front of him and the noise ceased. Into the darkness of the wood he fired the second barrel; and listened. He heard stray pellets rattling in the distance and the dragging of the gin as the retriever tried to lift it.

At dawn the crow that slept in the ivy-grown holly saw a new corpse hanging among the fitches and vairs which had run into one end of a drain-pipe, but never run out again. The crow said *aa-aa!* and flying to the gallows tree, picked out its eyes.

When daylight came the otter and her cubs were far from the wood, having arrived at new water, deep and dark and slow moving. They swam to an islet where rose sallows and ashpoles, and swaying at the trees' tops were rafts of twigs roughly pleached, being the nests of wild pigeons. The male birds were awake, and cooing to their mates, when the otter walked out of the water. Green sedges grew by the upper end of the islet, where sticks and roots of winter floods were lodged, and through them the otters crept. The mother trod down a place in the middle and bit off sedges for a couch, and afterwards, hearing a watery croak near her, she sank silently into the pool. Her head emerged by the nest of a moorhen which flew clumsily away from off six eggs, brown like the curling tips of sedge and speckled with dark blotches. These were carried back, one by one, to the cubs, who cracked them and sucked

the yolks, afterwards playing with the shells. Some- *Dove*
times Tarka whimpered and stopped play, for the *Islet*
bruise on his head was aching. Then the mother
licked it, and washed him all over, and he fell
asleep; and the sun had risen when she had cleaned
herself and nibbled the lead pellets out of her coat.

Time flowed with the sunlight of the still green
place. The summer drake-flies, whose wings were as
the most delicate transparent leaves, hatched from
their cases on the water and danced over the
shadowed surface. Scarlet and blue and emerald
dragonflies caught them with rustle and click of
bright whirring wings. It was peaceful for the otters
in the backwater, ring-rippled with the rises of fish,
a waving mirror of trees and the sky, of grey doves
among green ash-sprays, of voles nibbling sweet
roots on the banks. The moorhen paddling with her
first brood croaked from under an arch of stream-side
hawthorn, where the sun-shafts slanting into the
pool lit the old year's leaf-dust drifting like smoke
under water. The otter heard every wild sound as
she lay unsleeping, thinking of her lost one. The
cubs breathed softly, but sometimes their nostrils
worked and their legs moved, as though they were
running.

CHAPTER FIVE

WHEN TARKA AWOKE HE SAW A SMALL EYE quizzing him from among the ash-sprays. He stretched up his head and sniffed, and at the movement the eye disappeared. Ticking cries sounded from the middle of the tangle.

Hearing them, an ackymal that had been searching the stream-side hawthorn boughs for green caterpillars flittered to the islet and chittered beside the crackey. The ackymal had a mate in a stump hole, brooding over a family of thirteen in a nest of moss and feathers, and the crackey had a mate and a family of eight in a ball of grasses hidden in the side of a haystack. Both nests were hundreds of wing-flutters away, yet when the hens, both shorter than a man's finger is long, heard the cries of their songfolk, they left their young and hastened to join them. Their scolding was a summons to all small birds. Blackbirds flew in from the fields and let out shrill ringing cries which jerked their tails as they perched above the otters. Soon many small birds were gathered in the trees of the islet, and their mingled cries brought six larger birds, who sloped up one behind the other. They were among birds what the Irish are among men, always ready in a merry and audacious life to go where there is trouble and not infrequently to be the cause of it. Raising their crests and contracting their light blue eyes, the six jays screamed with the noises of tearing linen.

The cubs lay still, but the otter lifted up her head.

She had met jays before, and knew that men some- *The*
times go where the pretty crows are nagging. For *Crossing*
half an hour she was anxious, ready to take her cubs *Pool*
into the friendly water immediately the jay cries
became shorter; which would mean the coming of
the greatest enemy, man.

The birds became hungry. The crackeys and acky-
mals and ruddocks—Devon names for wrens and
tomtits and robins—flew away when the otters
neither heeded nor harmed them. The jays remained;
but when a sparrowhawk dashed into the trees in
search of a pigeon, they departed and mobbed the
hawk, helped by a pair of carrion crows.

Again the spirit of the green place was tranquil,
with peaceful doves cooing in the noonday's rest. All
the long day the sun swung over the islet until the
hilltops were fiery. Shadows lifted from the waters
and moved up the trunks of trees. They faded in
evelight. The pool darkened. Over the fields flew a
white owl, one of hundreds which like great blunt-
headed moths were quartering the pastures and
tilth of all the lands served by the Two Rivers. It
fanned above the vole-runs, where the craneflies rose
in flight from flower and bent. The reeling song of a
nightjar on a gatepost ran through the ground mist
not high enough to hide the flowers of ragged robin
and the hardening seeds of the flowering rush. The
pigeons settled at the tops of the ashpoles, and ceased
their clapping and flapping of wings.

A drop of water splashed, another and another.
The otter had withdrawn her head from the river,

Braund's wherein she had been harkening for stir of fin or
Hill wave of tail. Filling her lungs with new air, she slipped
Wood into the water and swam to the other end of the
islet, where a scour had been formed by the flood-
rains of the last south-westerly wind. Here the grown
family of the moorhen was paddling. When almost
under them, the otter saw the legs and the images of
legs joined to them, black in silhouette against the less
dark surface. She seized one of the moorhens and
drew it under, releasing it to bite it in her jaws, and
carried it back to her cubs, swimming with her nose,
whiskers, eyes, and part of the dead fowl out of the
water. The cubs were waiting, and seeing that she
had food, they ran to her and pulled it out of her
mouth, tearing away feathers and mewing with their
pads on the dead bird. When the otter returned to
the scour the moorhens were gone, so she dived and
sought fish.

Late at night she returned with the cubs to the
wood, and whistled for the lost one. She did not know
it was dead; she knew only her longing for it. Her
whistles went far in the still night, as she ran with
nose to the ground, stopping to whine when her
grief became acute. The cock on the apple bough
heard her and crew to the dog in the kennel, who
barked to its master. Hearing the bark, the otter took
her cubs away; and at the end of the night, when
they reached the big river, the lost cub was forgotten.

They hunted and ragrowstered for many days
under the high wooded hills, below which the river
wound and coiled like a serpent. When the moon

hung thin and bright in the dusk—the fourth he had *The*
seen—Tarka could swim thirty yards under water *Golden*
before he needed to put out his nose to breathe. In *Pool*
one of their haunts, the smaller cub caught a big
trout driven upwater by the bitch, and as she
dragged the flapping fish on the stones, Tarka seized
it above the tail. She snapped at his head, dropping
her bite to do so, and he dragged it away. She bit it
through the red-spotted back, and they tugged,
wrenching the fish into pieces which they ate held
in pads and munching with their heads on one side,
whereas before they had usually swallowed without
chewing. At any threat of piracy one whipped
round to eat facing another direction; very soon all
the trout was gone except a scriddick, or fragment,
of the tail.

There was no more yinny-yikkering when they had
fed, for then was the time for play. When Tarka had
drunk some water, he snapped playfully at the cub's
head, and inviting her by his manner to catch him,
romped through the shallow into the pool. Sometimes
he swam with only his hindlegs, as his mother did
when she was not close upon a fish, but when his
sister was so near to his rudder that she could touch
the tip of it, he used all four webs and swerved by a
swish of his rudder which swung him round in his
own length. In one of his turns she caught him and
they rolled in the water, pretending to bite each
other, and kicking as kittens do. And so it was that
Old Nog, the wisest heron of the Two Rivers, heard
the noise of bubbles breaking on the water as he

63

Beaford alighted by the pool side. He watched, prepared to
Weir jump-and-flap if there were danger. He saw a swirl
on the water, and the roll of two dark sleek bodies.
He waited. They rolled nearer. With neck and beak
held low—a two-pointed horn spear on a shaft hidden by long narrow feathers—he waded into water
over his knee joints. While he paused for a plunge of
the spear, which had pierced and held many a rat
and eel, the bitch's head arose a yard from him, and
at her sharp cry the cubs fell apart and swam under.
The heron, with a harsh squawk of anger and alarm,
jumped into the air and beat away slowly, with legs
stretched out behind him and neck tucked between
his lean shoulders. *Kaack!* cried Old Nog, as he flew
to his next fishing place.

For several nights after feeding, the cubs went down
to a mill-pool to ragrowster, always with the mother,
who delighted in playing tricks upon them. Once
she whistled the food-cry, and they ran in excitement
to her, only to find a large leaf laid on a stone. It
was fun, and they chased her. The pool, placid after
a dry month, was made turbid by the fragments of
leaf, stick, and stone stirred from the weedy bottom.
She let them catch her, and enjoyed the rage of her
little cubs who snarled so fierce and bit so hard, but
could not hurt her.

Early one morning the south-westerly wind arose
from off the Atlantic, and brought fast low clouds
over the land. A blown grey rain hid the trees on the
slopes of the valley. At night the young moon was
like a luminous grub spinning a cocoon around

64

itself in the sky. The river pushed to the sea with the *Dark* fresh, or brown flood-water, and at nightfall their *Hams* holt, rising three feet under a waterside alder, was *Weir* filled. The otters rode down on the fresh, over the spillway of the Dark weir, where branches were fixed amid long claws of water. They spread their legs and floated. The noise of the great waters filled Tarka with joy. A log rolled in front of him, and he scrambled on it, to jump off again with happy cries. He pretended that froth was fish, and turned over on his back, trying to clutch it. The river swilled him along, while he whistled in happiness. A memory of big fish was moved in the otter's mind by the smell of the fresh, and she was taking her cubs down to riverbend above Canal Bridge, where she and her mate had killed salmon and peal before the cubs were born.

During the journey the clouds were blown to the north-east, over the high and cold moorland, and when the otters had drifted under Rothern Bridge the moon was shining bright in a dark blue sky. Bubbles glinted around Tarka's head, where the water, hurrying too fast over shoals, tumbled back upon itself. Round a bend the river began to slow and deepen—it was dammed half a mile below by a concrete weir built diagonally from bank to bank. This was the head of the weir-pool. The otters drifted on, round another bend until they came to where the smooth and thundering fall-over of the bubble-whitened water slanted across the river, broken near the left bank by the plunge of breakers down the fish-pass. A mist hung over the river. An icicle stood

Beam in the moonlight below the fish-pass, a silver spark
Weir for an eye.

Below the fish-pass the water rushed in a foamy
spate. Above, it slid back and polished. Presently out
of the lower whiteness a silvery flicker shook and
vanished. The silver spark vanished and glinted
lower. Old Nog, peering below the pass, was so
excited that he nearly fell over the three long green
toes of each foot, in his haste to overlook more of the
water. A second fish tried to leap the weir; with sideways flaps of tail it struggled up the spillway, but the
claws of the water pulled it back. The moon in its
first bright quarter was smitten into a myriad shimmerings by the lower turmoil. Suddenly, it seemed,
the shimmerings were drawn together into a larger
quartered moon, which rose out of the water in a
silvery curve, and fell into the pool above, soundlessly
in the immense roar of the fall.

The otters were lying in an uvver, or hover, near
the right bank, away from the tug of the cascade
plunging down the fish-pass. The water in the uvver
turned quietly. On its surface revolved a wheel of
sticks, riveted by bubbles. The otters turned with it,
hanging rudders down in the current. When the
salmon leapt the weir, the bitch became rigid and
her nostrils widened; but before the burst of the
splash had dropped back, she had become supple
again. The back of her sleek head gleamed and was
gone. The cubs followed her, naturally so swift that
a human observer might have wondered what cry or
signal had been made by the otter.

They swam by the bank until the pull of the water *Railway* grew less, when the mother turned into midstream *Meadow* and sought the salmon by working upwater from bank to bank through the gloomy and tumultuous spate. The current forced them to swim with the webs of four feet. Tarka swam on her left flank and the other cub on her right. Sometimes he was flung sideways, or spun in another whirling wheel. He was swimming out of one when the bitch either scented the fish or saw the swift ream of its dorsal fin, for she turned and swam with the current, leaving them behind. Tarka turned after her, and was pursuing with all his strength when a narrow fish, larger than any he had ever seen, swished past him. A few moments afterwards the otter followed, but Tarka had to rise to breathe, and when he swam down again he was alone. He knew that hunted fish usually went upwater, so he swam against the current, swinging from side to side as he had learned by imitating his mother.

When, after several minutes, he could find neither mother nor sister, he climbed on the bank, where wet vegetation and sticks loading the lower branches of nut trees showed how quickly the fresh had risen, and was falling. Plashes of water covered the grassy depressions of the meadow, where moorhens were feeding; and Tarka was returning from an unsuccessful pattering after the birds when he heard his mother's whistle. She had been swept down the fish-pass and hurled against the concrete rim of the middle trough, where the water had pounded her until

Stikker- she had been flung out on the straight rush and left
see's gasping and coughing, on rocky shillets heaped
Wood against the lower bank by old floods. She was savage
in failure, and took her cubs over the plashy meadow
to a wood to find rabbits. In this wood she had never
heard the *iclack* of a sprung gin, so she had no fear.
But the rabbits told their fear by thumping their
hindlegs, and those which did not bolt into the open
ran to their buries and sat there quivering, with ears
laid back over shoulders. The otters followed them to
where they crouched, inert in terror, their faces
pressed into the earth where the tunnels stopped.
Twelve were dragged out squealing, and killed; three
being skinned by the bitch. While they were feeding
a harsh chattering came from one of the holes, with
two pricks of greenish light. Here stood Stikkersee
the weasel, who was in a rage because the water-
fitches were in his wood. Stikkersee was about half as
long as the otter's rudder, but he was not afraid of
her. He came within a yard of her nose and raved so
persistently at the smell of so much blood that she
turned away from the little beast's racket and went
back to the river.

When the moon had come to its full round shine,
Tarka was hunting his own food in the pools and
necks of the clear water running round the bend
above Canal Bridge, which rod-and-line men declare
to be the best fishing stretch of the Two Rivers. One
August night, after play under the oaken fender that
took the leat away from the pool, he had left his
mother but a short while and was running along the

bank, when a raucous cry in the darkness made him *Beam* halt. His paw was raised. His nostrils twitched. The *Pool* cry had come from the meadow, where tufts of rush-grass and sedge were left uncropped by cattle. It was followed by others—slurred and throaty notes which rose slowly into the air and ended in a sweet and liquid cry. The curlews, which were feeding with their young flown from the moors where they were born, were disturbed by something, and had cried the alarm. Tarka had heard curlews crying during many nights, but never before in such a way. He heard thuds in the ground; and from the river the warning whistle of his mother.

Remembering what had come with the ground thuds before, when the air of the hollow tree had shaken to the baying of hounds, Tarka ran swiftly to water. The otter had left the river and was standing on the bank, sniffing the night wind. A cloud like the seal of an otter drifted across the moon. Tarka slipped into the river, but returned to his mother, being curious. The alarm cries of the curlews had ceased, and other notes fell from the sky. In the riverside sedges two warblers began to speak to one another. They mixed hastily the notes of song and alarm, with the gentle under-song voice used only to their mates when brooding in the cradles woven to the green flags.

A low sound of a human voice came to Tarka, and a hound-like taint which raised the hair of his neck. Immediately the mother yikkered a threat, and with her cubs ran down the bank and hid among the sedges. Clouds hid the shine of the moon.

Beam On the bank, dark against the sky, appeared the
Pool figures of men, and a long-legged lurcher dog. The
men scrambled down to the river's verge. There was
a moment of quiet, when the trilling cries of the
flying curlews rose above the water-murmurs and the
wind in the trees.

A scratching noise and the flickering of a small light.
It went out. Another match was struck and shielded
by a hand, until it spread into a lurid flame, over-
casting with ruddy glow the dim shades of trees
across the water. The flare lit the faces of two men.
One held a pitchfork with gleaming prongs. They
stood still and watchful. Then a youthful voice ten
yards higher up the river said: "Fine li'l brown dog
going through the daggers, Shiner! Wish I'd took
hold of 'n."

Neither of the men answered. They were staring
intently at the water. Slowly the torch-bearer raised
an arm and pointed. The spear was poised, to quiver
over the man's head, while a ream skated over the
pool.

A hoarse voice whispered "Now!" and the fork was
plunged into the pool. A curved flash of fire scattered
its ripple. The torch-bearer threw down his torch and
waded into the water followed by the young man,
who had run down the bank when he had seen the
jumping salmon. They were groping for the fish,
guided by the agitated spear-shaft, when the man
yelled that one of the prongs had gone through his
hand. He held it up, dripping blood, and cursing that
the top of one of his fingers was knacked off.

The man on the bank picked up the torch—oily *Beam* rags tied to a stick—and held it as far out as he could *Pool* over the water without filling his boots. The youth cried out that he had got a grip on the sow's gills and that he couldn't hold it much longer. Before the man could get to him, he had dropped the fish, yelling that he had been bitten in the leg by the little brown dog.

On the moonlight bank, beside the black-and-red smoking rags, they tried to bind their wounds; and the uninjured man was bending down to pick up his empty sack when the lurcher dog began to growl. Its snarls increased; it ran forward; it yelped with pain and ran back past them, followed by two yellow, glowing eyes.

"Fine li'l brown dog you zee'd in the daggers," growled the poacher called Shiner, who had lost a finger-joint. "Us may as well keep whoam when they sort o' dogs be about!"

CHAPTER SIX

YELLOW FROM ASH AND ELM AND WILLOW, BUFF from oak, rusty brown from the chestnut, scarlet from bramble—the waters bore away the first coloured leaves of the year. Beeches preserved their tawny form in rain and hail, but yielded more and more to the winds. Sandmartins and warblers deserted their old haunts; kingfishers and herons remained. The reeds sighed in the songless days, the flags curled as they withered, and their brittle tops were broken by the rains.

Eels began to pass down to the sea. They were the females, travelling from ponds and lakes, from dykes and ditches and drains, from the hill streams of Dartmoor where the Two Rivers had their ancient source. The eyes of the eels grew larger as they were swept down in the turbid waters, as they writhed over wet grass, along cart ruts and drains. These eels were urged seawards by a common desire—to journey whither the shallow bed of the ocean broke off and dropped deep to its grave. Here among hulks rotting in seaweed, where strange fish carrying lights moved in the heaviest darkness, the eels of the world laid their eggs, and here they died, far under the floating weed of the Sargasso Sea whence as transparent, flat, ribbon-shaped creatures, they had set out for the inland waters. After their immense journey the elvers had reached the mouths of rivers and passed up to ponds and ditches, where those that were not killed by man, otter, heron, gull, waterfowl,

cormorant, kingfisher, dwarf owl, and pike, lived *Never-be-*
and grew until desire and instinct moved them *good*
to seek the eel's birthplace in the grave of the *Wood*
Atlantic.

The eels of the Two Rivers were devourers of the
spawn and fry of salmon and trout, and the otters
were devourers of eels. Tarka stood on the shillets of
the shallow stream while they twisted and moved
past his legs. At first he ate a small portion of each
capture near the tail, but when his hunger was gone
he picked them up, bit them, and dropped them
again. The more he killed the more he wanted to kill,
and he chopped them until his jaws were tired. It
was a slimy sport, and afterwards he washed for
nearly half an hour, quatting on a mossy rock.

While the eels were migrating the otters found their
food easily, as there was no hunting to be done. They
followed the eels down the river, eating them tail-first
as far as the vent, and leaving the head and paired
fins. They played away most of the night. The mother
took her cubs to a steep sloping bank of clay which
had been worn in past winters by many otters sliding
down it. Nine feet below was a pot-hole with seven
bubbles turning in the centre with a stick, and as
Tarka slid down headfirst he meant to seize the stick
and play with it. When he looked up through the
water it was gone, and many other bubbles rode
there, a silver cluster about the blurred image of
another otter. Hearing the strokes of an otter's rudder he looked in the direction of the sound, and saw
a strange cub, with the stick in its mouth, travelling

Otters at clay slide on river bank. (They also roll and tumble when playing.)

under the foamy current. Tarka followed the dim *Leaning* form until he reached a barrier made by an uprooted *Willow* pollard willow and broken branches lodged in the *Island* stream. He climbed on the trunk, shaking water from his ears and eyes, and ran back with jubilant whistles to the slide. There he saw the cub, the stick still in its mouth, standing with a grown otter. Tarka yikkered, and ran back to the water. The grown otter mewed to him, ran after him, licked his face, and purred in his ear. He tissed at her, and whistled to his mother, who came to him, but did not drive the stranger or the cub away.

The stranger had been the mother of many litters long before Tarka's mother had been born. Her fur was grizzled on pate and shoulders, and her muzzle was grey. Her canine teeth were long and yellow, and she had lost three of her incisors. She knew every river and stream that flowed north into the Severn Sea. She had roamed the high cold moors of three counties, and had been hunted by four packs of otter hounds. Her name was Greymuzzle.

She played with the otters at the slide, and remained with them when the low clouds became rosy in the east. That day all five hovered on Leaning Willow Island, and she curled beside Tarka, and washed his fur, treating him as though he were her own cub. Then she washed the other cub, who had a white-tipped rudder. Greymuzzle had met White-tip wandering alone three weeks before, and had remained with her ever since. There was friendship and sympathy between the two grown otters, for they never

Brima- yikkered or tissed at each other. Indeed, although *combe* Tarka's mother did not remember Greymuzzle, the *Brake* old otter had played with her and her cub brothers all one night in one of the duckponds near the estuary.

The rain was blown in grey drifts down the valley, and the river flooded the martin holes that riddled the sandy banks. Trees and branches and dead animals bumped towards the sea. So heavy the autumnal fresh that the otters could not see to hunt in the river. They travelled up the valley on land, feeding on little voles turned out of their drowned homes, and on rabbits which they caught in a warren in a wood where the corpses of herons, kingfishers, redthroated divers, cormorants, and shags were nailed to an oak tree. Some had been shot, others trapped. The cormorants and shags were beheaded, for the Two Rivers' Board of Conservancy paid one shilling for every head. The wings of the kingfishers were cut off their tiny bodies, for some women in towns were willing to pay money for the bright feathers, which they wore as ornaments on their hats.

After another gale the nests of old summer began to show in the woods above the winding river. Very beautiful were the wild cherry trees at the fall of their vermilion leaves. The gales of the October equinox stripped them off the branches and whirled them away. The otters went down again on another fresh, sometimes leaving the water to cross bends of marshy ground and fields, following trackless paths which otters had run along before fields were ploughed; before wild men hunted them for their skins with spears of fire-hardened wood. These paths were older *Annery* than the fields, for the fields were once the river's *Wood* wider bed, in the mud of which the heavy rudders had whilom dragged. They floated under Halfpenny Bridge, and lay by day in the reeds of the old canal bed. A dog disturbed them, and the next night they travelled inland, and sought a resting place in the hillside earth of badgers. The white-arrowed faces of the Brocks only peered and sniffed at them. A few dawns previously a fox had crept into the same earth among the hillside pines, but the badgers had turned him out, as he stank, and his habits were displeasing to their tidy ways. Had the fox crept there during the day, and his wheezing told them that he was being hunted by hounds, he would not have been bitten and driven out, but given shelter, for man was their common enemy.

The Brocks allowed the otters to sleep in one of their ovens—as countrymen call the chambers connecting the tunnels, for they were the size and shape of the cloam ovens wherein some Devon farmwives still baked bread. The otters were clean, and washed themselves before sleeping, and so the badgers were agreeable. At fall of night they left the earth together, Tarka keeping close to his mother, for the size and appearance of the old boar who had been snoring during the day on his bed of bitten grass and moss in the next oven made him uneasy. The badgers waddled down their paths trodden through the spindle-berry shrubs and blackthorns, but the otters made their own way among the brambles to the sloping top

Little of the hill. They ran along a row of sheep-nibbled
America rape to the skyline, crossed a road, and pushed
through the hedge-banks of many small fields. Travelling down a pasture, and through a wood of oak and
holly, they came to a pill, or creek, whose banks were
fissured by guts and broken by tidal waters. White-
tip suddenly galloped away over the mud, for she
recognized the Lancarse pill which carried the
stream coming down the valley from the Twin-Ash
Holt, where she had been born. It was low tide, and
the water ran below glidders, or steep muddy slopes.
They spread their legs and the water took them
under a road-bridge to the river, which ran through
a wide and shadow pool crossed by black round iron
pillars of the Railway Bridge—the Pool of the Six
Herons. Whenever Tarka crawled out to catch one
of the little birds feeding by the water-line, his feet
sank into mud and his belly dragged. Alarmed by
the otters the birds arose with cries which seemed to
awake echoes far down the river. These were the
cries of ring plover and golden plover, of curlew,
whimbrel, snipe, and redshank, and all the way down
into a dim starlit distance the cries were borne and
repeated.

The brown water rocked them down, and as they
were drifting in a wide curve Tarka saw something
which filled him with fear. The constellation of the
Plough, which had been before them, was now on
their left, with its starry shape touching the tops of
the trees far away. The stars were friendly, being of
the night and the water, but these strange lights were

78

Otter with fluke above Bideford Long Bridge, night, at slack tide.

The many times the size of the morning star. They
Long stretched in a twinkling line across the river, throwing
Bridge a haze above them, like the dawn which the otters
of the Two Rivers know as a warning.

Neither of the older otters was afraid, so Tarka
swam without diving. The lights made the three
cubs uneasy. As they drifted nearer, rumbling sounds
came on the night breeze which had arisen two hours
since with the flowing of the tide over the estuary bar.

Soon the sweep of the fresh lessened, for the tide was
pressing against the river. A wavelet lifted Tarka and
passed behind him, another curled like a long razor-
fish shell and broke over him. He shook the water
from his whiskers, and licked his lips, liking the
strange taste. He lapped and drank. The forerun-
ning press of the young tide lifted him up and down,
and chopped with playful foam at his pate. On every
ribbed shoal and mudbank the wavelets were lapping the stones and rocks, lapsing with faint trickling
sounds, and leaving domes of froth which trembled
and broke in the wind. As the otters swam down with
stronger strokes the mudbanks changed to sandy
shoals, and air bubbles out of ragworms' holes shook
up in the shallow water through which they paddled.
Long dark shapes rode on the water, swinging round
slowly in the tide, and the wavelets went flip flup
against them. Tarka was afraid of the salmon boats,
but the old otters ignored them. The lamplights on
the bridge were now very large and bright, and had
ceased to twinkle. They passed more boats at their
moorings. The rumbling noises of traffic on the

bridge were loud, and figures were seen. In front, *The* twenty-four arches, of different shapes and sizes, *Estuary* bore the long bridge. Greymuzzle dived, and the four followed her.

She had caught the scent of men and dogs blowing from the bridge, two hundred yards in front. Under water Tarka swam until he could swim no more, and rising quietly to vent, he turned his head to see if any danger were near, and swam on. He rose to breathe nine times before reaching the bridge, and the eighth rising brought him under one of the arches. He swam hard against the tide pouring between two piers.

This was the first time Tarka passed under the antient Long Bridge, which the monks built across their ford two centuries before the galleons were laid down in the shipyards below to fight the Spanish Armada. When the otters had passed under the bridge they had to swim hard, keeping near the right bank of the river to avoid the main flow of the tide. Flukes were caught in the estuary that night by the otters diving to deep water; they were not easy to find, for the dabs and plaice lay flat on the sand when they saw the dark shapes above them, and their sandy-speckled backs hid them. The otters raked the bottom with their paws, driving up the fish which they seized and took on the bank to eat.

In the nights that followed Tarka learned to eat crabs, cracking them with his teeth. With the other otters he sought the shellfish among the rocks below the stone quay of a fishing village at the meeting

Branton place of the Two Rivers, where often at night they
Pill were disturbed by the pailfuls of rubbish flung over
by the natives. Once a pailful of hot ashes came
down, burning both Tarka and White-tip.

By day the otters slept in the reeds of a duckpond
which they reached by drifting with the tide up the
other horn of the estuary, and turning into the Branton pill, where ketches and gravel barges were
moored. At dawn they left the salt water and ran
over the eastern sea-wall to the duckpond shaped
like a ram's horns. In the brackish waters of the
duckpond the otters took mullet which had been
washed in when the sea-wall had broken years before,
and rainbow trout put there by the owner. Old Nog
fished these waters, and at night many kinds of
wildfowl flapped and quacked beside the reeds;
mallard, widgeon, teal, coot, dabchick, and strays of
the duck family—shoveller, pochard, and golden eye.

On the fourth night of the otters' arrival at the
Ram's-horn duckpond, the swallows which settled
among the reed-maces at sunset did not sleep. They
twittered among themselves when the first stars
gleamed in the water, for they had received a sign to
leave the green meadows they loved so well. They
talked in their undersong voices—which men seldom
hear, they are so soft and sweet—while clinging to
the unburst heads of the reed-maces. They talked of
white-and-grey seas, of winds that fling away the
stroke of wings, of great thunder-shocks in the sun-
whitened clouds under, of wild rains and hunger and
fatigue to come before they saw again the sparkles in

82

the foam of the African strand. But none talked of *Ram's*- the friends who would fall in the sea, or be slain in *horn* France and Spain and Italy, or break their necks *Pond* against the glass of lighthouses, for the forktailed birds of summer had no thought of these things, or of death. They were joyous and pure in spirit, and alien to the ways of man.

During the day Tarka had been watching them, being curious. He had watched them sweeping above him with a windy rush of wings that darkened the sky, and had listened to their sharp cries as they dipped and splashed in the wind-ruffled water. As he was stretching himself before leaving his couch at sunset they flew like a great sigh up to the stars. *Krark! Krark! Krark!* cried Old Nog, standing grave and still in the shallow water at the pond's edge. It was the last English voice many of them would hear, the blue winged ones of summer, who had begun the weary migration from the land of thatched home- steads and old cob linhays.

Some days after the swallows had gone, Tarka heard a strange flute-like whistle while playing in the Ram's-horn duckpond. The five otters ceased their play and listened. The whistle came again, and Tarka's mother answered. The answering whistle was keen and loud. The bitch swam towards it, followed by Greymuzzle and White-tip. The whistle made Tarka cry in rage, *Ic-yang*, and when a dog-cub has cried thus he is no more a cub, but a dog-otter.

The night before, the otters had fished in the estuary by the sea-weedy hurdles and posts of a

Ram's-horn duckpond, Wrafton, with Burrows in background.

silted-up salmon weir, where in former times salmon *Ram's-* were left penned by the tide. They had returned to *horn* the duckpond across fields and dykes, along an otter *Pond* route, and on their trail an old dog-otter had followed.

Now he had trailed them to the duckpond, a big, flat-headed, full-thighed dog with great whiskers, more than double the weight of Tarka. He frightened the crier of *Ic-yang*, who crouched tissing with his sister when the stranger sniffed at her nose and then licked it. This action caused Tarka's mother to behave in a curious manner. Turning fiercely on the cub, she rolled her over, bit her, and chased her under water. Many bubbles were blown up. Tarka dived to see why this strange thing had happened, but the dog turned in a swirl of water to snap at his head. Tarka was so scared that he swam to the bank and crawled out among the dry thistles. Here, while the water ran from his fur, he whistled to his mother. He saw her swimming with her head out of water, with the strange dog behind pretending to bite her. She was heedless of her cub's cries, and dived with the dog in play. For hours Tarka ran on the grassy bank of the duckpond, following his mother as she played in the water. Once the dog rose to the surface with a mullet in his mouth, which he did not trouble to kill before leaving it to float on its side. Tarka whistled again and again, and at last the big dog left the water and chased the small dog for whistling to his mate.

Tarka ran away. He crossed over the sea-wall, and worked up the stony bed of the pill, catching the

Marstage flukes and green crabs which were feeding at the
Wall mouth of an open sewer. He met White-tip and
Greymuzzle, and together they returned to the
duckpond when the wildfowl flighted over. He was
swimming round one bend of the ram's horn when the
big dog heard the strokes of his hindlegs and swam after
him again. Tarka dived and twisted, and although
he was bitten twice in the neck and once through the
paw, he was not caught. His mother's training had
made him swift and strong. He quitted the water and
was pursued through grassy tufts and thistles and
bunches of frayed flags to the sea-wall, where the big
dog turned and whistled to his mate. Hearing
another whistle—it was really an echo of his own—
he galloped in rage back to the duckpond. Then
Tarka whistled, and the dog returned to kill him.
Tarka went up and over the sea-wall at his greatest
speed, across the mud and stones of the pill and to
the western sea-wall, where he stopped. He cried
Ic-yang! several times, but if the dog had returned in
answer to the challenge, it is doubtful whether Tarka
would have waited to drink the blood of his enemy.

Already his mother had forgotten, and perhaps
would never again remember, that she had loved a
cub called Tarka.

CHAPTER SEVEN

H E WAS ALONE, A YOUNG MALE OF A FEROCIOUS and persecuted tribe whose only friends, except the Spirit that made it, were its enemies—the otter hunters. His cubhood was ended, and now indeed did his name fit his life, for he was a wanderer, and homeless, with nearly every man and dog against him.

Tarka fished the pools and guts of the Branton pill, eating what he caught among the feathery and aromatic leaves of the sea-wormwood plants which grew in the mudded cracks of the sloping stone wall with the sea-beet, the scentless sea-lavender, and the glasswort. One night a restlessness came over him, and he rode on the flood-tide to the head of the pill, which was not much wider than the gravel barges made fast to rusty anchors half-hidden in the grass, and to bollards of rotting wood. The only living thing that saw him arrive at the pill-head was a rat which was swarming down one of the mooring ropes, and when it smelled otter it let out a squeak and rapidly climbed over the sprig of furze tied to the rope to stop rats, and ran back into the ship. Tarka padded out of the mud, and along the footpath on the top of the sea-wall, often pausing with raised head and twitching nostrils, until he came to where the stream, passing through a culvert under the road, fell into a concrete basin and rushed thence down a stony slope into the pill. Entering the water above the fish-pass, he swam under the culvert, following the

Caen stream round bends and past a farmyard, through
Bridge another culvert under a cart-road, and on till he
came to a stone bridge near a railway station. A horse
and butt, or narrow farm cart, was crossing the
bridge, and he spread himself out beside a stone, so
that three inches of water covered his head and back
and rudder. When the butt had gone, he saw a hole,
and crept up it. It was the mouth of an earthenware
drain, broken at the joint. He found a dry place
within. When it was quiet again, he went under the
bridge and fished up the stream, returning at dawn
to the drain.

He was awakened by the noise of pounding hooves;
but the noises grew remote and he curled up again,
using his thick rudder as a pillow on which to rest
his throat. Throughout the day the noises of hooves
recurred, for below the bridge was a ford where farm
horses were taken to water. Twice he crept down the
drain, but each time there was a bright light at the
break in the pipe, and so he went back. At dusk he
slipped out and went upstream again. Just above the
bridge was a chestnut tree, and under it a shed,
where ducks were softly quacking. He climbed on
the bank, standing with his feet in sprays of ivy, his
nose upheld, his head peering. The scents of the
ducks were thick and luring as vivid colour is to a
child. Juices flowed into his mouth, his heart beat
fast. He moved forward, he thought of warm flesh,
and his eyes glowed amber with the rays of a lamp
in the farmhouse kitchen across the yard. The
chestnut tree rustled its last few rusty leaves above

Caen Bridge, Braunton.

Corffe him. Then across the vivid smear of duck scent
Green strayed the taint of man; an ivy leaf trembled, a
spider's web was broken, the river murmured, and
the twin amber dots were gone.

Beside the stream was a public footpath and an
illuminated building wherein wheels spun and
polished connecting-rods moved to regular pulses
which thudded in the air like the feet of men running
on a bank. Tarka dived. He could not swim far, for
by the electric power station the river slid over a fall.
He swam to the right bank, but it was a steep wall of
concrete. Again he dived, swimming upstream and
crawling out on the bank. For many minutes he was
afraid to cross the railway line, but at last he ran
swiftly over the double track, and onwards until he
reached the stream flowing deep under a footbridge.

He had been travelling for an hour, searching the
uvvers of the banks for fish as he had learned in
cubhood, when on a sandy scour he found the
pleasing scent of otter. He whistled and hurried
upstream, following the scent lying wherever the
seals had been pressed. Soon he heard a whistle, and
a feeling of joy warmed his being.

A small otter was waiting for him, sitting on a
boulder, licking her coat with her tongue, the white
tip of her rudder in the water. As Tarka approached,
she looked at him, but she did not move from the
boulder, nor did she cease to lick her neck when he
placed his forepads on the stone and looked up into
her face. He mewed to her and crawled out of the
water to stand on hindlegs beside her and touch her

90

nose. He licked her face, while his joy grew to a *Buckland* powerful feeling, so that when she continued to *Meadow* disregard him, he whimpered and struck her with one of his pads. White-tip yikkered and bit him in the neck. Then she slid into the water, and with a playful sweep of her rudder swam away from him.

He followed and caught her, and they rolled in play; and to Tarka returned a feeling he had not felt since the early days in the hollow tree, when he was hungry and cold and needing his mother. He mewed like a cub to White-tip, but she ran away. He followed her into a meadow. It was strange play, it was miserable play, it was not play at all, for Tarka was an animal dispirited. He pressed her, but she yikkered at him, and snapped at his neck whenever he tried to lick her face, until his mewing ceased altogether and he rolled her over, standing on her as though she were a salmon just lugged to land. With a yinny of anger she threw him off, and faced him with swishing rudder, tissing through her teeth.

Afterwards she ignored him, and returned to the river as though she were alone, to search under stones for mullyheads, or loach. He searched near her. He caught a black and yellow eel-like fish, whose round sucker-mouth was fastened to the side of a trout, but she would not take it. It was a lamprey. He dropped it before her again and again, pretending to have caught it anew each time. She swung away from his offering as though she had caught the lamprey and Tarka would seize it from her. The sickly trout, which had been dying for days with the

Buckland Meadow lamprey fastened to it, floated down the stream; it had been a cannibal trout and had eaten more than fifty times its own weight of smaller trout. Tar from the road, after rain, had poisoned it. A rat ate the body the next day, and Old Nog speared and swallowed the rat three nights later. The rat had lived a jolly and murderous life, and died before it could fear.

The lamprey escaped alive, for Tarka dropped it and left White-tip in dejection. He had gone a few yards when he turned to see if she were following him. Her head was turned, she was watching. He was so thrilled that his whistle—a throat sound, like the curlew's—was low and flute-like. She answered. He was in love with White-tip, and as in all wild birds and animals, his emotions were as intense as they were quick. He felt neither hunger nor fatigue, and he would have fought for her until he was weak now that she had whistled to him. They galloped into the water-meadow, where in his growing desire he rushed at her, rolling her over and recoiling from her snapping of teeth. She sprang after him and they romped among the clumps of flowering rush, startling the rabbits at feed and sending up the woodcock which had just flown from the long low island seventeen miles off the estuary bar.

White-tip was younger than Tarka, and had been alone for three weeks before the old, grey-muzzled otter had met and taken care of her. Her mother had been killed by the otterhounds, during the last meet of the otter-hunting season, at the end of September.

Tarka and White-tip returned to the stream, where

among the dry stalks of angelica and hemlock they *Butts* played hide-and-seek. But whenever his playfulness *Water* would change into a caress, she yinny-yikkered at him. She softened after a while, and allowed him to lick her head, once even licking his nose before running away. She was frightened of him, and yet was glad to be with him, for she had been lonely since she had lost Greymuzzle, when a marshman's dog had chased them out of a clump of rushes where they had been lying rough. Tarka caught her, and was prancing round her on a bank of gravel when down the stream came a dog-otter with three white ticks on his brow, a heavy, slow-moving, coarse-haired otter who had travelled down from the moor to find just such a mate as the one before him. Tarka cried *Ic-yang!* and ran at him, but the dog-otter, who weighed thirty pounds, bit him in the neck and shoulder. Tarka ran back, tissing, swinging and swaying his head before he ran forward and attacked. The older dog rolled him over, and bit him several times. Tarka was so mauled that he ran away. The dog followed him, but Tarka did not turn to fight. He was torn about the head and neck, and bitten thrice through the tongue and narrow lower jaw.

He stopped at the boulder where White-tip had been sitting when first she had seen him, and listened to the whistles of his enemy. The water sang its stone-song in the dark as it flowed its course to the sea. He waited, but White-tip never came, so he sank into the water and allowed himself to be carried

The down past bends and under stone arches of the little *Burrows* bridges which carried the lanes. He floated with hardly a paddle, listening to the song of the water and sometimes lapping to cool his tongue. The wheels and rods of the power station turned and gleamed behind glass windows like the wings of dragonflies; over the fall he slid, smooth as oil. Slowly and unseen he drifted, under the chestnut tree, under the bridge, past the quiet railway station, the orchards, the meadows, and so to the pill-head. The current dropped him into the basin of the fish-pass, and carried him down the slide to salt water. With the ebb he floated by ketches and gravel barges, while ring-plover and little stints running at the line of lapse cried their sweet cries of comradeship. The mooring keg bobbed and turned in the ebb, the perches, tattered with seaweed, leaned out of the trickling mud of the fairway, where curlew walked, sucking up worms in their long curved bills. Tarka rode on with the tide. It took him into the estuary, where the real sea was fretting the sandbanks. He heard a whistle, and answered it gladly. Greymuzzle was fishing in the estuary, and calling to White-tip.

The old otter, patient in life after many sorrows and fears, caressed his bitten face and neck and licked his hurts. They hunted together, and slept during the day in a drain in one of the dykes of the marsh, which was watered by a fresh stream from the hills lying northwards. Night after night they hunted in the sea, and often when the tide was low they played in the

Pool opposite the fishing village that was built *The*
around the base of a hill. The north-east wind blew *Burrows*
cold over the pans and sandy hillocks near the sea,
but Greymuzzle knew a warm sleeping place in a
clump of round-headed club-rush, near the day-hide
of a bittern. She became dear to Tarka, and gave
him fish as though he were her cub, and in the
course of time she took him for her mate.

95

CHAPTER EIGHT

THE TREES OF THE RIVERSIDE WEPT THEIR LAST DRY tears, and the mud in the tidehead pool made them heavy and black; and after a fresh, when salmon came over the bar, beginning their long journey to spawn in the gravel where the rivers ran young and bright, broken black fragments were strewn on the banks and ridges of the wide estuary. In November the poplars were like bedraggled gull-feathers stuck in the ground, except for one or two or three leaves which fluttered on their tops throughout the gales of November.

One evening, when the ebb-tide was leaning the channel buoys to the west and the gulls were flying silent and low over the sea to the darkening cliffs of the headland, Tarka and Greymuzzle set out on a journey. They had followed the salmon up the river, and Greymuzzle had returned for a purpose. The bright eye of the lighthouse, standing like a bleached bone at the edge of the sandhills, blinked in the clear air. The otters were carried down amidst swirls and topplings of waves in the wake of a ketch, while the mumble of the bar grew in their ears. Beyond the ragged horizon of grey breakers the day had gone, clouded and dull, leaving a purplish pallor on the cold sea.

The waves slid and rose under the masted ship, pushing the white surge of the bar from her bows. A crest rolled under her keel and she pitched into a trough. On the left a mist arose off a bank of grey

boulders, on which a destroyer lay broken and sea- *Baggy*
scattered. It had lain there for years, in bits like
beetle fragments in a gorse-spider's grey web-tunnel.
One of the great seas that drive the flying spume over
the potwallopers' grazing marsh had thrown it up on
the Pebble Ridge. During the day Tarka and Greymuzzle had slept under the rusty plates, curled warm
on the wave-worn boulders rolled there by the seas
along Hercules Promontory.

Two hours after midnight the otters had swum five
miles along the shallow coast and had reached the
cave of the headland, which Greymuzzle had
remembered when she had felt her young kick inside
her. The tide left deep pools among the rocks, which
the otters searched for blennies and gobies, and other
little fish which lurked under the seaweed. They
caught prawns, which were eaten tail first, but the
heads were never swallowed. With their teeth they
tore mussels off the rocks, and holding them in their
paws, they cracked them and licked out the fish.
While Greymuzzle was digging out a sand-eel, Tarka
explored a deep pool where dwelt a one-clawed
lobster. It was hiding two yards under a rock, at the
end of a cleft too narrow to swim up. Four times
he tried to hook it out with his forepad, the claws of
which were worn down with sand-scratching, and
in his eagerness to get at it he tore seaweed with his
teeth. The lobster had been disturbed many times in
its life, for nearly every man of the villages of Cryde
and Ham had tried to dislodge it with long sticks to
which they had lashed hooks. The lobster had lost so

Seal many claws that after nine had been wrenched off,
Cavern its brain refused to grow any more. Its chief enemy was
an old man named Muggy, who went to the pool
every Sunday morning at low spring-tide with a
rabbit skin and entrails, which he threw into the
water to lure it forth from the cleft. The lobster was
too cunning, and so it lived.

The otters rested by day on a ledge in the cave
under the headland. Here dwelt Jarrk the seal, who
climbed a slab below them by shuffles and flapping
jumps. Sometimes Tarka swam in the pools of the
cave, rolling on his back to bite the drops of iron-
water which dripped from the rocky roof, but only
when Jarrk was away in the sea, hunting the conger
where the rocks of Bag Leap ripped foam out of the
tide.

The greatest conger of Bag Leap, who was Garbargee, had never been caught, for whenever it saw
Jarrk the seal, its enemy, it hid far down in the
crab-green water, in a hole in the rocks of the
deepest pool, where lay shell-crusted cannon and
gear of H.M. sloop *Weazel* wrecked there a century
before. When no seal was about, Garbargee hung
out of the hole and stared, unblinkingly, for fish,
which it pursued and swallowed. One morning as
Tarka, hungry after a stormy night, was searching
in the thong-weed five fathoms under the glimmering
surface, something flashed above him, and looking
up, he saw a narrow head with a long hooked preying beak and two large webs ready to thrust in
chase of fish. This was Oylegrin the shag, whose

98

oily greenish-black feathers reflected light. The *Bag*
smooth narrow head flickered as Oylegrin shifted *Leap*
his gaze, and a pollack below mistook the flicker
for a smaller surface-swimming fish. The pollack
turned to rise and take it, and the shag saw the
gleam of its side at the same time as Tarka saw it.
Oylegrin tipped up and kicked rapidly downwards,
faster than an otter could swim. Its tight feathers
glinted and gleamed as it pursued the pollack.
Garbargee also saw the pollack and uncurled a
muscular tail from its hold on a jut of rock. The
conger was longer than a man is tall, and thicker
through the body than Tarka. It weighed ninety
pounds. It waved above the weedy timbers, and as it
passed over, crabs hid in the mouths of cannon.

Bird, animal, and fish made a chasing arrowhead
whose tip was the glinting pollack; conger the flexible
shaft, otter and shag the barbs. Oylegrin swam with
long neck stretched out, hooked beak ready to grip,
while it thrust with webbed feet farther from the
bubbles which ran out of its gullet. The pollack
turned near Tarka, who swung up and followed it.
Oylegrin braked and swerved with fourteen short
stiff tail-feathers and one upturned web. The
pollack turned down a sheer rock hung with thong-
weed, but, meeting Tarka, turned up again and was
caught by Oylegrin.

The chasing arrowhead buckled against the rock,
in a tangle of thongs and ribbons and bubbles
shaking upwards. The giant conger had bitten the
shag through the neck. Wings flapped, a grating,

H

Sandy muffled cry broke out of a bottle of air. Tarka's
Cove mouth opened wide, but his teeth could not pierce
the conger's skin. The gloom darkened, for an
opaqueness was spreading where there had been
movement.

Now Jarrk the seal, who had been searching round
the base of the rock, saw an otter rising to the surface, and was swinging up towards him when he
saw a conger eel wave out the opaqueness, which was
Oylegrin's blood staining the green gloom. Garbargee held the shag in its jaws. The undersea cloud was
scattered by the swirls of flippers as the seal chased
the conger. Garbargee dropped the shag, and the
cleft of rock received its grey tenant. Jarrk swung up
with a bend of his smooth body, and lay under the
surface with only his head out, drinking fresh air, and
looking at Tarka six yards away. Wuff, wuff, said
Jarrk, playfully. *Iss, iss*, cried Tarka, in alarm. The
pollack escaped, and soon afterwards was feeding
with other fish on the crab-nibbled corpse of the shag.

It was not often that the otters went fishing in
daylight; usually they lay in the warm noonday sun
on the sand of a cove behind the Long Rock—a spur
of which was the plucking perch of Chakchek the
One-eyed, the peregrine falcon. One morning
Chakchek half-closed his wings and cut down at
Tarka, crying *aik-aik-aik!* and swishing past his head.
It was the cream-breasted tiercel's cry of anger. He was
a swift flyer and soon mounted to where his mate
waited at her pitch in the sky above the precipice,
scanning the lower airs for rock-dove, oyster-catcher,

finch, or guillemot. When they had swept away down *Bag*
the north side of the headland, Kronk the raven *Leap*
croaked thrice, deeply, and took the air to twirl with
his mate in the windy up-trends.

Near Sandy Cove was the Cormorants' Rock, where
five cormorants squatted during most of the daylit
hours, digesting their cropfuls of fishes. Each
cormorant, as it arrived with steady black flight,
would pass the rock about fifty yards, swing round
and fly back into the wind, alighting uneasily among
its brethren, some of whom had the tails of fishes
sticking out of their gullets. They held out their
wings and worked their shoulders to ease the fish
down into their crops. The top of Cormorants' Rock,
where they sat, was above the highest wave.

Bag Leap was a sunken reef stretching about half
a mile from the point, over which the tides raced.
Here the currents brought many seals, which had
followed salmon up the Severn Sea, on their return
home to Lundy Island. With them was a grey seal,
a stranger, who had come down from the north. For
several days the seals fished off the Leap, while Jarrk
roared among them and joined in their favourite
game of chasing the smallest seal, who was not black
and yellowish-brown like themselves, but a rare
silvery-white. They would swim round the rocks
looking for her, sometimes remaining under water
for nearly a quarter of an hour. Once when Tarka
was searching for a bass in four fathoms he met
Jarrk face to face, and the shock made him blow a big
bubble. He turned and kicked up to the light, while

Jarrk swum round him in a spiral. Jarrk was always gentle, for he had never an enemy to shock him into fear, and when Tarka tissed and yikkered at him, the scymitar-shaped lip-bristles of his broad muzzle twitched, his upper lip lifted off his lower jaw, he showed his yellow teeth, and barked. *Wuff, wuff,* said Jarrk, jovially. *Ic-yang,* yikkered Tarka. The seal snorted; then his back, stretched and gleaming, rolled under like a barrel.

When the seals left Bag Leap for the seventeen-mile swim to their island home, one remained with Jarrk. She was the stranger grey seal, and often while the other seals had been romping, she had been exploring the far dark end of the cave behind the Long Rock, where was a beach of boulders. Greymuzzle explored the beach for the same purpose, and sometimes otter and seal passed by each other in the pools. On one high-tide the seal swam into the cave, and did not return with the ebb. For three days she hid herself, and then she flapped down the sand and splashed into the sea, very hungry.

Many times during the rise and fall of tides the bitch-otter ran into the cave, and on the morning of the grey seal's return to the sea she swam round the Long Rock and crawled out of the surge among the limpet-studded rocks of Bag Hole. Three hundred and ten feet above her, perched on the swarded lip of a sand-coloured cliff, Kronk the raven watched her running round and over boulders. She reached the base of the precipice, and scrambled up a slide of scree, which had clattered down during the rains of autumn. Gulls wove and interwove in flight below the *Windy* raven, floating past their roosts in the face of the cliff. *Boulder* The scree had fallen from under the Wreckers' Path, made during centuries by the cautious feet of men and women descending after storms to gather what the sea had thrown on the boulders of the Hole. It was not much wider than one of the sheep-paths on the headland. Greymuzzle ran along it, and turning a corner by a lichened boulder, disappeared from the sight of Kronk. She had climbed here alone several times during the previous night.

Less than a minute afterwards the raven jumped leisurely over the edge, and opening his wings, rose on the wind, and turning, swept back over his perching place, over snares pegged by rabbit-runs in the grass, and to a shillet wall a hundred yards from the precipice. One of the brass snares Kronk was watching. It had been drawn tight about the neck of a rabbit since early morning; the rabbit had died after two hours of jumping and wheezing. It was cold; its fleas were swarming in agitation over its longer hairs. Kronk was waiting for a meal off the rabbit, but he did not like to go near it until he knew for certain that the trapper, whom he had watched setting the snare the afternoon before, had not tilled a gin beside it specially for Kronk. The raven knew all about the methods of trappers, and the gins and snares they tilled. Several times Kronk had sailed with the wind over the snared rabbit; he sailed without checking by tail or wing lest the trapper be spying upon him. In every other act of his life he was

Baggy as cautious, having learned many things about man in *Sheer* more than a hundred years of flying.

The raven was waiting for Mewliboy, the cowardly soaring buzzard hawk, to espy the rabbit; and when Mewliboy had ripped it open with one stroke of his hooked beak, the raven intended to call *krok-krok-krok* rapidly, and so summon his mate to help him deal with the buzzard, if he were not trapped. And if he had sprung a hidden gin, then it would be safe for Kronk. So the raven reasoned.

Greymuzzle came to the end of Wreckers' Path, and climbed up springy clumps of sea-thrift, among gull-feathers and mussel-shells and fish-bones, and ran along another path to the top of the precipice. She looked left and right, often pausing to sniff the air. She picked up a feather, ran with it a few years, and dropped it again. She cast round over the sward, peering into rabbit-holes, and pulling out dry stalks of thrift that the wind had blown there. Kronk watched her running, swift and low, along the narrow wandering lines pressed in the sward by the feet of rabbits; he saw her stop by the snared rabbit, bite on to its neck, and watched her tugging at it. *Crr-crr!* said Kronk to himself.

He jumped off the wall, which was covered with dry lichens dissolving the stones with acids, and circling above Greymuzzle, croaked a long, harsh note, meant to call the gulls. He dived at Greymuzzle, repeating the harsh cry, and very soon nearly fifty herring gulls were screaming about her. Alarmed by the noise, she ran back the way she had come; the

Greymuzzle on Baggy Point.

Sandy gulls followed, and Kronk had the rabbit to himself.
Cove Seeing him, the gulls returned, screaming and flying
as near to him as they dared. Kronk pecked and
pulled at his ease, knowing that the gulls would give
the alarm should a man come round either the
south or the north side of the wall, which hid approach.

Greymuzzle was slipping down the scree at the end
of Wreckers' Path, carrying a brown dry tussock of
sea-thrift in her mouth, when the remote crying of
gulls became loud above the cliff. *Quoc-quoc-quoac!*
many were muttering in anger. Several hundred
wheeled and floated above the otter. She heard a
soughing of wings, and looking up, saw the beak and
eyes of the raven growing larger as he plunged
towards her. He had taken nine long hops away from
the rabbit, and the tenth had taken him over the
precipice edge as a man, walking fast, had taken his
ninth stride round the northern wall, three hundred
yards off. Kronk opened his wings when half-way
down the cliff and sailed without a wing-beat round
the Point.

Mewing and scolding, the gulls floated higher in the
wind, and hearing them, the grey seal, who had been
lolling beyond the break of rollers, swam out twenty
yards and turned to watch the top of the cliff. She
knew that the tossing flight and the cries of *quoc-quoc-
quoac!* meant the presence of man.

Greymuzzle swam round the Long Rock with the
mat of roots in her mouth, and crawled out of the
sandy surge. Tarka was lying on his back, playing

with a smooth green flat pebble of glass that he had *Sandy*
carried from the bed of a pool. When he saw her, *Cove*
he turned on his pads—neither bone nor muscle
showed in action—and ran to see what she carried.
Greymuzzle lifted her burden out of his playful way,
but he jostled her, wanting to take it, and knowing
nothing of her purpose. He bit off three rootlets, and
at the mouth of the cave he ran back to his glass
pebble.

The seal watched with bleary eyes the man climbing
down, and his spaniel dog sitting three-quarters of
the way down the path, frightened to follow its
master farther. Tarka played with his pebble, hidden
behind the orange-lichened and towering wall of the
Long Rock. In a scattered and unled flock the gulls
drifted above the cliff. Over them Kronk the raven,
most powerful and black, cleaved the air on outspread
wings; sometimes he twirled on his back, recovering
immediately. He was practising the upward or
impaling lunge of beak that he had learned from his
father one hundred and thirteen years before. High
above the raven a small dark star twinkled and swept
in its orbit, twinkled and poised on its pitch.
Chakchek the One-eyed, slate-blue pinioned and
cream-breasted, was aloft. *Crr-crr*, said Kronk, as sea
and greensward turned up and over and upright
again. *Crr-crr-crr*, as the man disappeared round the
Long Rock, and Kronk sailed downwind to be over
him.

A thousand feet below the raven, Tarka tapped his
pebble of glass, green and dim as the light seen

Seal through the hollow waves rearing for their fall on the *Cavern* sand. The noise of waves, continuous and roaring on the rocks at low tide, was swelled by the echo beaten back by the cliff, and Tarka saw the man climbing round the Long Rock before he heard him. The man, jumping from boulder to boulder, did not see Tarka; but when he reached the sand he saw the trails of two otters. One trail led into the cave straitly, with regular five-toed prints, except where the track swerved from the impetuous and uneven trail of a galloping otter. Three rootlets of sea-thrift were dropped on the spurred sand. The strait trail led on; the other turned back to the wetted grey pebbles, where lay crab-shells, corks, fish-tails, and a piece of glass.

The man followed the strait tracks into the cave, into twilight, clambering over ice-cold rocks, and shining a light on the pools wherein drops glistened and struck loud in the stillness. He moved slowly, with glances over his shoulder at the diminishing circle of daylight. The roof of the cave was red and brown with the iron in the rock. Sometimes his foothold wobbled on a stone that in the motion of tides had worn a cup for itself. A hundred yards from its mouth the cave turned to the left, shutting darkness and sea-whispers together. The man went on, bending down to find his way by the light he carried. The pools became shallower, without life or weed; the roof lower and dry. A wailing cry ran along the walls. Holding the electric torch before him, he saw four pricks of light that moved, vanished, and

appeared again, one pair above the other. The wail *Seal*
went past him again, like the cry of a hungry infant. *Cavern*
On the grey boulder at his feet the wan light showed
a black mark, as of tar on bitten fish-bones—the
spraints of an otter.

In five minutes he had walked another fifty yards
into the cave. The pale yellow eyes shifted noiselessly
in front of him. The toe of his boot kicked something
that clattered on the stones, and looking down, he
saw a bone; and near it, other bones, skulls, and
shrunken hides. He picked up a jawbone, with
grinder teeth, cuspless and oblique, set along it.
Many seals had died in the cavern.

Again the wailing, not far away. The boulders
sloped upwards, and pressed one against another by
his feet, made a noise of *pob-pobble* that rang solidly
and echoed down the cave and up again. Before him
something white was stirring. Picking it up, he
stroked the soft, warm hair of a baby seal, putting his
finger in its mouth to stop the wailing. While he was
nursing it, he heard the hollow echo of a plunging
splash, a grumbling noise like *uch, uch!* and a slapping
as of the palms of great hands on flat rocks. Turning
his torch down into the gloom, he saw two dull red
orbs, and heard the angry bleat of a mother seal.

He carried the white calf to the inner wall of the
cave and laid it down; then hurried to the other wall,
where ledges formed natural steps. On the top ledge
an otter was crouching. By the shape of the head he
knew it was a bitch-otter; an old otter, with grey and
grizzled hairs on its muzzle. He climbed as high as he

Seal Cavern — Seal dared, and saw that it had made a couch of dry seaweed and grasses and thrift. He peered into the couch. The otter moved to and fro on the narrow ledge, tissing. He could see no cubs; nor did she appear to be in whelp.

Uch, uch! gasped the seal, exhausted and aching after her anguished journey over the boulders of the cavern. She had hurried by pressing the palms of her flippers on the ground and lifting her body forward by short jumps, moving fast as a walking man. She reached her cub and caressed it with her tongue, making sounds over it between sobbing and bleating. Then she turned her back to the man, and flung sand and pebbles at him with quick scooping strokes of her flippers. The man took from his pocket a wooden whistle, made from an elderberry stick, and played several soft notes upon it. The seal looked at him, enjoying the rude music. She lay still and happy with her calf, whose head was turned on one side as it sucked through the side of its mouth. The man played on, moving nearer to the seal. Slowly he bent down to stroke its head, and the seal licked his hand.

CHAPTER NINE

THE OTTERS WERE ALARMED BY THE COMING OF the man, and that night they left the headland, returning to the Burrows, and hunting rabbits in the great warren of the sandhills. A cold mist lay on the plains and in the hollows, riming the marram grasses and the withered stems of thistle and mullein, so that in the morning mildew and fungi in strange plant forms seemed to have grown out of the sand. On the coarser hairs of the otters' coats the hoar remained white, but on the shorter and softer hairs it melted into little balls of water. Everything except the otters and birds and bullocks was white. The sedges and reeds of the duckponds were white, so was the rigging of the ketches in the pill. The hoof-holes of cattle were filmed with brittle ice. In the cold windless air came distinct the quacking of ducks and the whistling of drakes as the wildfowl flighted from the ponds and saltings to the sea, where they slept by day.

The otters lay up near a cattle shippen, among reeds with white feathery tops. A dull red sun, without heat or rays, moved over them, sinking slowly down the sky. For two days and two nights the frosty vapour lay over the Burrows, and then came a north wind which poured like liquid glass from Exmoor and made all things distinct. The wind made whips of the dwarf willows, and hissed through clumps of the great sea-rushes. The spines of the marram grasses scratched wildly at the rushing air,

III

Ferny Hill which passed over the hollows where larks and linnets crouched with puffed feathers. Like a spirit freed by the sun's ruin and levelling all things before a new creation the wind drove grains of sand against the legs and ruffled feathers of the little birds, as though it would breathe annihilation upon them, strip their frail bones of skin and flesh, and grind them until they became again that which was before the earth's old travail. Vainly the sharp and hard points of the marram grasses drew their circles on the sand: the Icicle Spirit was coming, and no terrestrial power could exorcise it.

The north wind carried a strange thickset bird which drifted without feather sound over the dry bracken of Ferny Hill, where Tarka and Greymuzzle had gone for warmth. Its plumage was white barred and spotted with dark brown. Its fierce eyes were ringed with yellow, the colour of the lichens on the stone shippens. Mile after mile its soft and silent wings had carried it, from a frozen land where the Northern Lights stared in stark perpetuity upon the ice-fields. The thickset bird was an Arctic Owl, and its name was Bubu, which means Terrible. It quartered the mires and the burrows, and the gripe of its feathered feet was death to many ducks and rabbits.

Clouds moved over land and sea with the heavy grey drifting silence of the ice-owl's flight; night came starless, loud with the wind's rue in the telegraph wires on the sea-wall. As Tarka and his mate were running down to meet the flood-tide in the pill, a baying broke out in the sky; whiskered heads lifted *Horsey* fixed to harken. For a minute the otters did not move, *Marsh* while the hound-like baying passed over. The long skein of south-wending geese swung round into the wind, flying with slow flaps and forming a chevron that glided on down-held, hollow wings beyond the pill-mouth. Cries of golden plover, twined in the liquid bubble-link of the curlews' chain-songs, rose up from the saltings.

The white-fronted geese, eaters of grass and clover, had come before the blizzard howling its way from the North Star. A fine powdery snow whirled out of the sky at night, that lay nowhere, but raced over the mossy plains and hillocks, and in the burrows, faster than the grains of sand. Tree, dune, shippen, and dyke—all were hid in whirling white chaos at daylight. The next day thicker snowflakes fell, and out of the storm dropped a bird with white wings, immensely swift in flight, whose talon-stroke knocked off the head of a goose. It stood on the slain, holding by the black sickle-claws of its yellow feet; its hooked beak tore breast-bone and flesh together. Its plumage was brown-spotted like the plumage of Bubu—the hue of snow and fog. Every feather was taut and cut for the swiftest stoop in the thin airs of its polar ranging. Its full brown eyes glanced proudly as any Chakchek, for it was a Greenland falcon.

Beyond the shaped and ever-shifting heaps of sand, beyond the ragged horizon of the purple-grey sea, the sun sunk as though it were spent in space, a dwarf-red star quenching in its own steam of decay. The

Greenland falcon with wildfowl.

snow fled in the wind, over the empty shells of snails *Heanton* and rabbit skeletons lying bare and scattered, past *Marsh* the white, sand-stripped branches of dead elder-berry trees, and the dust of them aided an older dust to wear away the living tissue of the Burrows. Night was like day, for neither moon nor sun nor star was seen. Then the blizzard passed, and the snow lay in its still pallor under the sky.

And the sky was to the stars again—by day six black stars and one greater whitish star, hanging aloft the Burrows, flickering at their pitches; six peregrines and one Greenland falcon. A dark speck falling, the *whish* of the grand stoop from two thousand feet heard half a mile away; red drops on a drift of snow. By night the great stars flickered as with falcon wings, the watchful and glittering hosts of creation. The moon arose in its orbit, white and cold, awaiting through the ages the swoop of a new sun, the shock of starry talons to shatter the Icicle Spirit in a rain of fire. In the south strode Orion the Hunter, with Sirius the Dogstar baying green fire at his heels. At midnight Hunter and Hound were rushing bright in a glacial wind, hunting the false star-dwarfs of burnt-out suns, who had turned back into Darkness again.

Old Nog the heron, flying over the Ram's-horn Pond, saw Greymuzzle among the reeds, for she was the only dark thing in the white wilderness below. She was hiding a solitary cub by curling herself

Ram's- round it, so that her chin rested on her flank. During
horn the storm she had not left the couch of bitten reed
Pond and floss; the heat of her body melted the snowflakes.
For two days and a night she kept the snow from the
blind cub; and when the air was clear, a black frost
gripped the waters of the ponds, bound the drifts,
and hung icicles from drain and culvert. Then
Greymuzzle arose, and called to Tarka over the
ice. He answered from the northern horn of the
pond.

He had kept a fishing hole in the ice, which he bit
free as it froze. Fish were hard to see, for the top of the
water under the ice was a bad reflector of light to
the lower water. As it grew colder, the fish buried
themselves in the mud, and when Greymuzzle roved
in the brown dim water, she saw only her own vague
image following her above. More wildfowl flighted
to the estuary and the cries of birds when the tide
was flowing and covering the sandbanks were myriad
as the gold flickerings in the night sky. The otters
crossed the swift waters to the sandbanks where they
were feeding, swimming under the waves and rising
to breathe with only their wide nostrils above.
Greymuzzle swam up under a duck and seized it,
and the change of note in the quacking was heard
by the birds, who threw the alarm over the estuary.
Thousands of wings whipped jets on the water. The
wildfowler creeping up in his narrow boat pulled the
trigger of his gun too late—a long red flame sent a
blast of shot swishing over the head of Greymuzzle
as she dived. She swam to the mouth of the pill with

the duck in her jaws, and ate it on an icy litter of *The* twigs and seaweed left by the last high tide. *Great*

The next night the fishing hole was sealed, and no *Plain* longer marked by a ring of scales and bones, for the rats and crows had eaten them. Greymuzzle was scraping at a fish frozen in the ice when the sheet whanged and whined and creaked, then *boom!*, a crack ran across it, and water spirted in the fissure. When it was still, Orion was reflected there, with the red and green flashes of Sirius; but as Greymuzzle peered the starshine glazed, and mock-trees of the Icicle Spirit grew on the water.

The cold sharpened. To the estuary came sanderlings in white winter dress, who ran at the tide-line like blown sea-foam. Snow buntings followed, and went south with them. The flat-fish swam to warmer water beyond the bar, and often when the otters dived in the estuary they rose empty-mouthed to the surface, except perhaps for a green crab. Old Nog the heron grew so thin that he looked like a bundle of grey flags stripped by wind and clinging to two reeds. His inland fishing ponds were frozen, most of the streams ran under plates of ice, and the only food he could spear was to be found at low tide in the pools of the Shrarshook Ridge, where gravel had been dug.

The pans and plains of the Burrows were crossed by a thousand tracks, the prints of larks, finches, wagtails, crows, and gulls; the presses of weasels, rabbits, and stoats; the pads of badgers and foxes; the triple toes of herons and bitterns, like the veining

Black- of leaves. Many of the smaller birds were so weak
stone they could not fly, and their bodies were eaten by
Sands rats and weasels, which were eaten by the larger
owls and hawks.

Other otters from the Two Rivers came down to the
estuary, some of them cubs of ten or twelve pounds
in weight, who had kept together with their mothers.
Families of three and four and one of five—a bitch
and four cubs from the boggy moorland hill where
the Two Rivers began in the peat—came to the
duckpond along the otter path from the saltings, and
finding it frozen, went down the pill and out to the
coast. Tarka met White-tip with her mate by an
overturned hulk one night; she was scratching at
the webmark of a widgeon, frozen in the mud with
its scent. One look, and they had passed in the darkness.

Many of the dog-otters wandered solitary. Last of
all, slow and fatigued, after weeks of hunger, came
Marland Jimmy, the old dog with the split ear who
had played the funnel-game with Tarka's mother in
the deep clay pit. He limped along the otter-path,
which many pads had pressed into ice; the cysts
between his toes, inflamed by paraffin, were raw
and frostbitten. The tide was ebbing when he crawled
over the white sea-wall, and down the dark and
hard mud to the water, crackling the brittle ice-
forms of the glasswort. Hearing a whistle across the
pill, Marland Jimmy walked into the water and
swam. He kicked slowly, and the current carried
him aslant, amid plates of ice broken off by the last

tide. The trickles in the mud channers and salting *Branton* guts had already ceased. So black and bitter the *Pill* night that not even the whippering cries of golden plover were heard in the pill. The water ebbed in a blank silence of fixed star-points. Marland Jimmy swam across the pill and crawled out steaming. His breath froze on his muzzle, and his rudder was pointed with an icicle when he reached Tarka, a hundred yards along the bank. Tarka was rubbing his head and the side of his neck against a fish longer than himself, with gaps in its dull-shining length. A week before, Jarrk the seal had chased it over the bar, and as it turned past his head, he had taken a bite out of its belly. The dying salmon drifted with the tides until Greymuzzle and Tarka caught it in the pill. What a feast they had had! As soon as they had carried it steaming out of the sea, ice crystals had glittered on the scales.

Tarka rolled on the crisp snow while the aged otter tore at the fish, breaking off bone and frozen pink flesh. He moved from gills to tail, from tail to gills again gulping icy mouthfuls, wheezing with hard swallowing, and when he had breath, yikkering at Tarka to keep away. Tarka, warmed by his fullness, rolled and rolled, until he rolled into the water. *Hu-ee-ee-ic!* whistled Tarka.

The split-eared dog had gorged himself when Greymuzzle returned for another meal. He quaddled down the hard mud to where Tarka was sliding into the water. With a heavy rippling of his body, he ran to the top of the slide, and holding his legs rigid,

Branton slipped down on his ruined feet into the water. *Pill* Greymuzzle heard the happy whistles of the playing dogs, and slid with them until she heard the squeals of rats fighting by the broken carcass of the salmon. The noise made her remember her cub, for rats had squealed among the scrikkits of bones and scales around Tarka's fishing hole during the snowstorm. Tarka played on until he was hungry, when he went back to the salmon. Marland Jimmy played alone at the slide.

The ebb-tide moved along the sea-weedy perches stuck in the mud to mark the fairway. A mist was rising like steam from the top of the water, which moved slower with its weight of surface slush. The slush became clotted, and hardened, and suddenly ceased to move. The star-points dulled. Orion was stripped of his flashing, the green tongue of Sirius was mute, the Swan lost her lustre, the glare of the Bull faded.

Kack! croaked Old Nog, flapping up from the fish carcass as a fox slunk down to it. The tips of his open beak were red with the frozen blood of a speared rat, which was sticking in his gullet. In swaying flight, reed-like legs hanging with weakness, the heron set off for the gravel pools of the Shrarshook. *Kack!* he called to his mate, who was standing in the ebb to her knees, fifty yards beyond the slide. She did not move; nor did the tide.

Krark! called Old Nog at dawn, flying over the pill, and calling his mate again. *Hu-ee-ee-ic!* whistled Tarka to Marland Jimmy, who had not answered since the star-points had suddenly dimmed and *Branton* vanished off the water. *Hu-ee-ee-ic!*—a thin, hard cry *Pill* which Greymuzzle heard among the reeds of the duckpond. *Hu-ee-ee-ic!* travelling through the ice-blink in the pill, and out across the estuary.

Bubu stared down at Tarka walking over to the eastern sea-wall; fanned above him before beating away. The Arctic Owl perched fifty yards below Tarka's slide on something that swayed and creaked to its weight, but bore it upright. Staring around with several complete turns of its head, Bubu fixed orange-rimmed eyes on a mask set stiff before and below it. There was no movement; there was no life. The owl stared round again, and flew away, leaving its narrow perch swaying on reed-like legs, as though nodding to the head of Marland Jimmy gazing film-eyed out of the ice.

CHAPTER TEN

THE LITTLE THIN CUB, ON ITS COUCH AMONG THE reeds frozen and bent like the legs of dead spiders, greeted Greymuzzle with husky mewing whenever it heard her coming, and would not be comforted by tongue caresses. Frost had stricken its eyes. Greymuzzle prowled all day and all night when she was not warming and suckling her cub; and although she was so hungry, she still played with Tarka, sliding headfirst down a snowy hillock. They had to travel to the estuary for food, for every incoming tide piled up its floating floes at the pillmouth, with grinding shrieks and shuddering booms that sounded far over the Burrows. At low tide the frost welded them in a high and solid barrier.

Both otters had blistered their tongues by licking ice, and to ease their thirst, they rasped them against snow on the sea-wall in the middle of the day. Greymuzzle went into the village one night searching the gardens for food. She found the duckhouse under the chestnut tree in the farmyard above the bridge, and although she sought an entrance for more than an hour, she found none. The smell of the ducks was painful.

A fox slunk near her, passing with drooping brush and ears laid back, pad, pad, pad, in the snow.

Unable to get the ducks, she walked down the frozen pill to the estuary, meeting Tarka at the pillmouth, near the salmon-fishers' hut built on the shillet slope of the sea-wall. The fox followed her, hoping to get another meal of salmon. He followed *The* her until the dawn, and was near her at sunrise, *Shrars-* when she returned to the couch in the reeds of the *hook* duckpond. She winded him and ran him, and although he was chased by the marshman's dog when she had left off pursuit, the fox returned, knowing that she had young somewhere in the reeds. His name was Fang-over-lip, and he had wandered far in his hunger.

While the pallor of day was fading off the snow a skein of great white birds, flying with arched wings and long stretched necks, appeared with a measured beat of pinions from the north and west. *Hompa, hompa, hompa,* high in the cold air. Greymuzzle and Tarka were eating seaweed and shellfish on the Shrarshook, but when the swans splashed into the estuary, they slipped into the tideway and drifted with the flow to where the wild swans were floating. Fang-over-lip licked out some of the mussel shells they had dived for, and cracked up a crab's claws, before following along the beach.

The beams of the lighthouse spread like the wings of a star-fly above the level and sombre sands. Across the dark ridge of the Shrarshook a crooked line of lamps winked below the hill. In one of the taverns a sailor was singing a shanty, the tune of which came distinctly over the Pool. The swans moved up with the tide, the otters after them. They were thin and weak; for mussels, winkles, and sometimes a sour green crab were poor nourishment for an otter who, in careless times, had eaten a three-

Wild Swans off the Crow Neck, with White House in background.

pound sea-trout at a sitting and been hungry two *The* hours afterwards. *Crow*

The tide beyond the tail of the Shrarshook was divided by a string of froth made by the leap and chop of waters beginning to move north and south, along the arms of the sea stretching to the Two Rivers. The swans turned north, borne by the tide racing past Crow Island. They paddled out of the main flow, and turning head to tide, began to feed in the shallow over a sandbank. The otters drifted nearer, only their wide nostrils above water. When they were ten yards away from the nearest swan the nostrils sank, and chains of bubbles rose unseen above them. A swan saw a dark form under the water, but before it could lift out its head, Tarka had bitten on to its neck. Heavily its wings beat the water. Every curlew on the sandbank cried in a long uprising whistle, *cu-u-ur-leek, cur-r-r-leek!*, and the alarm flew up and down the estuary as fast as sound travelled. The treble whistle of the redshank was piped from shore to shore, the ring-plover sped over the water, turning and wheeling as one bird. Old Nog cried *Kra-r-rk!* Wind from the swans' wings scalloped the water and scattered the spray, and one struck Tarka a blow that made him float slowly away. But Greymuzzle hung to the swan's foot, even when her rudder was nearly out of the water as she was dragged along. The swan trumpeted afar its anger and fear. Bubu the Terrible flew towards the sound.

Before the Arctic Owl arrived Tarka was un-dazed and swimming to help his mate. Seeing and hearing

White the struggle, Bubu stretched his toes, opened his
House beak, and gave a loud and terrifying hoot; but when
Shingle he reached the conflict, fanning above like a shade
of chaos, there was nothing to see save only feathers
and bubbles. Silent as snow and fog, staring like the
Northern Lights, taloned like black frost, the
Arctic Owl flew over the Shrarshook and dropped
upon Fang-over-lip, but the snarl and the snap of
teeth drove him up again.

Across the pull of the tide, among the grating ice-
floes, the otters took the swan, whose flappings were
getting feeble as the death-fear grew less. Tarka had
bitten the artery in the neck. When the otters rested
the bird lay quiet on the water. It heard the wings
of its brethren beating out the flying song of swans,
Hompa, hompa, hompa, high and remote in the night.
It flapped thrice and died.

Tarka and Greymuzzle swam with the swan to the
shore, where they bit into the throat and closed their
eyes as they drank its hot blood. Soon mouthfuls of
feathers were being torn away but before they could
eat its flesh Fang-over-lip crept upon them. He, too,
was famished, having eaten only a mouse that night
—and that small biter of willow bark was but fur and
bone. With the boldness of starvation the fox rushed
upon them. The snarling brought a boar badger,
who had been digging for the roots of sea-beet in the
crevices of the stones of the sea-wall. The boar
lumbered down the slope, over the seaweed, and
across the shingle to where Fang-over-lip, with
fluffed-out brush and humped back, was threatening

the otters. The badger, who was called Bloody Bill *Ram's-*Brock by certain badger-digging publicans, had never *horn* before been so hungry. For two days the walls of his *Pond* belly had been flat. He had no fear of any animal. The otters bit his hide, but could not hurt him, as under the long grey tapered hairs his skin was nearly half an inch thick. Pushing them away and grunting he seized the swan in his jaws and dragged it away. He dropped it again to bite Greymuzzle; and then he stood absolutely still, except for his nose. Fang-over-lip did not move, nor did Greymuzzle, nor Tarka. Their heads were turned towards the cottage looming white on the sea-wall. A door had opened and closed.

The marshman had with him two bob-tailed cattle dogs, which rushed on the shingle. They found a circle of feathers. Downwind the wave-worn shells tinkled as though a wind had risen off the sea and was running over the beach towards the tarred wooden hospital ship. This was the sound of the fox's departure. Bloody Bill Brock was slower and clumsier, and his black bear-claws slipped on the boulders of the sea-wall's apron. Tarka and Grey-muzzle were lying in three feet of water, with only their ears and nostrils showing. They heard the pursuit of the badger, and some moments later the hoarse voice of a man. One dog yelped, two dogs yelped, and both returned to their master on three legs, while the thick-skinned badger continued his way with the swan on four sound legs.

Some hours later all of the swan, except the larger bones, feet, wings, and bill, was inside Bloody Bill

The Brock, who was snoring inside a sandy rabbit-bury,
Great where he slept for three days and nights.
Field Greymuzzle returned to the duckpond with only
seaweed and shellfish to nourish herself and her
cub. Unsteadily it dragged its little body towards her,
and opened its mouth to greet her. No sound came
from its mouth. Its legs trembled and could not carry
its head which hung over the couch of weeds. Its paws
were frost-bitten, its eye-sockets empty. Greymuzzle
stared at it, before lying down and giving the shelter
of her body. She spoke to it and took it in her paws
and licked its face, which was her only way of telling
her love. The cub tottered away, and sought the
milk which it could not find. Afterwards it slept,
until she left again to seek food in the wide daylight,
following the slot of deer across the snow. The hind,
which had come down from the high ground with a
herd and wandered away with her calf that had been
with her since its birth the previous May, caught the
scent of the otter and ran away, the calf beside her.
The otter followed, but turned away when she saw
a small bird crouching on the snow, unable to fly
further. She ate the fire-crested wren—a thimbleful
of skin, bone, and feather. After a vain prowl round
the garden of the marshman, she returned to the
duckpond, crossing the pill three hundred yards
below the place where men were breaking up, for
firewood, the hulk of an old dismasted ketch. In the
field she picked up the skull of a sheep and carried
it a few yards before dropping it. She had picked it
up and dropped it many times already.

The ice-talons set harder in the land. No twitter *Branton* of finch or linnet was heard on the Burrows, for those which remained were dead. Vainly the linnets had sought the seeds locked in the plants of the glasswort. Even crows died of starvation. The only noises in the frore air were of saws and axes and hammers, men's voices, the glassy sweep of wind in the blackened thistles, the cries of lambs and ewes, ravens' croaking, and the dull mumble of breakers on the bar.

Every day on the Burrows was a period of silence under a vapour-ringed sun that slid into night glowing and quivering with the zones and pillars of the Northern Lights. More wild red deer from Exmoor strayed to the Great Field, which even the rats had quitted. The deer walked into the gardens of the village, some to be shot stealthily, others to sleep into death. The shepherd of the marsh-grazing stamped at night round his fire, clad in the skins of sheep, and swinging his arms. Beyond the straw-and-sack-stuffed hurdles, foxes, badgers, and stoats slunk and prowled and fought for each other's bodies. Over the lambs in the fold flew Kronk the raven, black and croaking in the moonlight. *Ck!* cried Old Nog, tottering to the Shrarshook from the sandhills, where he hid shivering during the time of high-tides. The wind whined in the skeleton of his mate broken at the knees, near the skull of Marland Jimmy gaping at the crown, eyeless and showing its teeth in ice.

When two foxes and a badger had been shot,

Caen Greymuzzle went no more where ewes pared hollow
Farm the frozen turnips and suckled peacefully their
tail-wriggling lambs. One night, raving with hunger,
she returned to the wooden duck-shed in the farmyard by the railway station. High over the shed rose
the chestnut tree, black and bare and suffering,
with one of its boughs splitten by frost. Other
creatures had been to the duckhouse before her.

Fang-over-lip had started to dig a hole under the
rotten floorboards, but returning the night after, he
had smelt that during the day the hole had been
deepened and a gin tilled there to catch him by the
paw. When he had gone Bloody Bill Brock had
grunted to the duckshed and, putting head between
paws, had rolled on the metal tongue holding the
jaws apart. The gin had clacked harmlessly against
his grey hairs. The badger had scratched farther
down and up again, reaching the floorboards by
daylight; and departed, to return in the next darkness and to see a gin lying there with jaws as wide as
his back—a gin unhidden and daring him, as it were,
to roll across it. The gin's rusty jaws were open in
an iron leer, its tongue sweated the scent of man's
hand. Bloody Bill Brock, who had sprung many
gins in his life, grunted and went away.

There were no stars that night, for clouds loured in
the sky. As Greymuzzle walked on the ice upstream,
snow began to fall in flakes like the breast-feathers
of swans. From the estuary the scrambling cries of
thousands of gulls, which had returned with the
south-west wind, came indistinctly through the thick

and misty air. The South was invading the North, *Caen* and a gentle wind was its herald. The dreadful hoot *Farm* of Bubu was heard no more, for the Arctic Owl had already left the Burrows.

Greymuzzle walked under the bridge, and smelling the ducks, climbed up the bank. As she was walking past the beehives, she heard a sound that made her stop and gasp—the *ic-clack!* of a sprung gin. Tarka was rolling and twisting and jerking the heavy gin and chain off the ground. It held him. He lay still, his heart throbbing, blowing and tissing and slavering. The sight closed Greymuzzle's nostrils, so that she breathed through her open mouth. She called to him. The gin clanked, the chain clinked. She ran round him until Tarka's leaps, that wrenched the sinews of his leg, ceased in weakness, and he sank across the long rusty spring, blowing bubbles of blood out of his nostrils. A duck quacked loudly, and when its strident alarm was finished, the air held only the slight sounds of snowflakes sinking on the roof of the shed. They floated to rest on Tarka's fur, gently, and shrunk into drops of water. The chestnut tree suddenly groaned, and the corpse of a sparrow frozen for weeks to one of its twigs fell to the earth. It dropped beside Greymuzzle, and was flicked against the duckshed by a swish of her rudder as she stood over Tarka, gnawing in a fury the iron jaws of the gin.

Far away in the estuary gulls were running on the sandbanks through the yellow froth of wavelet-lap. Their jubilant and sustained cries told the winter's

Caen Farmyard.

end. Under the tree Greymuzzle rasped the bone of *Caen* the trapped paw with the sharp stumps of her broken *Farm* teeth. A rat passed near, brought by the smell of blood; it fled when it saw whose blood was wasting. Greymuzzle's face was torn, but Tarka did not know that he had bitten her.

She bit through the sinews, which were strong and thick, and Tarka was free. He rushed to the river. Greymuzzle remained, remembering her cub.

When the ducks heard the gnawing of wood, they began to run round inside the shed, quacking continuously. In the farmyard a dog in its kennel was barking loudly. There was an answering shout in the house that set the animal jumping against its chain. Both Greymuzzle and Tarka knew the sequence of barking dog and the shout of a man in a house! Greymuzzle stayed until the farm door opened, and then she ran away, splinters of wood in her bleeding mouth.

When the farmer came to the shed with his gun and lantern, he found his gin sprung and three toes of a paw lying in a red spatter about it. Seeing dots of blood leading away over the snow, he hurried to the cottage of one of his labourers and knocked on the door. He shouted, "I've got'n," as his father had shouted in the church door during a sermon half a century before, calling the men to leave and pursue the tracks of a fox through the snow.

The labourer and his two sons put on their boots warming on the slate hearth, and went out to the farmer. Armed with a dung-fork, the handle of a

Scur pickaxe, a ferreting crowbar, and the gun, they set
Farmyard out on the trail of the wounded otter. The lantern
showed the red dots leading over the railway crossing,
and on the snow by the station yard. "Come on,
you!" cried the farmer to three men going home
after the closing of the inn. It was ten o'clock. One
had a staff, and the others kicked up what stones they
could see.

The collie dog found the otters for them, in a shed
where Tarka had crawled for a refuge. Tarka stood
back in a corner on a heap of artificial manure sacks,
while Greymuzzle ran at the dog, tissing, and snapping her broken teeth. The lantern light made of her
eyes two tawny orbs of menace. Tarka found a hole
in the wall, while Greymuzzle fought the collie.
Weakened by starvation, she was not able to fight for
long, and as the farmer said afterwards, it was not
even necessary to waste a cartridge, when a dung-
fork could pin her down and a ferreting bar break
her head.

They carried the body back to the farm, where the
farmer drew a pint of ale for each of his helpers from
the XXXX barrel in the cellar. While they were
drinking "Best respects, Varmer," the collie dog
began to bark, and as it would not stop after several
cries of "Shut that rattle, you," the farmer went out
and gave it a kick in the ribs. The collie yelped and
went to kennel, but hardly had the farmer gone into
his kitchen again when it set up a furious barking.
It was banged on the head with the stag's horn
handle of a hunting whip, but even this did not

check its desire to tell its master that an enemy was *Branton* in the yard. It kept up an intermittent barking until *Marsh* the dawn, when it was flogged with its head wedged in the door. The farmer was a poor man and not very strong, and a sleepless night made him irritable. When he felt better he gave the dog the skinned carcass of the otter, and praised its courage and virtue in the Railway Inn, telling how it had warned him and how it had tracked the "girt mousey-coloured fitches" to the shed, where one escaped through a hole behind the sacks. He forebore to say how noisy his dog had been afterwards, deeming this a point not in its favour, for how was he, his natural senses dulled by civilization, to have known that an otter had remained all night in the farm-yard, waiting for the mate that never came.

Tarka was gone in the mist and rain of the day, to hide among the reeds of the marsh pond—the sere and icicled reeds, which now could sink to their ancestral ooze and sleep, perchance to dream;—of sun-stored summers raising the green stems, of wind-shaken anthers dropping gold pollen over June's young maces, of seeds shaped and clasped and taught by the brown autumn mother. The south wind was breaking from the great roots the talons of the Icicle Spirit, and freeing ten thousand flying seeds in each brown head.

Water covered the pond ice, deep enough to sail a feather, and at night every hoof-hole held its star.

After seven sunrisings the mosses were green on the

The hillocks, lapwings tumbled and dived and cried
ebb-tide their sweet mating cries, the first flower bloomed in
the Burrows—the lowly vernal whitlow grass, with
its tiny white petals on a single leafless stalk. Under
the noon sun sheep grazing in the marsh had silver
outlines. Linnets sat on the lighthouse telegraph wire,
wing to wing, and talking to the sky. Out of the
auburn breasts fell ravishing notes, like glowing
strokes of colour in the warm south wind.

And when the shining twitter ceased, I walked to
the pond, and again I sought among the reeds, in
vain; and to the pill I went, over the guts in the salt
grey turf, to the trickling mud where the linnets were
fluttering at the seeds of the glass-wort. There I
spurred an otter, but the tracks were old with tides,
and worm castings sat in many. Every fourth seal was
marred, with two toes set deeper in the mud.
They led down to the lap of the low water,
where the sea washed them away.

THE LAST YEAR

CHAPTER ELEVEN

BOGS AND HUMMOCKS OF THE GREAT KNEESET were dimmed and occluded; the hill was higher than the clouds. In drifts and hollows of silence the vapour passed, moving with the muffled wind over water plashes colourless in reflection. Sometimes a colder waft brought the sound of slow trickling; here in the fen five rivers began, in peat darker than the otter that had followed one up to its source.

Broken humps, rounded with grey moss and standing out of a maze of channers, made the southern crest of the hill. In the main channer, below banks of crumbling peat, lay water dark-stained and almost stagnant. The otter walked out and lifted his head, sniffing and looking around him. Drops from his rudder dripped into the water and the stirred fragments of peat drifted slowly as they settled. The river's life began without sound, in the darkness of peat that was heather grown in ancient sunlight; but on the slope of the hill, among the green rushes, the river ran bright in spirit, finding the granite that made its first song.

Tarka climbed up one of the humps of grey club moss and trod in its centre a bed soft and warm, yet cool for the paw thrust among the long, tight-growing fronds. The moss grew on and over a bush of heather, whose springy stems yielded to his curled body. He had travelled from the estuary, sleeping by day in riverside holts and marshes and feeding at night; remembering nothing, because the moor was

Cran- unfamiliar to his nose and ears and eyes. When his
mere paw ached, he licked it. It had been a happy journey
up the river swollen with snow water, hunting fish
and playing with sticks and stones, while mating owls
called through the darkness of valleys.

He slept curled in the moss until the last sun-
whitened wisps of clouds trailed away into space
above the northern slope of the hill, and the plashes
took light and colour. The sun awoke him and he
heard the twit of a bird—a little drab pipit alone in
the fen with the otter. It watched anxiously as the
otter warmed the dingy, yellow-white fur of his belly
in the sun and rolled to scratch his ears with a sprig
of heather. The pipit had seen no enemy like Tarka
before, and when the rolling otter fell off his bed and
splashed into the water below, the bird flew out of
the heather in straight upward flight, twittering as
it dropped, fluttering wings that seemed too feeble to
carry it higher than its first weak ascent. Up it
mounted, to fall back again, until it turned with the
wind and slanted down quickly into the heather.
Again the wilderness was to wandering air and water,
until webbed feet began to patter in the black soft
peat, past wan yellow tussocks of withered grasses,
and clumps of rushes dying downwards from their
brown tips.

Running in the plashes, treading the spider-like
tufts of red-rusty cotton grass, he came to a deeper
and wider channer fringed with rushes. Down a
crumbling sog of peat and into the still brown-clear
water. He swam its winding length, seeking eels under

140

the ooze which arose behind him in a swirl of heath *Cran*-fragments, dark and up-scattered by the kicks of his *mere* hindlegs. A minute's swimming and the channer widened into a shallow pit above whose broken banks the heather grew, on sprigs dispread and blasted under the sky. Some still bore the bells of old summer, that made a fine sibilance in the wry wind-music of the moor.

Tarka ran past a heap of turves, set around the base of a post marking Cranmere tarn, now empty, whither his ancestors had wandered for thousands of years. A fox had been walking there during the night, seeking the oval black beetles which, with moths, pipits, wheatears, and sometimes a snipe, were the only food it found in and around the fen. As Tarka ran out of the tarn a bird passed swiftly over his head gliding on down-curving dark wings and crying *go-beck, go-beck, go-beck!* when it saw him—one of the few grouse which lived and bred on the lower slopes under the wind. The bird had flown from a hut circle to the south, where seeds of gromwell were to be found. The gromwell had grown from a single seed carried from the lower tilled slopes of the moor on the fleece of a sheep, to which it had hooked itself. Gromwell seeds were the favourite food of the grouse around the source of the Two Rivers.

Tarka watched the bird until it glided below the hill, when he ran on again, finding nothing in the plashes moving only with images of sky and clouds and birds of solitude. Then the sun took the water, breaking brilliant and hot in every plash; the otter

Taw Head galloped with instant joy and sank in bog to his belly. He dragged himself on to a tussock of grass, rolled, shook himself, and set off again, roaming around the fen until he heard again the cry of running water. The cry came out of a hollow, whose sides were scarred by the sliding of broken hummocks —the faint cry of a river new-born. Through a winding channel in the turf, no wider than the otter and hidden by grasses growing over it, the little thread hastened, seeking its valley to the sea.

It fell over its first cascade and cast its first bubbles; and through a groove between hills it found a marsh where a green moss grew with rushes. Beyond the marsh, it ran strong and bright over its bed of granite gravel, everywhere glinting and singing. Over and under and past boulders of granite, splashing upon mosses whose browny-red seeds on the tall stalks were like bitterns standing with beaks upheld. Lichens grew on other boulders: silver with black undersides, and curled like strange pelts curing: grey-green in the shapes of trees and plants: bones with scarlet knuckles: horns of moose: shells and seaweeds. The lichens fastened to the granite were as the fantastic and brittle miniatures of strange and forgotten things of the moor.

By pools and waterfalls and rillets the river Taw grew, flowing under steep hills that towered high above. It washed the roots of its first tree, a willow thin and sparse of bloom, a soft tree wildered in that place of rocks and rain and harsh grey harrying winds. A black-faced sheep stood by the tree, crop-ping the sweet grass; and when a strange, small, *Ockside* flashing, frightening head looked out just below its *Hill* feet, the sheep stamped and bounded away up the hill to its lamb asleep by a sun-hot boulder. Tarka had caught a trout, the first in a mile of river; he ate it, drank, and slipped away with the water.

He caught sixteen fish in an hour, the biggest being three ounces in weight; and then he climbed upon a slab of granite and dozed in the sunlight. High above him a small bird was flying in sharp, irregular flight, mounting high to swoop towards the marsh. Every time it swooped it opened its tail against the rush of air, so that the feathers made a sound between the bleat of a kid and a dove's cooing. Its mate was flying near it. They were snipes, who had chosen for nesting-place a rush-clump in the marsh, and Tarka had disturbed them. He lay still in sleep, and they forgot that he was there, and flew down to find worms by pushing their long bills into the juggymire. When the sun sank behind the high tors, Tarka awoke and went down with the river. A small bullock, with long, black, shaggy hair, was drinking by a gravelly ford, and smelling the otter, it snorted and plunged away, alarming the grazing herd.

At night the stars were shorn of their flashes and burning dully through the cold vapour which drifted down from the hills. Everything was moistened— sprigs and faded bells of heather, young ruddy shoots of whortleberry, mosses, lichens, grasses, rushes, boulders, trees. The day rose grey and silent. When the sun, like an immense dandelion, looked over the light-smitten height of Cosdon Beacon, Tarka was returning along a lynch, or rough trackway, to the river. The grasses, the heather, the lichens, the whortleberry bushes, the mosses, the boulders— everything in front of the otter vanished as though drowned or dissolved in a luminous strange sea. The icy casings of leaves and grasses and blades and sprigs were glowing and hid in a mist of sun-fire. Moorfolk call this morning glory the Ammil.

The brimming light gladdened Tarka, and he rolled for several minutes, playing with a shining ball he found in the grass—the old dropping of a wild pony. Afterwards, running down to the water, he found a holt under a rock. It was cold and wet inside, and Tarka always slept dry when he could. He ran out again, liking the sun, and settled on a flat rock in the warming rays.

The rock was embedded below a fall, its lower part green with mosses hanging in the splashes. The mosses dripped and glistened. Tarka washed himself, the water-sounds unheard; he would have heard silence if the river had dried suddenly. The green weeds waved in the clear water with a calmer motion than the tail-fanning of idle fish. And then a sturdy, dark brown bird, with white throat and breast, lit on a stone down the stream, and pausing a moment, jumped down into the water. The dipper walked on the river bed, seeking beetles and shrimps and caddis-grubs. When its beak was crammed, it walked out of a shallow, flew up in a coloured rain of drops, and following the turns of the river, checked fluttering by

River Taw about three miles below Cranmere.

Watchet the rock whereon Tarka lay. It thrust its beak into
Hill the moss, six inches above the tumbling water. Rapid
notes, as of water-and-stones sharpened to music in a
singing bird's throat-strings, came out of the moss, a
greeting by the dipper's mate, who was brooding on
five white eggs in her wet nest. When she had swallowed the food, the water-ousel flew away upstream,
low over the water, following the bends of the river.
As he flew he sang, sipping his song from the stones
and the water.

The shadows moved, and the bright green weeds
of morning waved darkly in the river. Many times
the water-ousels flew to and from the nest, but they
did not see Tarka, he slept so still in the rocky cup
above them.

Tarka gave chase to a rabbit during the next night,
bolting it from a hillside clitter of rocks in a hollow
at the head of a cleave. Near the clitter a tall stone
reared head, shoulders, and body above the rocks
embedded there, in the outline of a sea-lion, smooth
and curved. The rabbit ran as far as a hole in the
north-western base of the stone sea-lion, but turned
back in terror as it smelt the dreaded smell of a fitch,
or stoat. The rabbit's wits went from it in a thin
squealing; its will to run away was gripped in the
base of its spine by a feeling of sickly fascination. Its
squeals caused an excited chakkering near it, and
almost immediately the fitch had it by the side of the
neck, and was dragging it into the hole. The fitch,
whose name was Swagdagger, was about to kill it
when Tarka ran through the opening. Swagdagger

146

loosened his bite to threaten the strange big invader, *Seal*
flicking his black-tipped tail and glaring at Tarka. *Stone*
One kick of the rabbit's hindlegs, so powerful for
running, could have broken Swagdagger's neck; but
it crouched still, its nervous force oozing away. Tarka
ran at it. Swagdagger faced him with an angry
chakker, and was nipped in the shoulder. The fitch
ran out through the opening, but turned outside and
gibbered in fury. Tarka looked once at the green
points that were the fitch's eyes, and went on with
his work. Swagdagger went away, to climb a granite
stone, and chakker into the night. The moon was
rising, dim in the mist, and the harsh notes echoed
about the grey stillness of the granite clitter. *Kak-h'*
kak-kak, he rattled, throwing his call one way, then
another. He was summoning the stoats of Belstone
Cleave.

Tarka had eaten half the rabbit when a strong
scent made him look round again. He saw in the low
opening several greenish dots, that stared and swung
about and stared again. He went on eating. Delicate
sniffs, sudden rustles and paddings, scratchings, a
quick sneeze—he peered for another way out,
wanting to be alone. He found a crack and explored
it with his nose, before beginning to scrape. He sucked
in the scent of fitch, for Swagdagger's mate had her
nest of young beyond the crack.

She had been hunting a rabbit three hundred yards
away when Swagdagger had climbed the stone, and
as soon as she heard the call, she galloped back. Other
fitches had run to the summons of Swagdagger.

L

Sharp-toothed, blood-thirsty, and without fear, they ran up and down by the opening, sniffing the delicious scent of fresh-slain rabbit, weaving quick bodies and lifting their small heads to sniff, sniff, sniff. The noises of teeth at work made a furious stir in the assembling tribe. The older dog-fitch yakkered with rage, as he wove in and out of the swift and impatient throng.

The little angry fitches in the cranny, beyond the nose of Tarka, heard the cry of their mother and spat at the enemy—all moving things unknown were enemies to the little fitches. She ran through the fitches outside in the moonlight and into the cave, jumping in her twisty way for a bite behind the otter's ear. Tarka shook her and tried to kill her, but she ran at him again, and with her ran Swagdagger and all the fitches who had come at his alarm. Tarka trod on stoats; he was pricked all over by the teeth of stoats; he chopped one through the ribs and back, but its biting did not cease; he chopped it again, trying to hold it by his forepaws, but though broken, it was alive and angry, and bit through the skin of his throat and hung there, as long as his rudder. He pushed through fitches into the moonlight, and the fitches followed him, including the four young ones who were excited and eager for play. The pack chased him, throwing their sharp tongues, all the rugged way down to the river, into which Tarka jumped with a splash. Three of them fell in after him, but they did not like the water and crawled out spitting and sneezing, tough and lithe and sinuous as

bines of honeysuckle. Unable to find the otter, the *Cheldon*
dog-fitches started a fight among themselves.   *Bridge*
As Swagdagger's mate went up the hill again with
her young running behind her, she met a badger, who
was going to drink in the river. The grey waddler,
animate granite, whose head was heavier than
her whole body, lumbered out of the way. He sought
no unnecessary trouble with fitches, and he had
eaten up the rabbit under the Seal Stone.

The river hurried round the base of the cleave, on
whose slopes stunted trees grew, amid rocks, and
scree that in falling had smashed the trunks and
torn out the roots of willows, thorns, and hollies. It
wandered away from the moor, a proper river, with
bridges, brooks, islands, and mills.
Soon the oaks above the river would break into leaf.
Magpies had topped their nests with thorns, and
buzzards were soaring long after owl-light. Kingfishers and dippers had hatched their eggs—there was
a dipper's nest, hanging dishevelled like a beard of
moss, under nearly every stone bridge spanning the
river. The innocent white flowers of the savage
blackthorn had withered brown and shaken into the
wind. Lent lilies—the wild daffodils of the woods
and meads—clasped with their blooms, shrivelled
and loving, the seeds of winter's hope. Already the
celandines were old thoughts of the spring, their
leaves hid by rising docks and nettles and flowering
dog's-foot mercury. Badger cubs had been taught to
use the latrines outside the tunnels. It was mid-April,

Colleton swallow-time in the West Country. Otter cubs romped in a big stick-heap resting on the nose of an island above a bridge, eager to play with the moon on the water. Their mother, who was Tarka's sister, attacked him when he looked on them in the stick-heap, and bit him in the shoulder, for she was most anxious, and did not remember her brother cub.

Though the birds scolded, the foxes snarled, and his own kind drove him away, Tarka had many friends, whom he played with and forgot—sticks, stones, water-weeds, slain fish, and once an empty cocoa-tin, a bright and curious thing that talked strangely as it moved over the shallows, but sank into the pool beyond, sent up three bubbles, and would play no more.

CHAPTER TWELVE

A T SUNSET, AS HE WAS CROSSING A SHOAL TO DEEP water under an old ash tree, he stopped at the taint of hounds lying on the scour pitted by their feet. Quietly he turned back to the water to swim sunken in the current, rising only to take in air. Round two bends he drifted, then landed and harkened. Ran up the bank, uncertain. Rose on hind feet, dripping and anxious. A dwarf owl making a peacock-like yowling in the woods beyond the meadow, the squeak of mice, the dry cough of an ewe. He ran back to the river, and after eating fish, he played with a rope of water twisting and un-twisting out of a drain, trying to catch it between his paws and bite it as it plattered on his face and chest.

An otter-path lay across the next bend, and he followed it to the middle of the field, where he hesi-tated. Strange smells lay in the dew. He scraped at a place in the grass where paper had been rammed by a pole, near orange peel covered by a loose tuft. He walked on, nose to ground, and smelt man, where hobnailed boots had pressed the turf and crushed cigarette-ends. He turned back, and would have gone straight to water if he had not heard the cry of a bitch-otter at the far end of the path. *Hu-ee-ee-ic!* he answered, and ran along to find her. Near the middle of the meadow he stopped as though he had trod on a gin. The taint of hounds lay thick with the scent of otter. Grasses were smeared with blood and spittle. His hair rose on his back. He blew through open

Oodmall mouth, swung his head about as though looking for *Ash Holt* hounds, and was gone, silent as his low moon shadow.

The river flowed darkly to the bend, where it broke shallow over shillets that scattered the moonlight. Tarka saw a movement at the tail of the shoal, where an otter was listening. She ran to him and licked his face, then she mewed, and ran on alone by the riverside. Tarka followed her. She was draggled and miserable. She caught a trout and called him, but when he reached her she yikkered and started to eat it herself. She mewed again, and ran into the water. And following her, Tarka returned to the scour opposite the ash-tree holt where that morning the hounds had plunged and bayed. All the way upstream she had been calling, and searching under banks, and on the beds of pools. At length she crawled on the scour with something in her mouth, and dropped it on the stones. She licked it from head to tail, and mewing again, sank back into the water and returned with another, which she laid with the first-found. Perhaps she could not count beyond two; perhaps White-tip had not known in her terror how many cubs she had dropped in the water, when the terrier had driven her out of her holt. The Master had seen them sinking in the pool, lit by a sun-shaft; and hounds were whipped off. They drew on up the river, and found the dog-otter, her mate, and killed him three hours later as he tried to cross a meadow to the wooded hillside.

The old dog and White-tip had wandered together since Tarka had been driven from her in the autumn.

Her first litter had been born in January, when the *South* river had frozen, and one day White-tip, returning *Molton* to the holt, had found them gone. She had called *Road* them, seeking everywhere, and in pain, but she had found none to suckle, for a badger walking on the ice had dug them out with his long black claws and eaten them. White-tip's grief had been so keen that soon it had grown less; and she had lain with her mate in the bracken of Ferny Hill.

And now White-tip was grieving again. For two nights, as she travelled down the river with Tarka, she would cease hunting, and run aimlessly on the banks, whining and searching. During the third night she left him and returned to the ash-tree holt, wherein she had been making ready a couch of reeds and grasses. Into the holt she carried a stone, laying it on the couch, and licking it, until a sudden cry called her outside again. She traced the cry to a stone on the shallow, and brought it in her mouth to the holt; soon the couch was filled with wet stones.

Tarka travelled on alone. As the river grew older, so the meadows and cornfields beyond its banks stretched a wider green over the age-long silt filling the valley's groin. Foxgloves claimed the hillsides wherever the oakwoods were felled, storing in their leaves the green power to raise red-purple spires to the midsummer sky. Seen by day from the hilltops, the river lay in its course like a viper broken by a buzzard's beak and claws, marked with brown on its twisted and bluish-white coils. Twin burnished lines were set by the river, touching its banks,

Junction straitly leaving it to its windings, and crossing it on
Pool stone bridges topped by tarred iron girders. Under
the girders jackdaws were building their nests of
sticks and sheep's wool and paper picked up in the
early morning from cottage gardens. The rolling
thunder over their heads did not disturb them, for,
like the otters, they had grown used to the noise of
trains in the valley.

Below one bridge the river slowed into a wide pool,
where the waters of a smaller south-flowing river
meditated before turning north with big brother
Taw. Tarka was cruising over the bed of the Junction Pool when the moon, shaking and distorted by
eddies above, was cut by dark and narrow slips. A
down-stroke of his strong rudder and a push off a
rock by his hindlegs swung him up for the chase of
shoaling fish. They darted away in a zigzag, turning
together, up and down and across the pool. Tarka
pursued one until he caught it, but as he was swimming to the bank he saw another, and followed it
with the fish in his mouth. He snicked it as it darted
back past his shoulder. Strokes of the heavy tapering
rudder over two inches wide at its base and thirteen
inches long, that could stun a fish by its blow, enabled him to turn his body in water almost as quickly
as on land.

He shook the fish out of his mouth as soon as he
had killed them, for now he was hunting for sport.
The dace glinted about the water, the slayer often
leaping after a fish that threw itself into the air and
jumped as it hit water again. A stain began to move

in the water, and a plaice flapped off the bottom *Junction* and swam in what it thought was the beginning of a *Pool* flood, when worms came swirling into the Junction Pool.   This sea-fish had lived a strange and lonely life in fresh water ever since it had been swallowed in the estuary by a heron and ejected alive from the crop a quarter of an hour afterwards when the bird, flying up the valley, had been shot by a water-bailiff.

The shape of an otter loomed in the water, and the plaice swam down again in a rapid, waving slant, perceived by a one-eyed eel that was lying with its tail inside a bullock's skull wedged in a cleft of rock. Thrust through the eel's blank eye-socket was the rusty barbed point of a hook, the shank of which stuck out of its mouth—a hook almost straightened before the line had broken. Tarka swam up behind the eel on its blind side, and opened his mouth wide to bite across the back.

The eel was longer than Tarka. It lashed its tail round his neck and bit on to his nose, when gripped below the paired fins. Bubbles were blown in two strings, one of them fine as charlock seeds, for the hook-shank was rammed up the otter's left nostril. Then the strings ceased, and stray bubbles arose, for the eel was throttling the otter. Tarka clawed it with his paws, but the small claws were worn by many weeks' scratching for trout in granite hides, and the eel's skin was slippery. Flattened on the pool's bed, the plaice watched the struggle of its two enemies.

Tarka knocked it with his paws, and scraped himself against stones and rocks, so that he could be free to

155

Skoop swim up and eat it. For three minutes until his breath
Water was gone, he tried to shake off the eel. Then he
kicked heavily and slowly up to the surface and tried
to climb out by the nearest land—a sheer bank. Its
head in the air, the eel lifted its bite on the otter's
bleeding nose and sank away down. Immediately
Tarka sprang half out of the water and with a *plop!*
like a round stone went after it, catching it below the
vent. The eel lashed again, and Tarka unbit. He
swam under and bit it at the back of the neck, and
again released it. The eel tried to wobble down to
the bullock's skull, but Tarka dragged it back; and
so he played with it, always avoiding the bite of its
big jaws. At length it grew feeble, and he took it to a
shallow, where, after walking round it and pretending
it was not there, he ate what he wanted of the tail-end.

When he had washed his face he went back into
the pool, harrying the dace until many score of the
silvery fishes floated away on their sides. He harried
them until the moon sank under the hill and he grew
tired of his sport. Then spreading his legs, he drifted
away out of the pool, past an island that divided the
river—a narrow island, shaped like an otter, with a
rudder of mud carved at its lower end by the swift
waters. Alders and willows grew on the island, many
broken by uprooted trees lugged down by floods.

Two hours later Tarka was hungry again, and
eating a two-pound trout, fat with easy feeding on
mullyheads, taken under the third railway bridge
after the Junction Pool. Below the bridge, on the
right bank, the river passed part of its old course,

now dry save for green-scummed pools, left by March *Shag-*
risings, among the shillets. The law of life was also *gery's*
the law of water—everlasting change. It had carved *Bed*
this deserted bed through the centuries, raised it with
shillets, and turned away to a newer course. Brambles, thorns, elderberry bushes, nettles, and briars
grew entangled along the silent waterway. It was
the haunt of grass snakes, frogs, mice, and a wild
sandy ram-cat without front paws. For the first three
years of its life the cat had been lean, feeding on rats
in and around a corn-mill and answering to the
name of Shaggery. During its fourth year it had gone
wild in the woods and grown fat on rabbits, until
caught in a gin. It limped back to the mill and
became tame again, but when the pad had rotted
away and the stump had healed, it had lain rough
in the woods. It was caught a second time, losing its
other paw. For two years it had lived in the old
river-bed, prowling forth at night and living on frogs,
mice, beetles, and carrion fish left by otters on the
banks and shoals. It moved by bounding hops from
its hindlegs, like a rabbit. Its claws had drawn up
above the ends of the short stumps, useful for a hug-
ging hold on its prey, but a hindrance in washing its
face. Sometimes otterhounds, tearing their way
through the undergrowth, had owned the scent of
this cat, whose hiding-place was in a deep rabbit
bury under a thorn brake.

Tarka ran over its scent, and followed it along
the old river-bed. The cat was sitting on a boulder,
from which it had been watching a vole-run below.

Tawstock Tarka stopped, surprised as the cat. Shaggery's ears flattened, its body increased into a loop of agitated fur, and it let out such a waul that Tarka's back began to twitch. The cry was loud, and slowly champed through teeth. It sank to a low grinding threat when Tarka stood up to sniff what was wauling at him. He steadied himself by touching the stone on which it stood and the ram-cat made a noise like one Tarka had heard before, when a pailful of hot embers had been shot over the village quay by the estuary. He fled remembering a burn. Alone again, the ram-cat lowered body on stumps, and lifted ears to listen for voles.

When the next night White-tip followed Tarka's trail along the dry bed, Shaggery was sitting above the bury, in an old mossy-damp magpie's nest. Again the waul and the grinding of teeth, again the spitting hiss, and again an otter hurrying back to water.

Tarka had gone under the last bridge above the tide, and the sun was rising when he crept out by a mud glidder and curled himself in a bed of green flags. Water ran clear and shallow on its rocky bed below the mud. Swallows flew to and fro over the river channel, winding deeper and broader through the meadows. All things were warmed in the sun. The grass and dock-leaves under the tide-wall were greenish grey with salt and silt dried on blade and stalk and leaf, after the sluggard tide's lapse. Seaweed, black and brittle, lay below the wall with scriddicks of old rush-tops and sticks among white flowers of scurvy-grass. The sun moved above the oakwood that sloped from the rocky bank across the *Mouse* river; the leaves of lower branches were blenched, *Hole* and weed-hung. A hot, broken glitter, like a flight of *Pit* silver birds, played lightly on the green flags where Tarka was lying. One brilliant beak of light slipped round a flag and pecked at his eye until he awoke, and yawned, and turned on his back. His nostrils lazily tested the wind that sometimes trembled the tips of the flags. It was a clean wind, and he lay content.

Three buzzards sailed over the river, one above the other, like the stars in Orion's Belt; the top bird moving with steady wings, the lower bird circling, and the lowest veering on broad vanes, cleaver-shaped, heavily with rolling sweeps into the lingering wind that eddied about the top of oak trees. The tree-trunks were dark; only from the high young branches had the sun struck colour, yellow and pale green.

A lustrous blue line was drawn against the dark forest of trunks as a kingfisher sped down-river. The buzzards drifted away south, their wings narrowing with a gold glister, and shrank into the sun.

Peet! The short, shrill cry came from a silver point drawing a ruddy line over the mud. With a fish in its beak the kingfisher sped up-river to its young in a sandy bank above the Mouse Hole Pool. Martins twittered along the river-bank, and hovered about the heads of bullocks, taking crisp-winged flies from their muzzles and between their horns. Tarka yawned, and dozed again.

A dark cloud arose over the crest of the oakwood,

New and the greenery of young leaves faded. Rain beat on
Bridge the flags. A million million drops in the river leapt
(*Taw*) to meet the drops fresh-risen from the Atlantic.
The cloud passed, and again the meadow was hot
and bright. The swallows flew up the river, quitting
at the coils its glitter and yellow kingcups, and fleeing
on across the green meadow to the road by the
bridge. Here, in the hollows of the broken road
surface, was to be found after rain a greyish mud
that set harder than the browny mud of the salty
scourings in the river. Only by the bridge was this
mud to be found, for the road sloped up and down
over the river, and the slopes were not tarred, lest
the feet of horses slip. The aerial masons were about
to build their nests on the rafters of shippen and
barn; they flew in pairs, singing their sun-songs.

Beside the bridge grew an elderberry tree, straight
and sturdy as a young oak in a park; one of the few
soft-cored elderberry trees in the country of the Two
Rivers that had not grown up a cripple of the winds.
Its leaves partly hid a motor-car, in whose closed
body, shut away from the wind and the sun of the
English spring, sat some men and women. They
were awaiting hounds before moving to the parapet
of the bridge, and perhaps, if a kill seemed certain
and early, to the meadow over the low wooden fence.
Other motor-cars stopped on the bridge. The swallows swooping over the stonework saw the sunlight
browned by the smoke of engines, and dived back
again over the grass. The baying of hounds above
the bridge became louder, for the otter had swum

through the lower stickle, and was travelling down- *Grattan's*
stream.   *Pit*

The hunted otter was White-tip. She had been
chased for nearly three hours. Always the cries and
tongues and legs had followed her, up the pools and
down the pools, from holt to holding, from holding
to shallow.

Tally Ho!

She saw faces and waving arms above the bridge,
but she did not turn back.

Light-laden drops rolled down the green flags as
their points drew down the sky. Tarka lay still,
watching. They rustled and broke with soft sappy
noises. White-tip was pressing through the bed of
flags. Her mouth was open. Tarka, who had been
listening for half an hour to the distant cries of men
and hounds, stared at the movement. A sudden
clamour ran down the river, loud and startling, for
Deadlock had found White-tip's deep seals in the
mud, where she had crept out of the water.

The two otters ran through the flags and slid down
the mud to the river again. Tarka spread himself in
the shallow flow, moving with light touches of claws
just over the rocks and stones of the bed. He moved
slowly, as an eel moves, as smooth as the water, and
with sinuous ease. Sometimes he crept out at the
edge of the mud, walked a few yards, and slipped
back into the water again. Hounds were crushing
the flags around his bed, and throwing their tongues
along his line.

Spady He swam through a long pool at his fastest pace,
Gut putting up his nostrils every fifty yards to breathe,
and down again immediately. He left the oakwood
behind him, and came to a narrow gut draining the
water of a small marshy valley, where bullocks were
grazing. The gut lay under trees above a rocky bank.
Its other bank was mud. Seaweed hung on the roots
of trees six feet above his head. Tarka walked up the
gut, as far as the first channer in its glidder, partly
hid by the broad strongly keeled leaves of river sedge.
He followed it into the marsh, and climbing out, ran
along a path trodden by cattle, through a gate and
down to a lower marsh, hidden from the opposite
bank by a tide-wall. The tongue of Deadlock spoke
across the river, and Tarka slipped into another gut.
He trod through brown mud to a black ooze, in
which he moved like an eel. The drain led under the
tide-wall to the glidder above the river. It led into
darkness, with light coming through the chinks of a
circular wooden trap, that kept the tides back from
the land. He sniffed at a chink, and waited in the
ooze.

For two hours Tarka lay behind the wooden trap,
while the noises of hunting moved away into remote-
ness. Slowly the sound of the low running river was
stilled into slack water. Tricklings, the lap and
slanting wash of ripple-ends, a turning drift of froth
and sticks below the mud—the sea was moving up
again. A heron alighted at the bottom of the muddy
glidder, and stalked gravely into water to his knees.
Flukes were rising off the silt, seeking food. The heron

bent down and peered. He stepped forward on one *Spady* foot, and speared with a swift plunge. Then he stared *Gut* up the river. A thin-drawn thread of sound in the air, looped to another and another and another; loosed as four gossamers floating by in the wind. It was the re-call to hounds. In the after-quiet the heron stalked to his spearing again. The murky water twired by the knee-joints of his thin green legs. Splash, flicker, and shaken drops—he swallowed fluke after fluke; but when twenty yards beyond the trap he straightened up his neck, stood on his toes, jumped hurriedly out of the water, and flapped away, pulling up his shanks after him and tucking his long neck and head between his shoulders. He had seen the heads of men.

Smells of the lower river, riding up with the young tide into the Mouse Hole Pit, had overspread the wishy washy otter-scent, and the pack was being taken back to kennels. The horn-like voice of the huntsman, as he talked to hounds by name, came to the otter through the chinks of the sodden elm-wood trap. They trotted on the opposite bank, happy at the huntsman's heels, led home by aged Harper, who had taught them all to mark an otter. Flews to flews with him was Deadlock, and at his stern, Blue-maid, old before her time, worn-out by swimming. Then came Pitiful, who worked hard and alone; whenever it was possible to go wrong, Pitiful went wrong; it was Pitiful who, whenever they passed by the dry river-bed, led them on the trail of Shaggery the ram-cat; if a hound were missing, it was always

M *163*

Spady Pitiful. Near her was Captain, a black-and-tan rough
Gut dog, who looked like a lurcher; the huntsman did
not take Captain to important meets, for Captain's
voice was like a knife whose edge is turned. He did
not throw his tongue, he screamed; and sometimes in
his excitement he babbled, flinging water-lies about.
Bite'm the terrier hurried among them, sometimes
sniffing in tufts, hoping to find a rat to shake; and
following Bite'm, like an easy-going, big, heavy boy
led by a sharp little quick-eyed tacker, came Rufus,
who cared more for a nest of field-mice than for a
joint or rib of rank otter. After Rufus on the tide-
wall ran Dewdrop, whose long fawn-coloured hair
was curly with wet. Her ears hung long and loose.
   Often while the trophies were being taken by the
huntsman those ears would flap between blue-
stocking'd legs, and teeth would slyly nip through
wool, as though it were brown fur of the worry. By
the Wharfdale bitçh—for Dewdrop was the only true
otterhound in the pack—ran Playboy and Actor,
whose dingy-white shapes were so alike that only
the huntsman could name them truly. Behind them
came Render and Fencer, who always tore at roots
of a holt with their teeth; Hemlock, with one eye
blind, the dark pupil grey-veined with the scar of a
blackthorn prick; Hurricane, the ancient Irish staghound with the filed canines; Barbrook and Bellman,
Boisterous and Chorister, Coraline, Sailoress, Waterwitch and Armlet, who always stood apart from the
pack during holt-marking and bayed moodily like a
lighthouse siren. Then came Sandboy, who fought

other hounds at the worry, and Grinder and Darnell *Spady* —hounds who had chased the fox. They trotted on *Gut* the tide-wall between the short, quick-stepping huntsman and the long-legged whip and kennel-boy, whose long loose striding had been formed in early years by crossing ploughlands on his way to school.

Twenty paces behind the pack walked the Master with two members of the Hunt. He was saying that it had been a great day, only lacking a kill to complete it, when old Harper stopped and lifted his muzzle. The air on the water, colder than the land air, was brimming over the sea-wall, and Harper had smelled an otter. Deadlock moved into the air-stream, threw up his head, whimpered, and ran down the grassy bank to the broken turf above the glidder. Sterns were waved like feathers. Deadlock leapt into the river, followed by half the pack. Pitiful started patiently to work the water-line of the mud, and Captain babbled in excitement as he lapped and swam.

The water was three feet deep. Hounds scrambled up the glidder, some slipping down, drawing long claw-lines on the harder clay beneath. They whimpered and scratched before the round wooden trap, and Armlet bayed them on from the bank above. Terrier Bite'm pushed his small eager body between their flanks, under their legs, whining and yelping. Five men waded the river, testing a footway with taps of iron-shod poles before them. Thinking that the otter they had hunted for more than five hours

Spady was hiding inside, and that the tired hounds would
Gut have no chance to kill even an exhausted otter in the
rising water, the pack was not withdrawn when
Bite'm was taken to the open end of the drain, where
Tarka's deep seals in the lower ooze showed like big
blackberries crushed in the mud. Bite'm was given
a pat on his ribs and gently shoved into the dark hole.
He crept in, quick and shivering.

The ooze sucked at Tarka's webs as he turned away
from the light-striped lid of the drain. His heart beat
as fast as water-drops drip without dribbling. The
hanging sodden door went *sug-plog-sug* as paws struck
it. He looked up and down, round and up again, for
a way of escape. He crawled in the ooze, away from
the immense din, and saw an enemy coming towards him an instant before he smelled it. *Is-is-iz!*

They met and joined and twisted into shapes
smoothed by ooze. The terrier got a grip on the
otter's rudder and hung on to it. Tarka bit and bit
and bit, quick as a striking viper, in cheek, shoulder,
flank, nose, and ear. Noises of bumping and squelch-
ing and snarling and tissing became louder when the
trap was lifted and light showed the red and black
shaking shapes. The otter's rudder, near the opening,
was seized and pulled by a hand. Another hand
gripped the terrier's scruff. The long black smooth
shape was lugged out of the drain, the terrier fixed
to it. Hounds were leaping and clamouring up at the
men. A hand held Bite'm's tail-stump, another hand
squeezed, trying to make him unclench. Tarka
writhed and contorted as he hung by his rudder;

Huntsman, Bite'm, and Tarka at the Spady Gut.

Spady his back became a bow, suddenly bending up, and *Gut* his teeth made a row of holes in a hand. The jerk made his rudder slip, and he dropped among boots, to squirm between legs and away down the glidder. He pulled Bite'm with him.

Hounds trod on him, snarling and thrusting. Tarka was hidden under their heads, picked up and thrown sideways, then dropped and picked up and shaken. Eight jaws held him at one time in the midst of a deep sullen growling. He was hid in the plunging of white and brown and black bodies. He bit Deadlock through the flews, and again in the nose, as he was lifted on other muzzles, Bite'm still joined to the base of his rudder. The pack bore him down to the tide, where the worry broke up. Heads were lifted again, and tongues thrown. Hounds stooped to water; some swam after Captain, who was cutting the air with his knife-edge voice.

But Tarka was gone, and so was Bite'm. The terrier came to the surface a minute later, forty yards away, and swam inshore, spluttering and gasping, the short hairs of the otter's rudder still between his teeth.

CHAPTER THIRTEEN

THE TIDE WAS FLOODING FAST IN MIDSTREAM. IT carried with it sunken branches that sometimes showed a stick, and turned under again. Tarka passed them as he swam into a riband of water returning under the steep and broken rock-face that was the river's left bank. The riband moved down again, feeling the roots of oak trees, and reclaiming the seaweed hung there since the morning ebb. The otter drifted to a root and rested his paws upon it, breathing through his mouth. Two pink nicks above his nose welled red immediately; so did his paws. He bled also from rudder, back, neck, flank, and shoulder. While he was among the hounds he had felt neither fear nor hurt, for the power of all his senses had been in movement to escape. Now his wounds smarted with the salt in the water, and he listened in a still dread for Deadlock's tongue. He lay still for a quarter of an hour.

No hound spoke. The water rose, and lifted him off the root, and carried him away. He drifted through the Mouse Hole Pit and beyond the oakwood to the deeper winding bed in the meadow, where oarweed hung dry on the lower branches of thorns, with sticks, grasses, sometimes the skeleton of a rabbit or bird. Dead brambles tangled in the thorns were swinging in the water, combing the scum of the tide. Cuckoo flowers grew above the top of the flood, their small pale gentle faces rising on tall stems from the dead

Two stumps of trees, some broken and wilting, trodden
Rock into the mud and asleep again.

Holt Through the soft pasture ground the river roamed,
coiling and uncertain. The tide-water filling it
gleamed dully like a seal's hide, greyish brown and
yellow freckled. The mud at its edges streamed with
tiny bubbles out of the ragworms' holes. It carried
Tarka with its other flotsam to the middle of its last
sea-bend, where the tide lay like a dead seal. Already
it had started to ebb. Tarka crawled into shallow
fresh water singing round stones, and reached two
rocks covered with green water-moss. Here he sat
and licked his wounds, and lapped the salt from his
mouth. Long shadows were on the grass, and the
faint-screaming swifts were high over the valley,
eager for the sunset and their mystic star-games.

Above the tide's head the banks were of brown soil
and upright under the broken turf. Seedling plants
of balsam were four inches high. Willows were green
and waving in the evening wind. Tarka walked
under the bank on dry shillets and sandy scours
washed loose of mud, until he reached the roots of a
big tree based at the tail of an eddying pool. He
crept into darkness, to a dry shelf within, and slept.

The high stars of mid-May were shining through
the branches when he came out of the holt, slow and
stiff and hungry. Below the two rocks the water
gushed in many clear rills. Tarka walked across a
bend, down a bank, over the shallow, and up the
other bank. He made a landloop that took him to
the bottom of the railway embankment, and pushing

through a low thorn hedge, he climbed the grassy *Barum* bank to the rails. Over the wooden sleepers he walked *Bridge* so that the stenches of oil and tar and cinder would mingle with his own scent, in case the enemies were trailing him.

At the next bridge, under which a dwarf owl nested, he left the track and went to water again. Working down the river, crossing from side to side and searching for fish under stones and in deep holes, he left the grassy sloping tide-walls behind and passed by boats resting on a ridge of gravel above a long road-bridge. Swimming with a fluke to the river-side, he could find no bank. The water lapped a stone wall. He swam under an arch of the bridge and ate the fish on a ledge of sand raised over an old galvanized-iron bath thrown away into the river. Below the bridge was a railway bridge, supported by round iron piers sunk into the gravel. A wave washed against the base of the pier near the right side of the river as he swam round it, hoping to find mussels clinging there. The sea was returning again. It poured over the ridges of sand, making a sound with every stone and shell and shillet tumbling before its eager spread. *Hu-ee-ic!* Tarka chopped at the froth, the new smarting of his wounds unheeded. *Hu-ee-ic!* The salt wave was of the sea, and the sea was the friend of otters.

As he was swimming down in a turbulent pool, Tarka saw a big fish turn before him. He raced after it. His hindlegs pushed forward under his body for the full double-thrust, and the arch of his back

Barum opened the big bite of Deadlock that had nearly *Yeo* touched the spine. He bled, but felt no pain in the joy of hunting a big fish. The mullet—one of many that had come up from the estuary, feeding in the muddy collar of the tide's head—nearly dashed into the stone wall of the quay in its terror. It saved itself by a leap that took it a yard into the air, and falling back, it sped swiftly down the river. Tarka followed it to where it had leapt, stood head and shoulders out of the water, while he looked round, before rolling under again. He swam up the base of the wall and turned back by the railway bridge, swimming three double-thrusts to the left, then three to the right, while watching for the glint of scales. He followed the wall until he came to an opening in the quay where the tide was rushing. Another fish turned in the turbid swirling water before him, and darted up the pill. Tarka swam up the narrow way, but seeing nothing, swung back into the wide river. He swam across the tide to the opposite bank by a shipyard, then returned along the piers of the bridge, searching by the stone sterlings.

The tide was pouring fast between the piers when he reached the wall again. Swimming along the wall he turned up the pill, and let the tide take him. With easy strokes he explored the water, swinging in a zigzag course from side to side. At the end of each crossing he threw head and shoulders out of the water, to breathe and survey before pushing off again with a thrust of hindlegs from the stones under the glidders. Many times he swerved off his course to peer round and under things that lay on the bed, *Pilton* broken kettles, cooking pots, basins, and battered *Bridge* oil-drums thrown away in the mud.

He saw fish-shapes in the water beyond and above him, and headed them again as they would dash back to the estuary. The mullet swam away from him at thrice his speed, but he followed surely. The spring-tide was now flowing at six knots and the mullet went up with the press of water. Tarka drove them under another bridge, past which, by some steps in the quay, water from a mill-leat was splashing under a culvert. Above this the walls of stone ended, and rows of weed-hung stakes leaned over the mud glidders. Following the westward curve of the pill, Tarka passed by a timber-yard, and after a minute's swimming, swung north again and then east. The creek was like a great hollow slug filling with water.

Above the next bridge the leading fish rushed back and skurried by him, missing his snap by a curve that gleamed all its side, and a flack of its tail that filled Tarka's mouth with air. It escaped with six of its grey brethren, but the last two were headed again. Tarka drove them up the straight and narrowing pill, through the collar of the tide and into still water, which was strange to the mullet, it was so clear and shallow.

Tarka was now a mile from the pill-mouth. The image of the bright moon rolled in shaken globules in the hollows of the brook's swift waters, blending as quicksilver. Every ten yards two clusters of small

Tacker bright beads arose out of the blackness and vanished
Pool in a dipping streak. Sometimes a delicate silver
arrow pointed up the brook and was tangled in a
fish-tail swirl. Every ten yards the whiskered head
looked up for direction—only the immediate fore-
ground was visible under water—and smoothly
vanished. Tarka swam with all his webs thrusting
together against the swift current, just above the bed
of the brook, ready to leap up and snap should the
fish try to pass him.

He swam under a bridge of the small-gauge railway,
whose shadow darkened the water. As he thrust up
his head to vent, Tarka saw beyond the shadow-bar
the white blur of water sliding over the sill of a weir.
Under water again, he looked from side to side more
quickly, for in this dark place the fish might easily
slip by him, although the water was not two feet
deep.

When midway through the shadow, his rudder
swished up sickle-shaped, slanting his body. His hindlegs touched stones; he sprang. The scales of the two
fish coming straight towards him in the darkness
reflected only the darkness, but he had seen a hair of
faintest light where the ream of a back-fin had
cut the surface and glimmered with the moon-
frosted slide. His teeth tore the tail of the leading fish,
which escaped—his rudder lashed for another turn,
his body screwed through the water, and struck upwards with teeth into the mullet's gorge. Tarka swam
into moonlight and dragged the five-pound fish
(despite its beats and flaps) on to a shillet heap under

the spillway of the slide. He gripped it with his paws *Swine* and stood over it and started to eat it, while its gills *Park* opened and closed, and it tried feebly to flap.

The chewing of its bony jaws soon made him impatient, and he fixed his teeth into the shoulder and tore away his bite. For five minutes he ate, then stretched up his head, with its spiky neck-hair raised, and excitedly assayed the air. *Hu-ee-ic!* His nostrils opened wide. *Hu-ee-ic!* White-tip looked over the weir-sill and slid down with the water. *Yinn-yinn-y-y-ikk-r!* she cried, through her white teeth, and pulled the fish away from Tarka who rolled on his back and tried to play with her tail. Then he rolled on his pads again and stared down through the rectangular space under the bridge, remembering the other fish.

He slid off the rock. White-tip ate two pounds of the mullet. Then she followed Tarka.

The leat, with its swift clear water and brown weed —like clusters of stoats' tails—ran parallel to the brook, a few yards away, and past a lime-washed mill with a ruined water-wheel. A fence made of old iron bedsteads was set in the leat's grassy bank, and here White-tip saw the dark shape of Tarka's head against the nobbled lines of framework. He was eating. Seeing her, he whistled. As she ran over the grass, she smelled the scales where he had dragged the fish. *Yinn-yinn!* she cried again, jumping on the fish and clutching its head in her paws. Tarka watched her. Then he licked the blood from his wounds and ran back to the pill. He was going after more big fish.

Swine Park In the meadow near the lime-washed mill was a dump of house-rubbish, tipped there by dust-carts, and spread about. A sow and her growing farrow were routing in the mess of rotten flesh and vegetable food, crunching up egg-shells and bones and cinders with eager delight. Here, while the moon was waning and the low mist was growing white, the otters returned to play a strange game. It was begun by White-tip making a splash before Tarka, to make sure that he would see her leave the water and climb the bank. When he followed, she ran around the meadow and back again, passing close by, but not once looking at him. After a while, they went back to the pill and romped like porpoises. Then they ran up the bank together and wandered off alone, up and down, passing and repassing many times through the squares of the wire fencing, without recognition or purpose, as though they were both mazed. To the water once more, a drink and a search for eels, and again the strange play in the meadow.

Each was pretending not to see the other; so happy were they to be together, that they were trying to recover the keen joy of meeting.

On the seventh round White-tip ran near a young pig that on sniffing her scent, jumped and grunted and squealed and then stood still. Every black jowl lifted from the pleasant garbage. Hot ears ceased to flap. White-tip moved, and ten pigs jumped, and squealed, and hurriedly bolted. The sow, a ponderous and careful animal with eyes sunken in fat, that had eaten two rats and a cat besides twenty pounds of other food that night, pointed her ringed snout at *Derby* the troublesome smell and moved her big shaking body towards it. White-tip threatened her, crying *Is-iss-iss!* If the sow had caught her, White-tip would have been eaten by sunrise, since she weighed only fourteen pounds and the sow weighed seven hundred pounds. She whistled to Tarka, who ran at the sow.

Seven hundred pounds of flesh returned from the fence with pricked ears and a tail-tip gone; and Tarka ate grass blades, although he was not hungry. He wanted to get the taste of sow out of his mouth.

All night the swifts had been racing over the valley, so high that not even the owls had heard their whistling screams. When these birds saw the golden fume of the sun rising out of the east, they poured down in three funnels to the lower airs of the valley. Their narrow wings made a whishing noise as they fell. Tarka and White-tip in the weir-pool lay on their backs and watched them as they linked into chains and chased away, some up the valley, others to the estuary. Suddenly the otter heads lifted, looked round, and sank together—they had heard the otter-hounds baying in the kennels on Pilton Hill.

In daylight they drifted down the mill-leat that drew out of the pool, passing from grassy banks to concrete, above which were walls and windows of houses and lofts where pigeons sat and croodled. Some of the older pigeons were already cocking red-rimmed eyes at the sky, for it was near the time of year when the peregrine falcons wheeled aloft the town of Barum, coming from the cliff eyries of Bag

Sawyers Bend Hole, Hercules Promontory, and the red cliffs along the Severn Sea.

A stag-bird, or farmyard cock, saw the otters from its perch on a bough over the leat, and cried *Wock-wock-wock-wick*, while its comb became redder. Then it saw nothing but water, and crowed in triumph among the hens. Tarka had not forgotten the time when a cock had crowed before.

The leat flowed under a road, and under a brick cliff that was one wall of the town mills, swirled back from the locked wheel and gushed under a penstock and through a culvert to the pill, from which the sea was ebbing. Tarka and White-tip swam over the drowned white flowers of scurvey-grass to the bend where timber lay, and climbing out, sought a hiding-place among the pile of oaken trunks. As they crept along a rough bole a rat squeaked, another squealed, and soon all the rats of the timber stack were squealing. An old buck saw Tarka and fled away, followed by others, who were either bucks or does without young. Some of the rats dived into the water, others ran to farther wood stacks, where lived families that fought with the invaders. Their squeals came out of the planks all the morning, while the ringing rasp of circular saws was loud in the sunlight. These rats were heard by the sawyers, and during the dinner-hour one went off to fetch his ferrets.

Tarka and White-tip were lying in a hollow trunk, curled side by side, their heads close together. The

178

hollow was damp; its crevices still held skulls and *Sawyers* leg-bones of mice and sparrows, that had looked at *Bend* Tarka when he was very young. There were also fishbones with a faint smell, but even these were beyond memory. In the autumn, long after the cubs had left its friendly hollow, the tree had been cut off from its roots and dragged by horses across the meadow and taken away, with other trees, to the saw mills.

Hidden in the pile of trunks, the otters heard the grumbling of the grist mill across the creek, with the noises of traffic and the voices of men. During the morning Tarka shook his ears, tickled by the irritant buzzing of a bluebottle-fly caught and fanged in a spider's web outside the hollow. Long after the fly was dead Tarka heard the buzzing, but without twitching his ears; for similar sounds now came from the bridge, where the motor-traffic crossed two roads. The noises were quieter when the sun was on the top of the sky, and the otters heard distinctly the chirping of sparrows. Then the chirping grew less, for the birds had flown to feed in the quieter roadways. Tarka ceased to listen for footfalls, and slept.

White-tip awakened before Tarka, by the time of an eye-blink. Light from a crevice above, between the trunks resting on the old tree, made two eyes to gleam like no eyes the otters had seen before. They were pink as some blossoms of the balsam, a flower that rose tall by the sides of the Two Rivers every summer. The pink eyes blinked and moved nearer, above a white body. The creature's strong smell,

N   *179*

Sawyers blent with the smell of man, its bold silence,
Bend its likeness to an otter, yet so curiously small,
made them move uneasily. It peered with its pallid
eyes, and sniffed at the tip of Tarka's rudder. Tarka
followed White-tip who was more nervous than he
was. As they were moving along a trunk, a rat
jumped upon Tarka's back and clung to his hair,
while screwing up its eyes and yinnering through
its bared teeth. It was crying aloud its fear, not of
the otter, but of the ferret. This tamed animal of the
weasel tribe, whose name was Zippy, followed the
rat in a quiet fury, and while Tarka was climbing up
through a gap between the first and second layer of
trunks, it leapt and bit the rat through the neck,
dragging it from its clutch on the bark and shaking
it as it drank its blood. Hearing another squeal,
Zippy left the limp and dying rat and rippled after
the squealer.

When White-tip looked from under the pile of
trunks, she saw a dog peering bright-eyed, its head
on one side, above her. A man stood beyond with a
cudgel. The dog stepped back three paces as she ran
out and yapped as the man struck at her with his
cudgel. White-tip turned back, meeting the sharp face
of the ferret under a log. She ran round the stack.

The broad sky, grey with heat beating down on the
dusty peninsula, dazed the eyes of Tarka, who was
stiff with wounds and bruises. He ran to the grassy
bank above the creek, slower than the man, who
struck him a glancing blow. The blow quickened
Tarka, and the man, eager to kill him, threw the

180

ground-ash stick at his head. It twirled past Tarka *Landkey* and scored a groove in the hot and hardening mud. *Brook* Tarka ran over the cracks beginning to vein the glidder, and sank into the water. He was seen from the bridge, moving round the larger stones like a brown shadow, slowly stroking with his hindlegs and never once rippling the waterflow, which was just deep enough to cover an old boot.

At night Tarka whistled in the creek, but heard no answer. He returned twice to the bend by the silent timber yard, where the eyes of rats were pricked in vanishing moonlight, but White-tip was not there. The flood tide took him two miles up the river again to the railway bridge where a pair of dwarf owls had their eggs, in a stolen jackdaw's nest. These owls, scarcely bigger than thrushes, flew both by day and night, feeding on flukes and shrimps, frogs, snipe, oak-webs or cockchafers, worms, rats, mice, butter-flies, and anything small they could catch and kill. When they saw Tarka under the bridge they wauled like Shaggery the ram-cat, they barked like foxes, they coughed like sheep, they croaked like bull-frogs. They flew over him as he walked up the gut that emptied a small brook from the east-lying valley beyond, blaking like herring gulls a yard above his head. When he was driven away from their eggs they hooted with soft pleasure, and left him.

Tarka walked under the road and climbed into a mill-pond, where three eels died. Travelling up the brook, under the mazzard orchards growing on the

Venn Pits northern slope of the valley, he reached a great hollow in the hillside, shut in with trees and luminous as the sky. Tarka saw two moons, one above trees, the other level and in front of him, for the hollow was a flooded limestone quarry. *Hu-ee-ic!* The sweet whistle, like the cry of the golden plover, only softer, echoed from the face of rock across the water. He swam down and down, and could not touch bottom. The sides of the quarry dropped sheer down into the still depths, except at the far end, where was a little bay under a knuckle of land.

He found no fish in the pit, and ran past the deserted lime-burners' cottages and kilns to the brook again. Climbing the right bank he ran over grass-grown hillocks of deads, or rejected shillets of slatey rock, to another drowned quarry. Sombre brakes of blackthorns grew in the slag-heaps near the ivy-covered chimney of the ruinous furnace, and willows bound with mosses leaned in the water, which was dark and stagnant. A tree-creeper had her nest in a crack of the tall chimney, which rocked in every gale, for only the ivy, whose roots had made food and dust of nearly all the mortar between the stones, held it upright against the winds. Every April for five years the tree-creeper's young had been reared within the crack, in a nest that always looked like a chance wind-wedging of dry grasses and little sticks. The crows and magpies never found the nest, so cunningly was it made each year.

Fish, big and slow-swimming, lived in the sombre waters of the pit, and Tarka chased one down to the mud forty feet under the surface, where it escaped. *Swim-bridge* It was a carp, more than fifty years old, and so wise for a fish that it knew the difference between a hook baited with dough-and-aniseed and one baited with dough-and-aniseed and cottonwool. Its habit, when it found a baited hook, was to expel through its mouth a flume of water on the dough until it was washed off and then it would swallow it; but dough stiffened with cottonwool was left alone.

Hu-ee-ic!

The sky was growing grey. Tarka could not catch a carp, and he was hungry. He went back to the brook.

Hu-ee-ic!

Only his echo replied, and he wandered on.

CHAPTER FOURTEEN

WHEN THE BEES' FEET SHAKE THE BELLS OF THE heather, and the ruddy strings of the sap-stealing dodder are twined about the green spikes of the furze, it is summertime on the commons. Exmoor is the high country of the winds, which are to the falcons and the hawks: clothed by whortle-berry bushes and lichens and ferns and mossed trees in the goyals, which are to the foxes, the badgers, and the red deer: served by rain-clouds and drained by rock-clittered streams, which are to the otters.

The moor knew the sun before it was bright, when it rolled red and ragged through the vapours of creation, not blindingly rayed like one of its own dandelions. The soil of the moor is of its own dead, and scanty; the rains return to the lower ground, to the pasture and cornfields of the valleys, which are under the wind, and the haunts of men.

The moor is to the deer, the badgers, the foxes, the otters, the falcons, and the hawks, pitiless despoilers of rooted and blooded things which man has col-lected and set apart for himself; so they are killed. Olden war against greater despoilers began to end with the discoveries of iron and gunpowder; the sabre-toothed tigers, the bears, the wolves, all are gone, and the fragments of their bones lie on the rock of the original creation, under the lichens and grasses and mosses, or in the museums of towns. Once hunted himself, then hunting for necessity, man now hunts in the leisure of his time; but in nearly all those

who through necessity of life till fields, herd beasts, *The*
and keep fowls, these remaining wildings of the moors *Forest*
have enemies who care nothing for their survival.
The farmers would exterminate nearly every wild
bird and animal of prey, were it not for the land-
owners, among whom are some who care for the
wildings because they are sprung from the same land
of England, and who would be unhappy if they
thought the country would know them no more. For
the animal they hunt to kill in its season, or those
other animals or birds they cause to be destroyed
for the continuance of their pleasure in sport—which
they believe to be natural—they have no pity; and
since they lack this incipient human instinct, they
misunderstand and deride it in others. Pity acts
through the imagination, the higher light of the
world, and imagination arises from the world of
things, as a rainbow from the sun. A rainbow may
be beautiful and heavenly, but it will not grow corn
for bread.

Within the moor is the Forest, a region high and
treeless, where sedge grasses grow on the slopes to
the sky. In early summer the wild spirit of the hills is
heard in the voices of curlews. The birds fly up from
solitary places, above their beloved and little ones,
and float the wind in a sweet uprising music. Slowly
on spread and hollow wings they sink, and their cries
are trilling and cadent, until they touch earth and
lift their wings above their heads, and poising, loose
the last notes from their throats, like gold bubbles
rising into the sky again. Tall and solemn, with long

The hooped beaks, they stalk to their nestlings standing
Chains in wonder beside the tussocks. The mother-bird feeds
her singer, and his three children cry to him. There
are usually but three, because the carrion crows rob
the curlews of the first egg laid in each nest. Only
when they find the broken empty shell do the curlews
watch the crows, black and slinking, up the hillside.

Soon the curlew lifts his wings and runs from his
young, trilling with open beak; his wings flap, and
up he flies to fetch song from heaven to the wilderness again.

A tarn lies under two hills, draining water from a
tussock-linked tract of bog called The Chains. The
tarn is deep and brown and still, reflecting rushes
and reeds at its sides, the sedges of the hills, and the
sky over them. The northern end of the tarn is morass,
trodden by deer and ponies. Water trickles away
under its southern bank, and hurries in its narrow
course by falls, runnels, pools, and cascades. One
afternoon Tarka climbed out of the rillet's bed,
scarcely wider than himself, and looked through
green hart's-tongue ferns at the combe up which he
had travelled. Nothing moved below him except
water. He walked up the hill, and saw the tarn below
him. He heard the dry croaking of frogs, and ran
down the bank that dammed the dark peat-water.
A yard down the slope he stopped.

A hen-raven, black from bristled beak to toes, hopped along the edge of the tarn when she saw him.
Tarka heard small plopping sounds and saw ripples
in the water, where bull-frogs had dived off the bank.

The raven took three hops to a pile of dead frogs, *Pink-* then stopped, crouched down, poked out her head *worthy* with flattened feathers, and gazed at Tarka. Her *Pond* small eyes flickered with the whitish-grey membranes of the third eyelids. The raven was not afraid of an otter.

She had been fishing for frogs by dapping the water with her beak. Hearing the noises, the bull-frogs swam to the surface and turned with bulging eyes towards the dapping. The raven made a dry and brittle croak. When the frogs heard it, the skin swelled under their necks, and they croaked a challenge, mistaking the noises for the struggle of a choking female. They swam within a few inches of the raven's beak. One, perhaps two, would leap out of the water, and then the raven opened her beak and caught one, perhaps two. She was very quick. She hopped with them to her pile, spiked them through the head, and walked quietly to another fishing place. She could carry eight or nine frogs in her craw at once to her nest of young in a rocky clitter near the head of the river Exe. When loaded, she flew with gaping beak.

Tarka lifted his head and worked his nostrils. The steadfast glance of the small eyes along the black beak pointed at him. He smelled the frogs, took three quaddling steps towards the raven, and stopped again. The raven did not move, and he did not like her eyes. He turned away. She hopped after him, and nipped the tip of his rudder as he slipped into the tarn.

Krok-krok-krok! said the raven, cocking an eye at the sky. Tarka lay in the water and watched her picking

Pink- up frog after frog and pouching them, before she
worthy jumped off the bank and flew over the eastern hill.
Pond When she returned, her mate was with her. They
soared above the tarn. Sometimes the cock-raven
shut his wings, rolled sideways, and twirled on open
wings again. *Krok-krok!* he said to the hen, seeing
below the form of the swimming otter, darker than
the dark tarn. The raven opened his beak wide, set
his wings for descent, and croaked *kron-n-n-nk* during
the slow, dipping swoop, in the curve of a scythe,
from one green-lined margin to the other. Then he
tumbled and twirled, alighting on the slope of the
hill, and walked down to the water to catch frogs.

Several times each day the two ravens flew to the
tarn. The cockbird talked to Tarka whenever he saw
him, and pestered him when he was sunning himself
on the bank. He would hop to within a few feet of him
with a frog in his beak, and drop it just to windward
of Tarka's nose. Once, when Tarka was playing with
a frog and had turned his back on it for a moment,
the raven picked it up and threw it to one side. Bird
and otter played together, but they never touched
one another. The raven, who was one of the three
hundred sons of Kronk, would drop a stick into the
tarn and Tarka would swim after it, bringing it to
the bank and rolling with it between his paws.
Occasionally the raven slyly pinched his rudder, and
Tarka would run at him, tissing through his teeth.
With flaps and hops the raven dodged him, flying up
out of his way only when driven to water.

Day after day Tarka slept in the rushes in the morass

at the north end of the tarn. Unless he was tired after *Hoar* the nightly prowl, the *kron-n-n-n-k* of the zooming *Oak Hill* raven would always wake him, and he would either run along the bank or swim by the weeds to play with the bird. One morning five ravens flew over the tarn, the hen leading three smaller ravens in line and the father behind them—a black constellation of Orion. They lit on the turf of the dam. The youngsters sat on the bank and watched their mother dapping for frogs. Tarka ran along the bank, amid guttural squawks and cronks, to play with them, but the parents stabbed at him with their beaks, beating wings in his face, and hustling him back to water. They flew over him when he bobbed for breath, and worried him so persistently that he never again went near a raven.

When the wind had blown the seeds of the cotton grass and the sedge drooped tawny under the sun, the curlews flew away to the seashore and the rivers. Little jerky flights of pipits crossed over the hollow in the hills, their twittering passed on, and the tarn lay silent as the sky. One afternoon in early September the silence stirred, and along the tawny hillcrest moved something like a leafless top of an oak-branch. It became a stag hastening with tongue a-loll to the wooded valleys of the south. Silence settled on the moor until the hill-line was broken by a long and silent file of staghounds running down from The Chains on the line of a deer. Tarka stood on his bed of rushes and watched them until they loped into the sky. When he had settled again a black cock

Hoar hurtled down the western hill and flew over the tarn,
Oak followed by a grey hen with her two heath poults.
Water Two horsemen in red coats slanted down the side of
the hill; and after them came a young farmer riding
bare-back a stallion with blown mane and flying
tail. Then came a grey hunter, carrying a man with
a face nearly as red as his coat. Others followed,
singly, and at long intervals, on weary horses.

That evening Tarka quitted the tarn, and journeyed over The Chains to water that hastened in a
bright thread out of the bog. It entered a narrow
goyal, and the moon was hid by the hill before him.
After a mile the water turned north, under the hill
whose worn grey feet it had broken for its bed. The
goyal widened by the Hoar Oak, whose splintered
stump, black as its shadow with the moon behind,
glistered with the tracks of slugs. Near the Hoar Oak
stood a sapling, caged from the teeth and horns of
deer, a little tree by the grave of its father.

And Tarka went down the Hoar Oak Water which,
under ridge and common, shattered the moon into
shards and lost them under the trees which grew
together in the lower valley. Its voice passed from
leaf to leaf, up through the woods where badgers
were seeking mice and black slugs, and to the night
over the autumn hills.

Where two waters met, to seek the sea together,
Tarka walked over the trail of otters, and recognizing the scent of White-tip, he followed up the water
the otters had travelled. Near the end of the night,
while he was swimming in a pool scooped in the

rocks below a fall, he saw an otter-shape before him. *East Lyn* It moved slowly with the sway of water, its head *Water* lolled on a stone. It had been drowned some hours. The whistles of otters playing at the fall, during the previous night, had been heard by the water-owner, who had set a gin under the wash of the fall, on a sunken ledge of rock where otters touched after the joyful pounding of the plunge. The otters had come back again.

Iron in the water sinks, and however long cubs call her, a bitch otter cannot swim with three legs for ever.

Tarka heard the clink of the chain as the swollen body rolled; and his bubbles blown of fear rose behind him.

At sunrise he had crossed two miles of woods and fields—stubble with lines of sheaves, stacked in sixes and tied in fours, fields of mangel and sweet turnip, where partridge crouched, and pasture given over to sheep—and found other water below Beggars' Roost hill. Ducks were paddling by a farm as he walked upstream, passing under a bridge, by which grew a monkey-tree with leaves as sharp as magpies' beaks. Cottages by the waterside and a mill were left behind, and he came to quiet meadows where only robins were singing. He crossed from side to side, looking for a place to hide during the sunlight. Half a mile above the mill he found a rock in the left bank of the stream, with a wide opening half under water. Hazels grew on the bank above. Their leaves took on the golden-green of spring in the beams of the low autumn sun as Tarka crept under the rock.

CHAPTER FIFTEEN

HE WAS AWAKENED BY THE TREMENDOUS BAYING of hounds. He saw feet splashing in the shallow water, a row of noses, and many flacking tongues. The entrance was too small for any head to enter. He crouched a yard away, against the cold rock. The noise hurt the fine drums of his ears.

Hob-nailed boots scraped on the brown shillets of the water-bed, and iron-tipped hunting poles tapped the rocks.

Go'r'n leave it! Leave it! Go'r'n leave it! Deadlock! Harper! Go'r'n leave it!

Tarka heard the horn and the low opening became lighter.

Go'r'n leave it! Captain! Deadlock! Go'r'n leave it!

The horn twanged fainter as the pack was taken away. Then a pole was thrust into the holt and prodded about blindly. It slid out again. Tarka saw boots and hands and the face of a terrier. A voice whispered, *Leu in there, Sammy, leu in there!* The small ragged brown animal crept out of the hands. Sammy smelled Tarka, saw him, and began to sidle towards him. *Waugh-waugh-waugh-wa-waugh.* As the otter did not move, the terrier crept nearer to him, yapping with head stretched forward.

After a minute, Tarka could bear the irritating noises no more. Tissing, with open mouth, he moved past the terrier, whose snarly yapping changed to a high-pitched yelping. The men on the opposite bank stood silent and still. They saw Tarka's head in sun-

Captain and Harper marking at the Ilkerton Holt.

Ilkerton light, which came through the trees behind them and
Water turned the brown shillets a warm yellow. The
water ran clear and cold. Tarka saw three men in
blue coats; they did not move and he slipped into the
water. It did not cover his back, and he returned to
the bankside roots. He moved in the shadows and
under the ferns at his ordinary travelling pace. One
of three watching men declared that an otter had no
sense of fear.

No hound spoke, but the reason of the silence was
not considered by Tarka, who could not reason such
things. He had been awakened with a shock, he had
been tormented by a noise, he had left a
dangerous place, and he was escaping from human
enemies. As he walked upstream, with raised head,
his senses of smell, sight, and hearing were alert
for his greatest enemies, the hounds.

The stream being narrow and shallow, the otter
was given four minutes' law. For minutes after
Tarka had left he heard behind him the short and
long notes of the horn, and the huntsman crying
amidst the tongues of hounds *Ol-ol-ol-ol-ol-ol-over!*
Get on to 'm! Ol-ol-ol-ol-over! as the pack returned in
full cry to the water. Hounds splashed into the water
around the rock, wedging themselves at its opening
and breaking into couples and half-couples, leaping
through the water after the wet and shivering terrier,
throwing their tongues and dipping their noses to
the wash of scent coming down.

Deadlock plunged at the lead, with Coraline,
Sailoress, Captain, and Playboy. They passed the

terrier, and Deadlock was so eager that he knocked him *Dusty* down. Sammy picked up his shivery body and followed. *Meadow* Tarka sank all but his nostrils in a pool and waited. He lay in the sunlit water like a brown log slanting to the stones on which his rudder rested. The huntsman saw him. Tarka lifted his whiskered head out of the water, and stared at the huntsman. Hounds were speaking just below. From the pool the stream flowed for six feet down the smooth slide up which he had crept. When Deadlock jumped into the pool and lapped the scent lying on the water, Tarka put down his head with hardly a ripple, and like a skin of brown oil moved under the hound's belly. Soundlessly he emerged, and the sun glistened on his water-sleeked coat as he walked down on the algae-smeared rock. He seemed to walk under their muzzles slowly, and to be treading on their feet.

Let hounds hunt him! Don't help hounds or they'll chop him!
The pack was confused. Every hound owned the scent, which was like a tangled line, the end of which was sought for unravelling. But soon Deadlock pushed through the pack and told the way the otter had gone.

As Tarka was running over shillets with water scarcely deep enough to cover his rudder, Deadlock saw him and with stiff stern ran straight at him. Tarka quitted the water. The dead twigs and leaves at the hedge-bottom crackled and rustled as he pushed through to the meadow. While he was running over the grass, he could hear the voice of Deadlock raging as the bigger black-and-white hound struggled through the hazel twigs and brambles and

o   *195*

Lynton honeysuckle bines. He crossed fifty yards of meadow,
Road climbed the bank, and ran down again on to a tarred
road. The surface burned his pads, but he ran on,
and even when an immense crimson creature bore
down upon him he did not go back into the meadow
across which hounds were streaming. With a series
of shudders the crimson creature slowed to a stand-
still, while human figures rose out of it, and pointed.
He ran under the motor-coach, and came out into
brown sunshine, hearing above the shouts of men
the clamour of hounds trying to scramble up the high
bank and pulling each other down in their eagerness.

He ran in the shade of the ditch, among bits of news-
paper, banana and orange skins, cigarette ends and
crushed chocolate boxes. A long yellow creature
grew bigger and bigger before him, and women rose
out of it and peered down at him as he passed it.
With smarting eyes he ran two hundred yards of the
road, which for him was a place of choking stinks
and hurtful noises. Pausing in the ditch, he harkened
to the clamour changing its tone as hounds leaped
down into the road. He ran on for another two
hundred yards, then climbed the bank, pushed
through dusty leaves and grasses and briars that
would hold him, and down the sloping meadow
to the stream. He splashed into the water and swam
until rocks and boulders rose before him. He climbed
and walked over them. His rudder drawn on mosses
and lichens left a strong scent behind him. Deadlock,
racing over the green-shadowed grassland, threw his
tongue before the pack.

In the water, through shallow and pool, his pace *Cherry-* was steady, but not hurried; he moved faster than *bridge* the stream; he insinuated himself from slide to pool from pool to boulder, leaving his scent in the wet marks of his pads and rudder.

People were running through the meadow, and in the near distance arose the notes of the horn and hoarse cries. Hounds' tongues broke out united and firm, and Tarka knew that they had reached the stream. The sun-laden water of the pools was spun into eddies by the thrusts of his webbed hindlegs. He passed through shadow and dapple, through runnel and plash. The water sparkled amber in the sunbeams, and his brown sleek pelt glistened whenever his back made ripples. His movements in water were unhurried, like an eel's. The hounds came nearer.

The stream after a bend flowed near the roadway, where more motor-cars were drawn up. Some men and women, holding notched poles, were watching from the cars—sportsmen on wheels.

Beggars' Roost Bridge was below. With hounds so near Tarka was heedless of the men that leaned over the stone parapet, watching for him. They shouted, waved hats, and cheered the hounds. There were ducks above the bridge, quacking loudly as they left the stream and waddled to the yard, and when Tarka came to where they had been, he left the water and ran after them. They beat their wings as they tried to fly from him, but he reached the file and scattered them, running through them and disappearing. Nearer and nearer came Deadlock, with Captain

Barbrook and Waterwitch leading the pack. Huntsman, *Mill* whippers-in, and field were left behind, struggling through hedges and over banks.

Hounds were bewildered when they reached the yard. They ran with noses to ground in puzzled excitement. Captain's shrill voice told that Tarka had gone under a gate. Waterwitch followed the wet seals in the dust, but turned off along a track of larger webs. The line was tangled again. Deadlock threw his belving tongue. Other hounds followed, but the scent led only to a duck that beat its wings and quacked in terror before them. A man with a rake drove them off, shouting and threatening to strike them. Dewdrop spoke across the yard and the hounds galloped to her, but the line led to a gate which they tried to leap, hurling themselves up and falling from the top bar. A duck had gone under the gate, but not Tarka.

All scent was gone. Hounds rolled in the dust or trotted up to men and women, sniffing their pockets for food. Rufus found a rabbit skin and ate it; Render fought with Sandboy—but not seriously, as they feared each other; Deadlock went off alone. And hounds were waiting for a lead when the sweating huntsman, grey pot-hat pushed back from his red brow, ran up with the two whippers-in and called them into a pack again. The thick scent of Muscovy ducks had checked the hunt.

Tarka had run through a drain back to the stream, and now he rested in the water that carried him every moment nearer to the murmurous glooms of the glen below. He saw the coloured blur of a kingfisher *Riddaway* perching on a twig as it eyed the water for beetle or loach. The kingfisher saw him moving under the surface, as his shadow broke the net of ripple shadows that drifted in meshes of pale gold on the stony bed beneath him.

While he was walking past the roots of a willow under the bank, he heard the yapping of the terrier. Sammy had crept through the drain, and was looking out at the end, covered with black filth, and eagerly telling his big friends to follow him downstream. As he yapped, Deadlock threw his tongue. The stallion hound was below the drain, and had re-found the line where Tarka had last touched the shillets. Tarka saw him ten yards away, and slipping back into the water, swam with all webs down the current, pushing from his nose a ream whose shadow beneath was an arrow of gold pointing down to the sea.

Again he quitted the water and ran on land to wear away his scent. He had gone twenty yards when Deadlock scrambled up the bank with Render and Sandboy, breathing the scent which was as high as their muzzles. Tarka reached the waterside trees again a length ahead of Deadlock, and fell into the water like a sodden log. Deadlock leapt after him and snapped at his head; but the water was friendly to the otter, who rolled in smooth and graceful movement away from the jaws, a straight bite of which would have crushed his skull.

Here sunlight was shut out by the oaks, and the roar of the first fall was beating back from the leaves.

Glen Lyn The current ran faster, narrowing into a race with
Clitters twirls and hollows marking the sunken rocks. The
roar grew louder in a drifting spray. Tarka and
Deadlock were carried to where a broad sunbeam
came down through a break in the foliage and lit the
mist above the fall. Tarka went over in the heavy
white folds of the torrent and Deadlock was hurled
over after him. They were lost in the churn and
pressure of the pool until a small brown head appeared and gazed for its enemy in the broken honey-
comb of foam. A black and white body uprolled
beside it, and the head of the hound was thrust up
as he tried to tread away from the current that would
draw him under. Tarka was master of whirlpools;
they were his playthings. He rocked in the surge
with delight; then high above he heard the note of
the horn. He yielded himself to the water and let it
take him away down the gorge into a pool where
rocks were piled above. He searched under the
dripping ferny clitter for a hiding place.

Under water he saw two legs, joined to two waver-
ing and inverted images of legs, and above them the
blurred shapes of a man's head and shoulders. He
turned away from the fisherman into the current
again, and as he breathed he heard the horn again.
On the road above the glen the pack was trotting
between huntsman and whippers-in, and before them
men were running with poles at the trail, hurrying
down the hill to the bridge, to make a stickle to stop
Tarka reaching the sea.

Tarka left Deadlock far behind. The hound was

feeble and bruised and breathing harshly, his head *Glen Lyn* battered and his sight dazed, but still following. *Bridge* Tarka passed another fisherman, and by chance the tiny feathered hook lodged in his ear. The reel spun against the check, *re-re-re* continuously, until all the silken line had run through the snake-rings of the rod, which bent into a circle, and whipped back straight again as the gut trace snapped.

Tarka saw the bridge, the figure of a man below it, and a row of faces above. He heard shouts. The man standing on a rock took off his hat, scooped the air, and holla'd to the huntsman, who was running and slipping with the pack on the loose stones of the steep red road. Tarka walked out of the last pool above the bridge, ran over a mossy rock merged with the water again, and pushed through the legs of the man.

Tally-ho!

Tarka had gone under the bridge when Harper splashed into the water. The pack poured through the gap between the end of the parapet and the hill-side earth, and their tongues rang under the bridge and down the walls of the houses built on the rock above the river.

Among rotting motor tyres, broken bottles, tins, pails, shoes, and other castaway rubbish lying in the bright water, hounds made their plunging leaps. Once Tarka turned back; often he was splashed and trodden on. The stream was seldom deep enough to cover him, and always shallow enough for the hounds to move at double his speed. Sometimes he was under the pack, and then, while hounds were massing for the

Lynmouth worry, his small head would look out beside a rock ten yards below them.

Between boulders and rocks crusted with shellfish and shaggy with seaweed, past worm-channered posts that marked the fairway for fishing boats at high water, the pack hunted the otter. Off each post a gull launched itself, cackling angrily as it looked down at the animals. Tarka reached the sea. He walked slowly into the surge of a wavelet, and sank away from the chop of old Harper's jaws, just as Deadlock ran through the pack. Hounds swam beyond the line of waves, while people stood at the sea-lap and watched the huntsman wading to his waist. It was said that the otter was dead-beat, and probably floating stiffly in the shallow water. After a few minutes the huntsman shook his head, and withdrew the horn from his waistcoat. He filled his lungs and stopped his breath and was tightening his lips for the four long notes of the call-off, when a brown head with hard dark eyes, was thrust out of the water a yard from Deadlock. Tarka stared into the hound's face and cried *Ic-yang!*

The head sank. Swimming under Deadlock, Tarka bit on to the loose skin of the flews and pulled the hound's head under water. Deadlock tried to twist round and crush the otter's skull in his jaws, but he struggled vainly. Bubbles blew out of his mouth. Soon he was choking. The hounds did not know what was happening. Deadlock's hindlegs kicked the air weakly. The huntsman waded out and pulled him inshore, but Tarka loosened his bite only when

he needed new air in his lungs; and then he swam *The*
under and gripped Deadlock again. Only when *Severn*
hounds were upon him did Tarka let go. He vanished *Sea*
in a wave.

Long after the water had been emptied out of
Deadlock's lungs, and the pack had trotted off for
the long uphill climb to the railway station, the gulls
were flying over something in the sea beyond the
mouth of the little estuary. Sometimes one dropped
its yellow webs to alight on the water; always it flew
up again into the restless, wailing throng, startled
by the snaps of white teeth. A cargo steamer was
passing up the Severn Sea, leaving a long smudge of
smoke on the horizon, where a low line of clouds
billowed over the coast of Wales. The regular
thumps of its screws in the windless blue calm were
borne to where Tarka lay, drowsy and content, but
watching the pale yellow eyes of the nearest bird.
At last the gulls grew tired of seeing only his eyes,
and flew back to their posts; and turning on his back,
Tarka yawned and stretched himself, and floated at
his ease.

CHAPTER SIXTEEN

SWIMMING TOWARDS THE SUNSET TARKA FOUND a cleft in the high curved red cliff, and on the crest of a wave rode into the cavern beyond. The broken wave slapped against the dark end as he climbed to a ledge far above the lipping of the swell, and curled himself on cold stone. He awoke when the gulls and cormorants were flying over the sea, silent as dusk, to their roosts in the cliff.

The straight wavelets of the rising tide were moving across the rock pools below the cleft, where under green and purple laver-weed crabs and prawns were stirring to feed. The weed, so placid before, was kicked and entangled by the searching otter. The crab he climbed out with was bitter, and leaving it, he swam into deep water.

A herring shoal was coming up with the evening tide, followed by a herd of porpoises, which when breathing showed shiny black hides through the waves. Fishermen called them errin-ogs. Once these warm-blooded mammals had ears and hair and paws, but now their ear-holes were small as thorn-pricks, and their five-toed paws were changed into flippers. Their forefathers, who had come from the same family as the forefathers of otters and seals, had taken early to water, shaping themselves for a sea-life while yet the seals were running on land. Their young, born under water, needed no mother's back to raise them to the air of life, for ancestral habit had become instinct.

An old boar porpoise flung himself out of a trough

near Tarka and fell with a clapping splash on its *East*
back, to shale off the barnacle-like parasites boring *Cleave*
into its blubber. Near the boar swam a sow porpoise,
suckling her little one, who, towed along on its back,
breathed during every rise and roll of its mother.
Tarka caught his first herring and ate it on a rock,
liking the taste, but when he swam out for more, the
under-seas were vacant.

For a week he slept in the disused lime-kiln on the
greensward above the Heddon water, that lost itself
in a ridge of boulders above the tide wash. While he
was exploring the fresh water a storm broke over the
moor, and the roaring coloured spate returned him
to the sea. He went westwards, under the towering
cliffs and waterfalls in whose ferny sides he liked to
rest by day. Once he was awakened by a dreadful
mumbling in the wind far above him. As he lifted
his head he heard a whishing noise, as of falcons in
swoop. Flakes of scree clattered and hurtled past
him; then a stag, and three staghounds. The bodies
smashed on the rocks, and were of silence again.
Soon the cries of seabirds and daws were echoing out
of the cliffs. Ravens flew down, and buzzards, and
the air was filled with black and white and brown
wings, with deep croaking, wailing, and shrill
screaming. They jostled and fought for an hour, when
a motor-boat, holding a red-coated figure, came
round the eastern sheer and drove them into flight.
The gulls mobbed Tarka when they saw him slipping
down from his resting ledge, but he found the sea and
sank away from them. That night, quatting on a

rock and eating a conger, the west wind brought him
the scent of White-tip.

At dawn he was swimming under the sea-feet
of the Great Hangman; and he followed the trail
until sunrise was shimmering down the level sea and
filling with aerial gold the clouds over the Welsh hills.

At dusk the shore-rats on Wild Pear Beach, searching
the weed-strewn tide-line, paused and squealed
together when their sharp noses took the musky
scent of water-weasels. They ran off chittering as
terrible shapes galloped among them. A rat was
picked up and killed in a swift bite. The cub did not
want it for food; he killed it in fun. He ran into the
sea after White-tip, who had been taking care of
the cubs since their mother had been trapped under
the waterfall.

Six hours later Tarka ran up Wild Pear Beach and
his thin, hard cries pierced the slop and wash of
waves on the loose, worn, shaley strand. He followed
the trail over the weeds to the otters' sleeping place
under a rock, and down again to the sea. In a pool
off Briery Cave he scented otter again, for at the
bottom of the pool lay a wicker pot, holding something that turned slowly as the ribbons of the thong-
weed lifted and dropped in the water. The long blue
feelers of a lobster were feeling through the wicker-
work; it was gorged, and trying to get away from the
otter cub it had been eating. The cub had found no
way out of the cage it had entered at high tide, in-
tending to eat the lobster.

Hu-ee-ic! Tarka did not know the dead. Nothing *Rockham* answered, and he swam away, among green phos- *Bay* phoric specks that glinted at every wave-lop.

Autumn's little summer, when day and night were equal, and only the woodlark sang his wistful falling song over the bracken, was ruined by the gales that tore wave and leaf, and broke the sea into roar and spray, and hung white ropes over the rocks. Fog hid cliff-tops and stars as Tarka travelled westwards. One night, as he was drinking fresh water from a pool below a cascade, he was startled by immense whooping bellows that bounded from the walls of mist and rebounded afar, to return in duller echoes as though phantom hounds were baying the darkness. Tarka slipped into a pool and hid under lifting seaweed; but the sounds were regular and harmless, and afterwards he did not heed them. On a rock below the white-walled tower of Bull Point lighthouse, whose twin sirens were sending a warning to sailors far out beyond the dreadful rocks, Tarka found again the trail of White-tip, and whistled with joy.

Travelling under the screes, where rusted plates of wrecked ships lay in pools, he came to the end of the land. Day was beginning. The tide, moving northwards across Morte Bay from Bag Leap, was ripped and whitened by rocks which stood out of the hollows of the grey sea. One rock was tall above the reef— the Morte Stone—and on the top pinnacle stood a big black bird, with the tails of fish sticking out of its gullet. Its dripping wings were held out to ease its tight crop. The bird was Phalacrocorax Carbo,

The Morte Stone and Isle-of-Wight Parson meditating.

called the Isle-of-Wight Parson by fishermen, and it *The* sat uneasily on the Morte Stone during most of the *Morte* hours of daylight, swaying with a load of fishes.

Tired and buffeted by the long Atlantic rollers, Tarka turned back under the Morte Stone, and swam to land. He climbed a slope strewn with broken thrift-roots and grey shards of rock, to a path set on its seaward verge by a fence of iron posts and cables. Salt winds had gnawed the iron to rusty splinters. The heather above the path was tougher than the iron, but its sprigs were barer than its own roots.

Over the crest of the Morte, heather grew in low bushes, out of the wind's way. There were green places where among grass cropped by sheep grew mushrooms mottled like owl's plumage. The sky above the crest was reddening, and he found a sleeping place under a broken cromlech, the burial place of an ancient man, whose bones were grass and heather and dust in the sun.

Tarka slept warm all day. At sunset he ran down to the sea. He worked south through the currents that scoured shelly coves and swept round lesser rocks into the wide Morte Bay. Long waves, breaking near the shallows, left foam behind them in the shapes of dusky-white seals. Bass were swimming in the breakers, taking sand-eels risen in the sandy surge. A high-flying gull saw a fish flapping in the shallows, with ribbon weed across its head. The gull glided down, and the ribbon weed arose on low legs, tugging at the five-pound fish, and dragged it on to firm, wet sand. *Hak-hak!* cried the gull, angrily. *Tu-lip, tulip!*

Wool- the ring-plover arose and flickered away in a flock.
combe Other gulls flew over, and dropped down. Tarka
Sands feasted among the noise of wings and angry cries.
When he was full, he lapped fresh water trickling
over the sand in a broad and shallow bed. *Hu-ee-ic!*
He galloped up the sand, nose between paws. He
ran up into the sandhills, where his passing sowed
round orange-red seeds from the split dry pods of the
stinking iris. Over a lonely road, among old stalks
of ragwort and teasel, and up a steep bank to the
incult hill, pushing among bracken, furze, and
brambles, following the way of White-tip. He found
the head of a rabbit which she had caught, and
played with it, whistling as he rolled it with his paws.

Already larks were ceasing to sing. When he reached
the top of Pickwell down, eastern clouds were ruddy
and Hoaroak Hill, seventeen miles away as the falcon
glides, was as a shadow lying under the sky. He
descended to a gulley in the hills, a dry watercourse
marked by furze bushes, and thorns, and hollies,
growing down to sandhills by the sea. The gulley
lay south-west; the trees lay over to the north-east,
bitter and dwarfed by salt and wind. Under a holly
bush, bearer of ruined blossoms and spineless leaves,
whose limbs were tortured by ivy thicker in trunk than
its own, the otter crawled into a bury widened by many
generations of rabbits, and lay down in the darkness.

The wind rushed up the gulley, moving stiffly the
blackthorns which squeaked as they rubbed against
each other. Dry branches of elderberries rattled and
scraped as though bemoaning their poverty. Gulls

veered from hilltop to hilltop, calling the flock *Weest* standing far below on the sands that gleamed with *Gulley* the dull sky. The dark base of the headland lying out in the Atlantic was flecked along its length with the white of breaking waves. The sea's roar came with blown spray up the gulley. Tarka slept.

He awoke before noon, hearing voices of men. Mist was drifting between the hills. He lay still until a man spoke at the day-dim opening of the bury. An animal moved down the tunnel, whose smell immediately disturbed him. He remembered it. The animal's eyes glowed pink, and a bell tinkled round its neck. Tarka crawled farther into the bury and ran out of another hole, that was watched by a spaniel sitting shivering and wet, behind a man with a gun on the bank above. The spaniel jumped back when it saw Tarka, who ran down the gulley, hastening when he heard a bark, a shout, and two bangs of the gun. Twigs showered upon him, and he ran on, hidden by the thorny brake. Two men clambered down the banks, but only the spaniel followed him, barking with excitement, but not daring to go near him. It returned to its master's whistle. Tarka hid under a blackberry bush lower down, and slept among the brambles until darkness, when he left the shelter and climbed up the hillside.

He ran under a gate to a field beyond, crossing a rabbit's line, he followed it through hawthorns wind-bent over the stone bank, to the waste land again. The rabbit was crouching under the wind in a tussock, and one bite killed it. After the meal Tarka

Skirr drank rain-water in a sheep's skull, which lay among
Cottage rusty ploughshares, old iron pots, tins, and skeletons
of sheep—some broken up by cattle dogs, and all
picked clean by crows and ravens. Tarka played
with a shoulder-blade because White-tip had touched
it in passing. He ran at it and bit the cold bone
as though it were White-tip. He played with
many things that night as he ran across field and
bank.

Following the trail he came to a pond in a boggy
field below a hill. Moorhens hid in terror when he
swam among them. He caught and played with an
eel, which was found dead next morning on the bank,
beside the seals pressed in the mud by his clawed feet,
and the hair-marks of his rolling back. *Hu-ee-ic!*
Tarka ran under a culvert that carried a trickle to
a smaller pond in the garden of a rectory. *Hu-ee-ic!*
while clouds broke the light of the moon.

He climbed round the hatch of the pond, sniffing
the tarred wood, and crept under a gap in the wall
which ended the garden. The stream flowed below
a churchyard wall and by a thatched cottage, where
a man, a dog, and a cat were sitting before a fire of
elm brands on the open hearth. The wind blew the
scent of the otter under the door, and the cat fumed
and growled standing with fluffed back and twitching tail beside her basket of kittens. The otter was
scraping shillets by a flat stone under a fall by the
road, where farmers' daughters crouch to wash
chitterlings for the making of hogs'-pudding. An eel
lived under the kneeling stone, fat with pig-scrap.

Its tail was just beyond the otter's teeth. White-tip *Milkaway* had tried to catch it the night before. *Lane*

Hu-ee-ic!

The cottage door was pulled open, the spaniel rushed out barking. A white owl lifted itself off the lopped bough of one of the churchyard elms, crying *skirr·rr*. An otter's tiss of anger came from out of the culvert under the road. Striking a match the man saw, on the scour of red mud, the twy-toed seal, identical with the seal that led down to the sea after the Ice Winter.

Tarka was gone down the narrow covered way of the culvert, amid darkness and the babble of water. The stream ran under a farmhouse, and through an orchard, under another culvert and past a cottage garden to the watermeadow below. Wood owls hunting far down in the valley heard the keen cries of Tarka.

Hu-ee·ic!

Often the trail was lost, for the otters had left their seals on bank and scour before the rain had pitted and blurred them.

Tarka followed the stream. At the beginning of Cryde village the water was penned above the curve of the road. the pond being kept back by a grassy bank where stood a hawthorn clipped like a toadstool. Swimming round the edge among flags and the roots of thorns and sycamores, he saw a head looking at him from the water, and from the head strayed a joyous breath. He swam to it—a snag of elm-branch stuck in the mud. White-tip had rubbed

Down
End against it when swimming by. Tarka bit it before swimming round the pond again to sniff the wood of the penstock. He climbed out and ran along the bank, by the still mossy wooden wheel of the mill. They heard his shrill cry in the inn below. A cattle dog barked, and Tarka ran up a narrow lane which led to the top of a hill. In hoof-mudded patches he found the trail again, for the otters had run the same way when alarmed by the same dog. The trail took him under a gate and into a field, over a bank where straight stalks of mulleins were black in moonlight, to land that had forgotten the plough, a prickly place for an otter's webs. Sea-wind had broken all the bracken stalks. Suddenly he heard the mumbling roar of surf and saw the lighthouse across the Burrows. He galloped joyfully down a field of arrish, or stubble. He travelled so swiftly that soon he stood on the edge of sandy cliffs, where spray blew as wind. He found a way down to the pools by a ledge where grew plants of great sea stock, whose leaves were crumbling in autumn sleep.

The trail led over the sandhills with their thin stabbing marram grasses, and to the mossy pans behind them, where grew privet bushes and blunt-head club-rushes. The way was strewn with rabbit skulls and empty snail shells. Tarka crossed the marsh of Horsey Island—where grew Russian thistles, sprung from a single seed blown from the estuary off a Baltic timber ship years before—until he came to the sea-wall, and below the wall, to the mouth of the Branton pill. The tide took him slowly

Tarka crossing the Burrows on his way to the estuary.

Ram's- in a patch of froth which the meeting waters had
horn beaten up, the gossip of the Two Rivers. He ran
Pond over the eastern sea-wall, and along the otter path
to the Ram's horn pond.

Hu-ee-ic!

He swam to the wooden bridge by the boat-house,
and to the withies on the islet.

Hu-ee-ic!

He hunted the brackish waters until the stars were
dimmed by dawn, when he pressed through the
reeds by a way he had trodden before, but forgotten,
and slept on an old couch where lay bones, and a
little skull.

CHAPTER SEVENTEEN

ALL DAY THE WIND SHOOK THE RUSTY REED-
daggers at the sky, and the mace-heads were
never still. Before sunset the couch was empty.
The purple-ruddy beams stained the grass and the
thistles of the meadow, and the tiles of the cattle-
shippen under the sea-wall were the hue of the sky.
Westward the marchman's cottage, the linhays, the
trees, the hedges, the low ragged line of the Burrows,
were vanishing in a mist of fire.

The tide was ebbing, the mud slopes grey, with
ruddy tricklings. In the salt turf below the sea-wall
great cracks wandered with the fire of the sky. Ring-
plover and little stints ran by the guts, and their
slender peering images quenched the flame in the
water. Bunches of oarweed on each sodden perch
dripped their last drops among the froth and spinning holes of the gliding tide. The mooring buoys
rolled and returned, each keg gathering froth that
the current sucked away under its lowest stave. By an
old broken wicker crab-pot, only its rib-tops up, a
small head showed without a ripple, moving with the
water. Men were walking on the deck of a ketch
below; other men were sitting at oars in a boat under
the black hull waiting for their mates. A dog began
to bark, then it whimpered, until it was pushed over
the gunwale. It met the water in a reddish splash.

Men climbed down to the boat, oars were dipped,
and the dog swam astern, breathing gruffly and
whining. The otter head, drifting nearer, sank when

Luke's a man pointed with his pipe-stem. Fifty yards below,
Hut by the chain sagging and lifting from the bows of the
Island riding ship, the head looked up again beside the
broken wicker-work. "Artter," said the man who had
pointed, and forgot it. They were going to drink beer
in the Plough Inn.

Their voices became faint as they walked on the
wall. Flocks of ring-plover and little stint flickered
and twisted over the mud and the water. A late
crow left the saltings, as a sedge-owl swept on long
wings over the drooping yellow grass of the wall, and
slunk away across the water.

Where the pill merged into the estuary the mud
was scoured, leaving sand and gravel. Below the
stone setts and pebbles of the wall's apron, whose
cracks held the little ruddy winter leaves of the sea-
beet, was an islet of flat stones, apart from the wall
by a narrowing channel where water rushed. On
the stones stood Old Nog, watching for shapes of fish.
The broken crab-pot bumped and lurched along the
channel, and the heron straightened his neck when
he saw a fish jump out of its crown. He peered in the
dusky water, where weeds moved darkly, and saw the
fish darting before a tapered shadow. It was green
and yellow, with a streamer flying from its back. Old
Nog snicked the gemmeous dragonet from before the
otter's nose, shook it free of his beak, caught it in a
jerk that pushed it into his gullet, and swallowed it
while the otter was still searching.

Tarka saw a blur of movement above, and swam
on under water to the wide sea,

Colour faded; the waves broke grey. Across the *Horsey* marsh a shining fly had lit on the white bone of the *Weir* lighthouse. A bird flew in hooped flight up the estuary, wheeled below the islet, and began feeding. It saw Tarka, and out of its beak, hooped as its wings in downward gliding, fell a croak, which slurred upwards to a whistle, and broke in a sweet trill as it flew away. Other curlews on the sandbanks heard the warning, and to the far shore the wan air was beautiful with their cries.

Rows of hurdles, black and weed-hung, stood out of the water farther down the estuary. They were staked on three sides of a pool, while every rising tide flooded over the tops of the fences. It was an old salmon weir. The hurdles had been torn away so many times by the dredging anchors of gravel barges and ketches, whose crews were friendly with poor net fishermen, that the owner had let the weir fall ruinous. Herons fished from the hurdles, and at low tide crows picked shellfish off the stakes, and flying with them to the islet, dropped them on the stones.

At half tide Old Nog flew to the seventh hurdle up from the western row, where, unless gorged or in love or disturbed by man, he perched awhile during every ebb-tide. He stood swaying and sinuating his neck; the grip of his toes was not so strong as it had been in his early tree-top life. While he was trying to stand still, before jumping to the rim of the sand-bank awash below him, a salmon leapt in the lagoon, gleaming and curved, and fell back with a thwack on the water. Old Nog screamed, and fell off the

Horsey hurdle. Three heads looked up, and dipped again.
Weir Old Nog walked along under the hurdles, watching the
water. The salmon was many times Old Nog's own
weight, but it was a fish, and Old Nog was a fisher.

Tarka was drifting past the weir when he heard the
whistle of White-tip beyond the hurdles. His head
and shoulders rose out of the water; he listened.

Hu-ee-ic!

White-tip answered him. Her cry was like wet
fingers drawn over a pane of glass. Tarka's cry was
deeper, more rounded, and musical. He ran across
the strip of wet sand, clambered over the hurdles,
and down to the lagoon. He touched water, and a
ripple spread out from where he had disappeared.
His seals in the sand crumbled as they welled water.

Ka-ak! Old Nog ejected the living dragonet in his
excitement, for the salmon had leapt again, a glimmering curve. The teeth of White-tip clicked at its
tail. Three otter heads bobbed, flat as corks of a salmon net. They vanished before the double splash fell.

The salmon passed through the cubs, cutting the
water. They turned together. Tarka drove between
them and slowed to their pace, keeping line. Then
White-tip, who was faster than Tarka, overhauled
them, and the old otters took the wings. The line
swung out and in as each otter swam in zigzag. The
eager cubs swam in each other's way. Once more
the salmon rushed back against the current, straining
through the top hurdles, where the water was deeper
and safer. Tarka met it; and the thresh of its turning
tail beat up splinters of water. The line of otters

forced it into the shallow by the lower hurdles. *Horsey* They swam upon it, resting in two feet of water, but *Weir* it escaped past one of the cubs.

Soon the tide dropped back from the top row of hurdles and the water was cleared of sand. A race poured steadily through a gap in the sand-bank, spreading wider as it drained the lagoon. In the penned and slack upper water the salmon was lying, its fins and tail so still that shrimps rose out of their hiding-places in the sand beside it. While it rested in the water, its gills opening and closing, a dark squat thing was walking on the sand towards it, using its fins as feet. It was the shape of an immense tadpole, covered with tatters of skin like weed. Its head was as broad as a barrel, gaping with a mouth almost as wide. Its jaws were filled with bands of long pointed teeth, which it depressed in the cavern of its mouth when it came near the salmon. Out of the middle of its head rose three stalks, the first of which bore a lappet, which it waved like a bait as it crept forward. It was a sea-devil, called rod-and-line fish by fishermen. During the spring tide it had left the deep water beyond the bar where usually it lived, and moving up the estuary, had been trapped in the hurdle weir.

It crept forward so slowly that the salmon did not know it for an enemy. The close-set eyes behind the enormous bony lips were fixed on the salmon. Chains of bubbles loomed beyond, with otter-shapes; the salmon swirled off the sand, into the cavern of jaws; the teeth rose in spikes and the jaws shut.

The Crow Thrice the old otters worked round and across the dwindling lagoon in search of the fish, and then they forgot it, and went down with the tide. Stars shone over the estuary, the cries of wading birds were wandering as the air. The otters drifted down, passing the cottage glimmering white on the sea-wall, passing the beached hulk of the hospital ship, silent and dark but for a solitary candle in a port hole. The tide took them to the spit of gravel, crowned by sandhills bound with marram grasses, called Crow Island, and here they left the water for a ragrowster. While the cubs were rolling and biting, Tarka and White-tip played the game of searching and pretending not to find. They galloped up the sandhills to slide to the hollows again. They picked up sticks, empty shells of skate's eggs, old bones and feathers of sea-birds, corks from the jetsam of the high tide, and tossed with them in their paws. They hid in the spines of the tussocks, and jumped out at each other.

The lighthouse beams shone on the wet sands down by the water, and across the Pool the lights of the village lay like wind-blown embers. *Craa-leek, cur-lee-eek!* The curlews saw them as they swam the shallow water to the top of the Shrarshook. White-tip and Tarka ate mussels down by the black-and-white Pulley buoy, and the cubs followed them to the pools of the lower ridge.

Salmon, feverish to spawn in the fresh waters of their birth, were "running" up the fairway, and with the flow came a seal, who tore a single bite from the belly of each fish it caught, and left it to chase

222

others. Tarka brought one of the wounded fish to the *Horsey* rocks, and the otters scratched away scales in their *Pit* haste to eat its pink flesh. They sliced from the shoulders, dropping pieces to feel the curd squeezed from the corners of their mouths. Tarka and White-tip ate quietly, but the cubs yinnered and snarled. Their faces were silvery with scales when they left the strewn bones. Being clean little beasts they washed chins and whiskers and ears, and afterwards sought water to drink in the pond behind the sea-wall cottage.

Among the reeds the four otters lay, dozing and resting, while rain pitted the grey sheet of water and wind bent down the stalks of the wild celery that grew in the marsh When the clouds became duller they left the pond, and saw the tide lapping almost over the top of the wall, coloured with the fresh from the rivers.

Mullet had come up with the tide, and a school of nearly a hundred found a way through a drain-lid under the sea-wall of the pill. At the end of the night the otters, who had been gorging on eels in the mires —reed-fringed dykes in the grazing marsh, filled with fresh drinking water from the hills—found them in the pit in the corner of Horsey marsh. For two hours they chased and slew, and when every fish was killed Tarka and White-tip stole away on the ebb to the sea, leaving the young otters to begin their own life.

The next night was quiet and windless, without a murmur of water in the broad Pool, on which the

Beam lights of the village drew out like gold and silver eels.
Weir Sound travels far and distinct over placid water, and
fishermen standing in groups on the quay, after the
closing of taverns, heard the whistling cries of the
young otters, a mile away on Crow Island, lost on
the shingle where the ring-plovers piped. They were
heard for three nights, and then the south-west gale
smote the place and filled the estuary with great seas.

Black bits of old leaves turned and twirled in the
flooded weir-pool above Canal Bridge, like the rooks
turning and twirling high in the grey windy sky.
The weir in flood was an immense loom in sunlight;
the down-falling water-warp was whitey-yellow with
bubbles; to and fro across the weir moved the air-
hollows, a weft held by a glistening water-shuttle.
Below, the bubble-woven waters were rended on
the shillets; they leapt and roared and threw up
froth and spray. A branch of a tree was lodged on
the sill; the rocks had stripped it of bark. Sometimes
a lead-coloured narrow shape, longer than a man's
arm, would appear in the falling water-warp, moving
slowly against the torrent with sideways flaps of tail
until washed back into the lower river again, which
roared and heaved like fighting polar bears. The sun
lit the travelling air-hollow under the sill of the weir.
The salmon never reached the sill. Some fish tried
to swim up the fish-pass, but the pound of the flood
was mightier on the steps. Above in the weir-pool a
bird was swimming, low in the water, watching with
small crimson eyes for trout. Its beak was sharp as a

Salmon at fish-pass of Beam Weir, in heavy Torridge fresh.

Beam rock-splinter. Above the water it was brownish-
Weir black, foam-grey beneath—a great northern diver in
winter plumage. When Tarka saw it first it was rolling from side to side and stretching out first one
wing then the other. The otter on the bank alarmed
the diver, who tipped up and vanished quick as the
flash of a turning fish, hardly leaving a ripple. When
it appeared again the otter was gone. It lay in the
water, nearly a yard long, with head and neck
stretched out, and swam rapidly up-river. At the top
of the pool it saw another otter, and uttering a wailing cry of alarm, it splashed along the water to rise,
making a dozen oar-like dips with the tips of its wings.
With neck out-stretched it took the air and flew
round the curve of the river, with wing-beats quicker
than a heron's.

Tarka and White-tip had come from the wood in
daylight, lured to play by the sun and the flood.
Tarka dropped over the sill, the whitey-yellow turmoil bumped and tossed him below. A minute later
a narrow lead-coloured shape pushed slowly up the
concrete spill-way, and behind it the darker, sturdier
shape of an otter. Fish and animal made slow and
laborious head-way; they seemed to be hanging in
the warp; and then White-tip dropped over in the
smooth and glistering water's bend. They instantly
disappeared. The racing churn carried them on its
top to the bank thirty yards below, and there left
them on stones; and there, an hour later, a thirty-
pound fish, clean-run, its gills crusty with ocean
shellfish, was found by the water-bailiff, with bites

torn from behind its shoulder—the mating feast of *Lancarse* otters. *Yeo*

November, December, January, February were past —but otters know only day and night, the sun and the moon. White-tip and Tarka had followed the salmon up the big river, but at the beginning of the new year they had come down again. Drifting with the ebb under Halfpenny Bridge, they crossed the marsh and came to the Pool of the Six Herons, out of whose deep middle reared the black iron piers of the Railway Bridge. Just below the Railway Bridge, the muddy mouth of the Lancarse Yeo was washed and widened by the sea, and in here, on the flood tide, the otters turned. White-tip was way-wise in this water, having known it in cubhood. She was going back to the Twin-Ash Holt above Orleigh Mill, where she had been born.

With the tide the otters drifted under the road bridge to a holt in an old rabbit bury above high water mark. It was fallen in, and the home of rats, so they left it, and travelled on in daylight. A mile from the pill-mouth the water ran fresh and clear. After another mile they came to the meeting of two streams. White-tip walked up the left stream, and soon she reached the slide where she had played during many happy nights with her cub-brothers; and climbing up, she was in the remembered weir-pool. It was narrow, and nearly hidden by trees. Past six pines, and round a bend, where two ash trees leaned over the brook. Ivy grew on one, moss on the other. Floods had washed the earth from their top

Q

Duntz roots, carving a dark holt under the bank. White-tip *Brook* had forgotten the baying and yapping and thudding one day long ago, when an iron bar had broken a hole in the roof and scared the five of them into the water. She had remembered the bass at night round the bridge piers in the Pool of the Six Herons, the frogging places in the Archery Marsh, the trout and the mullyheads in the *Duntz* brook, the eels in the mill-pool; and she had come back to them.

The soft elderberry tree broke into leaf, with the honeysuckle; the wild cherry blossom showed white among the oaks. The green shovels of the celandine dug pale gold out of the sun, and the flowers were made. Oak and ash remained hard budded; these trees, enduring the ancient, were not moved to easy change like lesser growths.

On the first day of March Halcyon the kingfisher, speeding up the brook, hit the sandy bank with his beak, and fell away. His mate followed him, knocking out another flake of earth, and thus a perching place was made. They picked out a tunnel with their beaks, as long as a man's arm, with a round cave at the end in which seven round eggs were laid, shiny and white, among bones of fishes and shucks of water-beetles. Then the river-martins came back to their old drowned homes in the steep sandy banks above the springtime level of the brook. In the third week of March the carrion crow, secure in her nest of sticks atop one of the six pines growing over the pool below the Twin-Ash Holt, watched the first chipping of her five eggs, watched the tip of a tiny beak chip, chip, chipping a lid in a green black- *Lancarse* freckled shell. The crow sang a song, low and sweet, *Pill* in the tree-top. White-tip heard the song as she suckled her cubs in the Twin-Ash Holt. Every night Tarka came up from the Pool of the Six Herons to see her.

March winds brought the grey sea-rains to the land, and the river ran swollen, bearing the floods of its brooks and runners. Salmon, languid from spawning, dropped tail-first over the sills and down the passes of the weirs, and Tarka caught them easily in the eddies and hovers, and dragged them on the bank. He took bites from the infirm and tasteless flesh, and left the fish uneaten. Many of the salmon that reached the sea alive were taken in the nets of fishermen rough-fish-catching, in the estuary Pool, to be knocked on the head and thrown back—for the fishermen hated the water-bailiffs who upheld the Conservancy Bye-laws protecting salmon out of season, and secretly killed the fish because of their hatred. The fishermen did not believe that salmon spawned in fresh water, where the rivers were young, but regarded it as a story told to prevent them fishing for salmon throughout the year.

Oak and ash broke their buds, and grew green; the buzzards repaired their old nests, and laid their eggs. The heron's young, after days of flapping and un-happy crying, flew from their tree-top heronry in the wood below Halfpenny Bridge. And one evening in June, between the lights, Old Nog and his mate sailed down to the pool by the Railway Bridge to

Pool of give the four fledglings their first lesson in fishing.
the Six Curlews saw the dark level wings gliding over the
Herons mudbanks, and cried the alarm, being afraid of the
sharp beaks. Every year Old Nog and his mate
taught four fledglings to spear fish in the pool, which
lay placid when the sea had lapsed.

Six herons stood in a row eighty yards above the
bridge, in the sandy shallow at the head of the pool.
Kack! Kack! Kack! Kack!—the young birds squawked
with eagerness and delight. Dusk deepened over the
wide and empty river, the pool shone faintly with the
sky. Down by the round black piers of the bridge
something splashed. Old Nog raised his head, for he
had been awaiting the splash. It was a sign that the
bass in the pool were beginning to feed.

Splash, splatter, splash. Soon many fish were rising
to take the shrimp-fry on the surface. They were
hungry after the daytime rest, having gone up with
the tide to Halfpenny Bridge, and returned to the
pool without feeding, while men on the banks fished
with lines of rag-worm-baited hooks. Usually the
men went home to supper, with empty baskets,
before the fishes' feeding time. Then to the quiet pool
came that wise fisher, Old Nog, with his family,
standing motionless while the bass swam into the
shallow water;—splash, splatter, splash, as they
turned on their gleaming sides to take the shrimp-fry.
Old Nog peered with beak held low, and snicked—
Kack! Kack! Kack! Kack! cried the four small herons,
beating vanes and falling over long toes in their
eagerness to gulp the silvery fish.

230

The Iron Bridge, Lancross.

Pool of Gark! said Old Nog, swallowing the bass, and *the Six* thrusting his beak and long feathered neck at the *Herons* four. *Gark!* They got out of his way; never before had he spoken so severely to them. One saw the flicker of a fish in the water, and stepped towards it; the bass saw the enemy, and sped into deeper water. *Gark!* said Old Nog, sharply, and they stood still.

Sucking noises arose out of the pool as it grew darker. These were the feeding noises of male eels, thin and small and mud-coloured, whom the larger blue females would meet in the autumnal migration. In wriggling rushes the eels sought the shrimp-fry in the shallows, and whenever one passed near a beak—*dap!* it was snicked, lifted from the water as a writhing knot, and swallowed.

The Railway Bridge loomed low and black against the glimmer of sky and water. Splash, splatter, the bass were moving about the pool. Two or three lay trout-wise, in the slight downward current by each round iron pier, watching the surface above them for the dark moving speck of a shrimp. The splashes of their jumps echoed under the girders.

A summer sandpiper flew over the bridge, crying in the darkness, for it had been alarmed while feeding under the mud slopes of the empty pill. It was answered by a curlew on the gravel bank above the herons.

Immediately below the bridge the brook poured its little fresh stream into the pool; raising up little ridges of sand, sweeping them away again with sudden little noises. Splash, splatter, the bass were feeding in the weed on the stone piling below the bridge- *Pool of* end. Patter, patter, five dark shapes moving on the *the Six* soft wet sand of the pill's mouth—the pattering *Herons* ceased, and the brook slurred its sand-sounds as they slid into the pool. White-tip had brought her four cubs from the Twin-Ash Holt.

The vigorous splashing of the bass was lessening, for many fish were gorged with fry. A whitish shine by the stone piling, and one had risen to seize a shrimp in its large mouth—splash, flicker, splatter, bubble. A dark shape crawled out of the water with the bass. Three lesser shapes followed, yikkering on the stone piling. White-tip turned back into the pool.

Krark! Kak! Ark! Kak! Kack! Kack! Kack! Kack! Kak! Kak! Gark! Kack!

With heads upheld and watching the herons talked among themselves. They saw three cubs fighting over the fish on the piling; and two heads in the water between the first and second pier. Tarquol, the eldest cub, was following White-tip, for he liked to do his own hunting; and it was in the Pool of the Six Herons that the strange big otter, who chased him in and out of the piers, never biting or sulking, was to be found. Tarquol, who had two white toes on one of his paws, was stronger than the other cubs, and often hurt them in play without knowing it.

The bass, staying in the flumes around the piers with fin and tail, watched the dim forewater above them. All was dark beside and below them. Tarquol and White-tip swam one on either side of a pier, deeper than the bass, whose narrow shapes were dark

The Kelt and plain above them. A fish darted around the pier
Pool before White-tip, and was taken by Tarquol. He ate
it on the quick-sand of the right bank, away from
the cubs. The sharp point of the back fin pricked his
mouth.

The otters caught eels in the shallow edges of the
pool, watched by the hungry herons, whose harsh
continuous cries told their anger. When the cubs had
eaten enough they played on the sand, running on
and on until they were behind the six birds, on the
ridge of gravel where snags were part buried.
Curlews—the unmated birds which had not gone to
the moors—flew off the glidders, and away up the
tidal reaches of the river.

Hu-ee-ic!

Tarquol, playing with the rotten crown of an old
bowler hat—fishermen always kept their bait in old
Sunday chapel-going hats—heard the whistle, and
dashed back to the pool. *Krark!* cried Old Nog, flying
up before him, his toes on the water. *Kak! Kack!
Kack! Kack! Kack!* as his mate and youngsters followed. Old Nog flew over the bridge, but seeing and
hearing the tide flowing up, he wheeled and beat up
the Yeo valley. The five herons followed him, but
he dived at them, screaming *Gark! Gark!* Old Nog
was weary after many weeks of hunger, of disgorging
nearly all he caught into the greedy maws of four
grown fledglings, and often, the greedy maw of his
mate. *Krark!* a cry of satisfaction. Old Nog flew
alone.

Every night for a week the otters came to the pool

at low water, until the tides, ebbing later and later, *Canal* and so into daylight, stopped the fishing. One *Bridge* evening, when the Peal Rock in the river below Canal Bridge was just awash after a thunderstorm, Tarka and White-tip and the four cubs followed a run of peal as far as the weir-pool, staying out until after sunrise, when several fish were taken in the water, then low and clear again. The Twin-Ash Holt was far behind them, so they slept in a holt under an oak, which was entered by an opening two feet below the water-level. The next night they went on up the river, catching and eating fish on the scours and shoals, then hastening back to water again.

Tarquol swam near Tarka; the cub was lithe and swift as his parent, and sometimes snatched fish from his mouth. They rolled and romped together, clutching rudders and heads and pretending to bite; their joyful whistles went far down the river, heard by Old Nog as he sailed by in the wasting moonlight.

Paler the moon rose, and at dawn White-tip went down with the cubs and Tarka wandered on alone; but he turned back again, calling her to Canal Bridge to play one last game.

Hu-ee-ic!

They played the old bridge game of the West Country otters, which was played before the Romans came. They played around the upper and lower cut-water of the middle pier, while the lesser stars were drowned in the heavenly tide flowing up the eastern sky, and the trees of the hill-line grew dark, and larks were flying with song.

Dark Hu-ee-ic!

Hams Tarquol followed Tarka out of the river and along the otter-path across the bend, heedless of his mother's call. He followed up the river and across another bend; but, scared of the light, returned to water and sought a holt under a sycamore. Tarka went on alone, up three miles of river, to a holt in a weir-pool shadowed by trees, where peal were leaping. The sun looked over the hills, the moon was as a feather dropped by the owl flying home, and Tarka slept, while the water flowed, and he dreamed of a journey with Tarquol down to a strange sea, where they were never hungry, and never hunted.

Deadlock.

CHAPTER EIGHTEEN

A T HALF-PAST TEN IN THE MORNING A COVERED motor-van stopped at the bridge below the Dark Pool. From the driver's seat three men got down, and at the sound of their footfalls deep notes came from the van. Hearing the hounds, the two terriers—Biff and Bite'm—held by a girl in jacket and short skirt of rough blue serge, yapped and strained against the chain.

Motor-cars were drawn up on one side of the road. The men, women, and children who had come to the meet of otterhounds stood by them and talked or lounged against the stone parapets of the bridge. Some men leaned on long ash poles, stained and polished with linseed oil and shod with iron and notched from the top downwards with the number of past kills, two notches crossed denoting a double-kill. The women carried smaller and slenderer poles, either of ash or male bamboo. There were blackthorn thumbsticks, hazel-wands, staves of ground-ash; one boy held the handle of a carpet-sweeper, slightly warped. He had poked the end in some nettles, lest the wooden screw be seen by other boys. It had no notches.

Faces turned to the hound-van. Huntsman and his whipper-in each lifted a rusty pin from the staples in the back of the van and lowered the flap. Immediately hounds fell out and over each other, and to the road, shaking themselves, whimpering, panting with pink tongues flacking, happy to be free after the crush and heat of the journey from kennels. They *Town* were admired and stroked, patted and spoken to by *Mills* name; they scratched themselves and rolled and licked each others necks; they sat and looked up at the many faces—old Harper solemnly, with eyes sunk by age, the younger hounds, still remembering their walking days, going to seek their human friends, and sniff and nuzzle pockets where biscuits, cake, and sandwiches were stored. The kennel-boy and whip called them by name and flicked gently near the more restless with his whip: Barbrook and Bellman, Boisterous and Chorister, Dewdrop, Sailoress, Coraline, and Waterwitch; Armlet, who lay down to sleep, Playboy and Actor, Render and Fencer; Hemlock the one-eyed, with Bluemaid, Hurricane, Harper, and Pitiful, the veterans; Darnel and Grinder, who sat behind Sandboy. Then two young hounds of the same litter, Dabster and Dauntless, sons of Dewdrop and Deadlock.

And there Deadlock, his black head scarred with old fights, sat on his haunches, apart and morose, watching for the yellow waistcoat of the Master. His right ear showed the mark made by the teeth of Tarka's mother two years before, when he had thrust his head into the hollow of the fallen tree. The swung thong of the whip idly flicked near Deadlock; he moved his head slightly and his eyes; from upper and lower teeth the lips were drawn, and looking at the kennel-boy's legs, Deadlock growled. The hound hated him.

People were watching. The whipper-in felt that the

Town hound was making him ridiculous, and flicked Dead-
Mills lock with the lash, speaking sharply to him. The
hound's growls grew more menacing. Between his
teeth the hound yarred, the dark pupils of his eyes
becoming fixed in their stare. Then seeing Dabster
trotting off to the bridge the whipper-in gladly went
after him. Deadlock looked away, ignoring all eyes.

Other cars descended the hill above the bridge and
stopped on the left of the road. For a week in the
early summer of each year, known as the Joint Week,
a neighbouring Hunt visited the country of the Two
Rivers, bringing their own hounds with them, so
that the home pack might rest every other day of the
six hunting days. Other otter-hunters came from their
rivers which flowed into the seas of Britain west and
south and east. Their uniforms were coloured as the
dragon-flies over the river. There were grey pot-hats,
dark blue jackets and stockings, and white breeches
of the Cheriton; the grey hats and breeches and
stockings and red coats of the Culmstock; the cream-
collared bright blue coats and stockings and cream
breeches of the Crowhurst from Surrey, Kent, and
Sussex; men of the Dartmoor, all in navy-blue, from
pad-pinned cap to black brogues, except for white
stock round the throat; the green double-peaked
caps, green coats, scarlet ties, white breeches, and
green stockings of the Courtenay Tracey from Wessex.
A man like a great seal, jovial and gruff among
laughing friends, wore the gayest uniform, in the
judgment of two ragged children. It blazed and
winked in the sunlight, scarlet and blue and brass.

The Meet at Town Mills, below Torrington.

Dark Shortly after half-past ten o'clock eleven and a half
Hams couples of hounds and two terriers, nearly throttling
Bend themselves in eagerness to press forward, were trotting behind the huntsman through the farmyard to
the river. The huntsman repeated a cooing chant at
the back of his nose of *C-o-o-o-o-orn-yer! Co-o-o-o-orn-*
yer! W-wor! W-wor! with names of hounds. They
trotted with waving sterns, orderly and happy, enjoying the sounds, which to them were promise of
sport and fun if only they kept together and ignored
the scent of duck, cat, offal, mouse, and cottage-
infant's jammy crust. They pattered through the
farm-yard in best behaviour; they loved the huntsman, who fed them and pulled thorns out of their
feet and never whipped them, although he sometimes dropped unpleasant medicine at the back of
their tongues, and held their muzzles, and stroked
their throats until they could hold it there no longer,
but had to swallow. The *W-wor! W-wor!* and other
cooing dog-talk was understood perfectly; they
caused even Deadlock to forget to growl when young
Dabster, avoiding a kitten, bumped into him. For the
two strongest feelings in Deadlock, apart from those
of his private kennel life, were blood-thirst for otters
and his regard for the huntsman.

They jumped down the bank into the river, leaping
across the shallows to the left bank, and working
upstream to the occasional toot of the horn. Almost at
once Deadlock whimpered and bounded ahead. Tarka
had touched there, on the shillets, six hours before.

They came to the groove in the right bank between

two hazel stoles, where Tarka had climbed out to *Forda* cross the meadows to the weir, for the river-course *Holt* was like a horseshoe. The grasses still held enough scent for the hounds to own, and they followed the trail to the wood that grew steeply up from the water. A crow, that had been waiting on the weir-sill for beetles and little fish to pass in the gentle film of water near its feet, heard them as they splashed up the leat and flew to the top of a tall tree to watch hidden in the leaves. The crow had seen Tarka as he swam from the leat into the Dark Pool at five o'clock in the morning. Then he had loudly cawed, calling his mate to annoy the otter; now he kept quiet. Hounds swam up the pool.

A furlong above the weir was a ford, where, in summer, horse-drawn butts go for the gravel heaped up by winter floods. By the ford was a tree, and under the roots of the tree was a holt. Deadlock, Render, and Fencer swam to the tree, whimpering, splashing scratching, and tearing at roots with their teeth. Soon the pack was trying to break into the entrance. They did not obey voice, horn, and whip at once, but had to be urged away by taps of whip-handles on ribs, and by individual commands. *Go'r'n leave it! Go'r'n leave it* cried one of the honorary whips in a yarring voice, to Deadlock and Render who remained. A little shivering sharp-nosed terrier, uncollared, peered with cock-ears and whined on the bank above. The entrance of the holt was under water, and Biff's collar was slipped round her neck again.

The honorary whip, a retired senior officer of the

Hounds marking at holt, while whipper-in rates a hound rioting after rabbit in background.

army, prodded with his pole among the roots, and *Dark* finding soft earth, tried to force the pole to the back *Hams* of the holt. The water moved away in a yellow *Weir* muddy wound. He worked until he was hot. He stopped, pushed his hat back from his forehead, and rubbed it with his goatskin glove. "Where's that chap with the bar?" Below the holt, at intervals of ten to fifteen yards, men were gazing into the sun-dappled water of the Dark Pool. Voices sounded high above, where on the road cut in the rock many of the cars were waiting.

A man came hastening down the cart-track with the iron digging bar. A hole was worked in the ground over the holt, while a sportsman in the Cheriton uniform banged the turf with the length of his pole. The hole was made deeper, the bar worked backwards and forwards, and plunged hard down.

The Master, leaning his chin upon his hands clasping the top of his pole, saw a chain of bubbles rise a yard from the bank, and steadily lengthen aslant the river. Sweeping off his grey hat, he scooped the air with it, crying *Tally-ho!* Hounds poured down the track and splashed into the river, giving tongue and stirring up the gravel silt. Through shadows of trees lying on the water the lit dust drifted. Many hounds swam mute, striving hard to take the lead, urged by the cries and gestures in front of them.

The chain drew out from one bank to another, in stretches of fifty and sixty yards, until by the sill of the weir a ripple was made by a brown head that sank immediately; but was viewed.

Town *Yoi-yoi-yoi-yoi! Ov-ov-ov-ov-ov-ov-over! Tally-ho! He's*
Mills *gone down the leat!*
Leat

The dark green weeds were bended and swayed
silently by the slow glide of the water. The leat was
deep, with a dark brown bed. It had been dug to
carry water to the elm wheels of the two mills by the
bridge a mile below. Now the larger wheel had been
replaced by a turbine, which used less water. Leaves
rotted on the leat's bed, the water brimmed almost
into the meadow. Tarka swam through the dark
green swaying weed, and over the dark brown bed.
When he swung up to breathe his nose showed in the
ripple like a dead leaf turned up in the current, and
settling down again. He swam under the crinkled
top-scum by the heavy oaken fender, which was
raised to let the water through. A trout darted by
him as he passed under the fender, and he caught it
with a sudden turn of his body.

Trees made the leat shadowy; ferns hung over it;
the taloned brambles stretched down to the water.
It flowed in the low ground of the valley, bending
like the river below it. It left the meadows, the tall
grasses, and the reddening sorrel, and flowed through
a jungle of rushes and grasses, briars and hazel
bushes, where the webs of spiders were loaded with
bees, flies and grasshoppers. Only a weasel could
run on the banks. The blue flowers of borage and
confrey grew in the jungle, where the buds of the
dog-rose were opening.

Sometimes a swift, cutting the air with alternate

246

strokes of its narrow black wings, dashed a ripple as *Town* it sipped and sped on. Willow wrens flitted in the *Mills* ash-sprays lower down, taking insects on the leaves. *Leat* A chiffchaff sang its two-note song. By a briar raking the water the otter's head was raised; he listened and swam to the bank. Hounds spoke remotely; he knew Deadlock's tongue among them. He climbed out of the leat, the trout still in his mouth, and pushed through the undergrowth, among nettles and marsh-wort, and over soft damp ground. Robins ticked at him, wrens stittered. Burrs and seeds tried to hook to his hair, finding no hold. Warble flies tried to alight on his back and suck his blood; the rushes brushed them off. He ran in a loop back to the leat, and slipped into the water above the hounds, who had gone down. He swam up for a quarter of a mile, then rested by an alder root and listened to the pack running over his land-trail. He looked round for a stone whereon to eat the fish, but hearing Deadlock's tongue, he lay still.

From the wooded hillside above the distant bank of the river came the knock of axes on the trunk of an oak tree, the shouts of woodmen, a sudden crack, the hissing rush and thud of breaking branches, and then quietness, until began the steady knocks of boughs being lopped. After a while Tarka did not hear these sounds—he was listening in another direction. He scarcely heard the shooting buzz of sun-frisked flies over the leat. He felt no fear; all his energy was in listening.

Chiff-chaff, chiff-chaff, chiff-chaff sang the bird among

Dark the ash trees. And soon the voices of men, the tearing *Hams* of brambles against coats, boots trampling and snap- *Wood* ping the hollow green stalks of hog-weed and hemlock. Tarka saw their heads and shoulders against the sky, and swam on up the leat.

His scent was washed down by the water, and the hounds followed him. He crept out on the other bank, on soft ground littered with dead leaves, which lay under crooked oak trees. He ran swiftly up the slope and entered a larch plantation, where the sky was shut out. The narrow lines of thin straight boles stood in a duskiness as of midsummer night. All sound was shut out; nothing grew under the trees. A wood owl peered down at him as he ran among the brittle fallen twigs; it peered over its back and softly hooted to its mate. The plantation was silent again.

Tarka sat by a bole in the middle of the Dark Hams Wood, listening through the remote sough of wind in the branches to the faint cries below. The smell of the sap was strong in his nostrils. He dropped the fish. Sometimes he heard the querulous scream of a jay, and the clap of pigeon-wings as the birds settled in the tree-tops.

For nearly twenty minutes he waited by the tree, and then the hunting cries swelled in the narrow groves of the wood. The owl flapped off its branch, and Tarka ran down the leat again, passing the hounds nine lines of trees away from them. Sunlight dazzled him when he ran out of the plantation. Then he saw many men and women before him.

Tally Ho! *Town*

Tarka ran round them and dived into the leat. *Mills*
When first he had swum down, the water had brimmed to the meadow, floating the green plants in its
slow-gliding current; now the bank glistened with a
sinking watermark, and only the tags of the starwort
were waving. Trout darted before him as he swam
against the water flowing faster. Often his head
showed as he walked half out of water beside the
starwort. He reached the square oaken fender, where
only a rillet trickled. It rested on the bed of the leat,
penning the water above.

Tally Ho!

Tarka turned and went down the leat again. He
reached water deep enough to cover him before he
met the hounds who, hunting by the sense of smell,
did not see him moving as a dark brown shadow
through the channels in the weeds. Hounds passed
him, for the wash—or scent on the water—was still
coming down.

Tarka swam down to the mill end of the leat,
which was dark with the brown stains of stagnant
life on its muddy bed. Trees kept the sun from it. A
runner, or streamlet, from other woods joined it
at this end, and waited in the pool to pass through
the grating to the mills. Tarka swam under the culvert of the runner, but finding shallow water he
returned and looked for a hole or drain in the banks.
Shafts of sunlight pierced the leaves and dappled the
water. A broad shade lay before the grating, where
oak planks, newly sawn, were stacked over the water.

Wheel The ringing rasp of a circular saw cutting hard wood
House suddenly rang under the trees, overbearing the
shaken rumble of millstones grinding corn. Specks of
wood settled on the water beyond the shade, where
Tarka rested, staying himself by a paw on a rusty
nail just above the water level.

He waited and listened. The sawdust drifted past
him, and was sucked away between the iron bars of
the grating. The noise of the saw ceased. He heard
the hounds again, coming down the leat. A voice
just over his head cried, *One o'clock!* Footfalls hurried
away from the saw. The hatch was closed, the
trundling wheel slowed into stillness. Tarka heard
the twittering of swallows; but he was listening for
the sound of the horn. Deadlock speaking! Up the
leat waterside plants were crackling as feet trod
them down. Voices of the whips, one harsh and
rating, were coming nearer. Heads and shoulders
moved over the culvert. When the leading hound
swam into the pool, throwing his tongue, Tarka
dived and found a way through the grating, where
one iron bar was missing—a space just wide enough
for an otter. He drew himself on to the hatch and
walked slowly up the wet and slippery wooden
troughs to the top of the wheel. He quatted low and
watched the grating. Hounds swam along it and
Deadlock pushed his black head in the space of the
missing bar. His flews pressed the iron and stopped
him. He bayed into the cavern where the ancient
water-wheel dripped beside the curved iron conduit
of the modern water turbine. The place was gloomy;

250

but in a corner, framed in a triangle of sunlight, *New*
three ferns hung out of the mortar—spleenwort, *Bridge*
wall-rue, and male fern. Five young wagtails filled a (*Tor-*
nest built on the roots of the male fern; the nestlings *ridge*)
crouched down in fear of the baying.

Drops from the elmwood troughs dripped into the
plash hollowed in the rock under the wheel. Tarka
sat on the topmost trough, his rudder hanging over
the rim of the wheel. He heard the shrill yapping of
terriers on leash; the shuffle of feet on the road over
the culvert; the murmur of voices. Poles were pushed
among the layers of planks; feet of hounds pounded
the deep water as they swam under the timber baulks.
He listened to their whimpers; smelt their breath.
After a time the noises receded, and he heard *chik-ik*,
chik-ik—the cries of the parent wagtails, waiting on
the roof with beakfuls of river flies. Tarka licked his
paws and settled more comfortably in the sodden
elmwood trough. Sometimes his eyes closed, but he
did not sleep.

At two o'clock he heard voices in the gloomy wheel-
house. The men were returning to work after dinner.
The hatch was lifted. Water gushed in and over the
trough. The wheel shuddered and moved. Water
gushed in and over each trough as it was lowered on
the rim, and the wheel began its heavy splashing
trundle. Tarka was borne down into darkness and
flung on the rock. Under the troughs he crept, to the
shallow stream that was beginning to flow through a
lower culvert to the river. Sunlight dazed him. The
bridge was ten yards below.

New The parapet before and above him was a smooth
Bridge line across the sky, except for a wag-tail's pied body,
(*Tor*- the tops of three polybody ferns, the head and
ridge) shoulders of an old grey-bearded man in a blue coat,
and a black empty beer-bottle.

Tally-ho!

CHAPTER NINETEEN

TARKA BECAME ONE WITH THE RIVER, FINDING HIS course among the slimy stones so that his back was always covered. He rose beside the middle pier, whose cutwater was hidden by a faggot of flood sticks. Under the sticks was dimness, streaked and blurred with sunlight. Tarka hid and listened.

His paws rested on a sunken branch. The water moved down, clouded with the mud-stirrings of the leat. He lay so still that the trout returned to their stances beside the stone sterlings.

B'hoys, b'hoys! Com' on, ol' fellars! Leu in, ol' fellars. Com' on, all 'v yer!

The stain spread into the pool below the bridge. Hounds whimpered and marked at the stick-pile. Their many tongues smote all other sounds from Tarka's ears. He knew they could not reach him in his retreat, and so he stayed there even when a pole, thrust into the heap, rubbed against his flank. Then over his head the sticks began to crack and creak, as a man climbed upon them. The man jumped with both feet together on the heap. Tarka sank and turned downstream. Cries from the lower parapet; thudding of boots above. The chain of bubbles drew out downstream.

Tarka swam to the left bank, where he touched and breathed. He heard, in the half-second his head was out of water, the noise that had terrified him as a cub —the noise as of an iron shod centipede crossing the shallows. Way down the river was stopped by a line of upright figures, standing a yard apart and stirring

Otter and Stickle. (The dog is not a hound, but a cattle-tyke looking on.)

the water with poles. Tarka heard the noise under *The*
water, but he swam down until he saw before him *Rolle*
the bright-bubbled barrier. He swung round and *Straight*
swam upstream as fast as three and a half webbed
feet could push him.

He swam under the heap of sticks again, enduring
the massed tongues of marking hounds until the
creaking and thudding over his head drove him to
open water again. He swam under an arch, turned by
the lower sterling, and swam up another arch, to a
backwater secluded from the main stream by the
ridge of shillets made by the cross-leaping waters of
the runner in flood. An ash tree grew over the backwater, but Tarka could find no holding in its roots.
He swam past the legs of swimming hounds and
went down again.

Tally Ho!

He swam through the plying poles of the stickle, and
ran over the shallow, reaching safe water before the
pack came down. He was young and fast and strong.
Hounds were scattered behind him, some swimming,
others plunging through the shallows below the
banks, stooping to the scent washed on scour and
shillet, and throwing their tongues. He could not
see them, when swimming under water, until they
were nearly over him. He swam downstream, never
turning back, touching first one bank to breathe,
and then swimming aslant to the other. Once in the
straight mile of river under the Town on the Hill, he
emerged by a shallow almost by Deadlock's feet;
instantly he turned back. Farther down, by a jungle

Taddi- of balsam, whose top drought-roots were like the red
port toes of a bird, he left the river and ran on the bank,
under trees. He had gone thirty yards on the hot
land when Render and Deadlock crashed through
the jungle of hollow sap-filled stalks after him.
Although his legs were short—it was difficult to see
them when he ran—he moved faster than any of the
men hunting him could run. He left the land a
hundred yards above Taddiport Bridge, by a bank
where shards of Roman tiles were jutting.

Below the bridge was a ridge of shillets, long and
wide as the broken hull of a sailing ship. Alders and
willows grew here, and tall grasses that hid the old dry
twigs and reeds on the lower branches of the trees.
Floods had heaped up the island. The wet marks
of Tarka's feet and rudder soon dried on the worn
flakes of rock; but not before the larger pads of hounds,
making the loose shillets clatter, had covered them.

Leu-in! Leu-in, b'hoys. Ov-ov-ov-ov-over!

Tarka's feet were dry when he took again to water,
after trying to rid himself of scent on the stones so
hot in the sun. He passed plants of water-hemlock
and dropwort, tall as a man, growing among the stones,
some sprawling with their weight of sap. He swam
on down the river, passing Servis Wood, over which
a buzzard, pestered by rooks, was wailing in the sky.
The rooks left it to see what the hounds were doing,
and wheeled silently over the river. Their shadows
fled through the water, more visible than the otter.

A thousand yards from Taddiport Bridge, Tarka
passed the brook up which he had travelled with

256

his mother on the way to the Clay Pits. He swam *Drum-*
under a railway bridge, below which the river hur- *met's*
ried in a course narrow and shaded. An island of elm *Mill*
trees divided the river bed; the right fork was dry— *Brook*
hawkweed, ragwort, and St. John's wort, plants of
the land, were growing there. Tarka swam to the
tail of the island, and climbed up the dry bank. The
place was cool and shady, and filled with the stench
arising from the broad leaves and white flowers of
wild garlic growing under the trees. Tarka trod into
a thick patch, and quatted low.

Hounds passed him. He listened to them baying in
the narrow channel below the island.

Deadlock clambered up the dry bank, ran a few
yards among the grasses, threw up his head, sniffed,
and turned away. Tarka held his breath. Other
hounds followed, to sniff and run down the bank
again. Tarka listened to them working among the
roots under the island bank, and across the river.
He heard the chaunting voices of huntsman and
whippers-in; the noises of motor-cars moving slowly
along the hard-rutted trackaway, the old canal-bed,
above the right bank of the river; the voices of men
and women getting out of the motor-cars; and soon
afterwards, the scrape of boots on the steep rubble
path down to the dry, stony bed.

Tarka had been lying among the cool and stinking
garlic plants of Elm Island for nearly five minutes
when he heard gasping and wheezing noises at the
top of the island. The two terriers, Bite'm and Biff,
were pulling at their chains, held by the kennel boy.

Elm Island Their tongues hung long and limp, after the two-mile tug from the mills over sun-baked turf, dusty trackway, and hot stones, to Elm Island. Just before, while tugging down the path, Bite'm had fainted with the heat. A lapping sprawl in the river had refreshed the couple, and now they strove against the collars pressing into their windpipes.

Tarka started up when they were a yard from where he lay. The kennel-boy dropped the chain when he saw him. Tarka ran towards the river, but at the sheer edge of the island he saw men on the stones six feet below. He ran along the edge, quickening at the shout of the kennel-boy, and had almost reached the island's tail when Bite'm pinned him in the shoulder. Tissing through his open mouth, Tarka rolled and fought with the terriers. Their teeth clashed. Tarka's moves were low and smooth; he bit Bite'm again and again, but the terrier hung on. Biff tried to bite him across the neck, but Tarka writhed away. The three rolled and snarled, scratching and snapping, falling apart and returning with instant swiftness. Ears were torn and hair ripped out. Hounds heard them and ran baying under the island cliff to find a way up. The kennel-boy tried to stamp on and recover the end of the chain, for he knew that in a worry all three might be killed. White terriers and brown otter rolled nearer the edge, and fell over.

The fall shook off Bite'm. Tarka ran under the legs of Dabster, and although Bluemaid snapped at his flank he got into the water and sank away.

Tally Ho! Tally Ho! Yaa-aa-ee on to 'm!   Rothern
By the bank, fifty yards below Elm Island, stood *Bridge*
the Master, looking into water six inches deep. A
fern frond, knocked off the bank upstream, came
down turning like a little green dragon in the clear
water. It passed. Then came an ash-spray, that
clung around the pole he leaned on. Its leaves bent
to the current it stayed, it swung away, and drifted
on. A dead stick rode after it, and a fly feebly struggling—and then the lovely sight of an otter spreading
himself over the stones, moving with the stream,
slowly, just touching with his feet, smooth as oil
under the water. A twenty-pound dog, thought the
Master, remaining quiet by the shallow water
listening to the music of his hounds. There was a
stickle below Rothern Bridge.

The hounds splashed past him, stooping to the
scent. Tarka's head showed, and vanished. He swam
under Rothern Bridge, whose three stone arches,
bearing heavy motor-transport beyond their old age,
showed the cracks of suffering that the ferns were
filling green. A sycamore grew out of its lower
parapet. Deeper water under the bridge; the frail
bubble-chain lay on it. A cry above the bridge; a
line of coarser bubbles breaking across the stickle,
where six men and two women stood in the river.

Tarka's head looked up and saw them. He lay in
the deep water. He turned his head, and watched
hounds swimming down through the arch. He dived
and swam up; was hunted to shallow water again,
and returned, making for the stickle. The water was

s   259

Beam threshed in a line from shillet-bank to shillet-bank,
Pool but he did not turn back. As he tried to pass between
a man in red and a man in blue, two pole-ends were
pushed under his belly in an attempt to hoick him
back. But Tarka slipped off the shillet-burnished
iron and broke the stickle. The whips ran on the
bank, cheering on the hounds.

*Get on to 'm! Hark to Deadlock! Leu-on! Leu-on!
Leu-on!*

A quarter of a mile below Rothern Bridge the river
slows into the lower loop of a great S. It deepens
until half-way, where the S is cut by the weir holding
back the waters of the long Beam Pool. Canal Bridge
crosses the river at the top of the S.

Where the river begins to slow, at the beginning of
the pool, its left bank is bound by the open roots of
oak, ash, alder, and sycamore. To hunted otters
these trees offered holding as secure as any in the
country of the Two Rivers. Harper, the aged hound
—he was fourteen years old—knew every holt in the
riverside trees of Knackershill Copse, and although
he had marked at all of them, only once had he
cracked the rib of an otter found in the pool.
Leeches infested the unclear water.

Tarka reached the top of the pool. Swimming in
the shade, his unseen course betrayed by the line of
bubbles-a-vent, he came to the roots of the sycamore
tree, where he had slept for two days during his
wandering after the death of Greymuzzle. He swam
under the outer roots, and was climbing in a dim

light to a dry upper ledge when a tongue licked his *Sycamore* head, and teeth playfully nipped his ear. Two pale *Holt* yellow eyes moved over him. He had awakened the cub Tarquol.

Tarka turned round and round, settled and curled, and closed his eyes. Tarquol's nostrils moved, pointing at Tarka's back. His small head stretched nearer, the nostrils working. He sniffed Tarka's hair from rudder to neck, and his nose remained at the neck. It was a strange smell, and he sniffed carefully, not wanting to touch the fur with his nostrils. Tarka drew in a deep breath, which he let out in a long sigh. Then he swallowed the water in his mouth, settled his ear more comfortably on his paw, and slept; and awoke again.

Tarquol, the hairs of his neck raised, was listening at the back of the ledge. He was still as a root. The ground was shaking.

Go in on 'm, old fellars! Wind him, my lads! B'hoys! B'hoys! come on, b'hoys, get on to 'm.

The otters heard the whimpers of hounds peering from the top of the bank, afraid of the fall into the river. They watched the dim-root opening level with the water. Footfalls sounded in the roots by their heads; they could feel them through their feet. Then the water-level rose up and shook with a splash, as Deadlock was tipped into the river. They saw his head thrust in at the opening, heard his gruff breathing, and then his belving tongue. Other hounds whimpered and splashed into the river.

Pull him out, old fellars! Leu-in there, leu-in, leu-in!

Sycamore Tarka quatted on the ledge; he knew that Deadlock
Holt would follow him wherever he swam in water.
Tarquol, twisting and weaving his head, ran down
on roots to the water, dragging his rudder for a dive;
but a whitish light alarmed him and he ran up to the
ledge again. The whitish light was reflected from the
breeches of a wading man. A voice sounded near
and hollow. Then a pole pushed through the opening between two roots. Its end was thrown about,
nearly striking Tarquol's head. It was pulled out
again, and the whitish light moved away. Tarka
heard the whining of Bite'm.

Hands held and guided the terrier past the outside
root. Tarquol tissed again as the dim light darkened
with the shape of the enemy, whose scent was on the
hair of Tarka's neck. Bite'm whined and yapped,
trying to struggle up to the otters. His hind feet slipped off the roots, and he fell into the water below.
Plomp, plomp, plomp, as he trod water, trying to
scramble up the side.

Again the opening grew dark with arms holding and
guiding another terrier, and Biff began to climb.
Wough! wough! wough! Soon she fell into the water.
The terriers were called off. Tarka settled more
easily, but Tarquol could not rest. Hounds and
terriers were gone, but still the voices of men were
heard. The sound was low and regular, and Tarka's
eyes closed. Tarquol quatted beside him, and for
many minutes neither moved. Then the murmur of
voices ceased with footfalls along the bank coming
nearer, and stopping above.

Heavy thuds shook down bits of earth on the otters' *Beam* heads and backs. The huntsman was pounding the *Pool* holt-top with an iron digging bar. Tarquol tissed, moving to and fro in fear of the great noises. Tarka slipped into the water, climbed out again, then submerged himself, only his nose and whiskers being out of the water. On and on went the pounding, until he could bear it no longer. He rolled over, and swam out of the holt. Tarquol followed him. He saw Tarka's chain rising bright before him. He turned upstream and was alone.

Seventy yards from the holt he rose under the bank to rest, and heard the baying of hounds. He dived again and went on upstream at his greatest speed. At his next vent he knew that the terrible beasts were following him. He swam out of the pool, turned back again, saw their heads in the water from bank to bank, became scared, and left the river. Galloping across the meadow faster than he had ever run in his life, with the hunting cries behind him and the thudding hooves of bullocks cantering away from hounds on his left, Tarquol came to sheds where farm machines were stored, and going through a yard, he ran through a gap in a hedge into a garden, where an old man was picking off the tops of his broad beans in a row, muttering about the black-fly on them. Tarquol passed him so near and so swiftly that the granfers short clay pipe dropped from between his gums. He muttered in the sunshine and pondered nearly a minute. Hardly had he stooped to pick up his pipe when a great black and

Granfer Goad's Garden white hound crashed through the hedge and ran over his tettics and sun-dried shallots, followed by three more hounds, and after them a couple, and then his garden was filled with them.

Git'oom!

The hounds were gone, leaving him staring at his broken beans.

Tarquol had run round the walls of the cottage and into a farmyard, scattering fowls in terror before him. One of the hens, who was broody, ran at him, and leapt at his back, pecking and flapping. Tarquol kicked a little dust behind his straight rudder. At full speed he ran into a pigsty, where a sow was lying on her side with a farrow of eleven tugging at her. Seeing him, they stopped tugging, stared together, squeaked together, and scampered away into corners. The sow, too fat to get up quickly, tried to bite Tarquol as he rippled from corner to corner. The baying of the pack grew terribly loud, and still Tarquol darted about the sty, seeking a way of escape. The sow, after many grunts, flung herself on her trotters and bundled her flabby mass to the door, unlocking her dirty teeth to bite Deadlock, who had just arrived. Squealing with rage, her bristly, mud-caked ears flapping on her chaps, she chased him out of the sty, followed him back into the yard, and scattered the rest of the pack. Tarquol had run out behind the sow. He gained three hundred yards before hounds found his line again. He ran with the sun behind him for two hundred yards over grass, then he turned and went through a thorn hedge,

climbed the railway embankment, and ran up over *Furze-*
Furzebeam Hill, leaving an irregular trail. He ran *beam*
for three miles on land, hiding among the dry spikes *Hill*
of gorse, and under branches. Sometimes he mewed
in his misery.

Hounds ran far ahead of the men and women.
Eventually the pack—with the exception of Pitiful,
who was lost—hunted him back to the railway line,
to where he was crouching low in the thorn hedge.
A bird with a loud rasping voice, and a beak like a
bent iron nail, clacked and chattered on a briar
rising out of the hedge. It was a bird of property, or
red-backed shrike, and Tarquol was quatting by its
larder of bumble-bees, grasshoppers, and young
harvest mice impaled on thorns. The mice were dead,
but the bees still moved their legs.

Tarquol ran out of the thorns just before Render's
muzzle pushed into his hiding place; but hounds
leapt the low hedge and overtook him, before he had
gone very far on his short, tired legs. Deadlock
seized him and shook him and threw him into the air.
Tarquol sprang up as soon as he fell, snapping and
writhing as more jaws bit on his body, crushed his head,
cracked his ribs, his paws and his rudder. Among
the brilliant hawkbits—little sunflowers of the meadow—he was picked up and dropped again, trodden
on and wrenched and broken, while the screaming
cheers and whoops of sportsmen mingled with the
growling rumble of hounds at worry. Tarquol
fought them until he was blinded, and his jaws were
smashed.

Death of Tarquol.

THE LAST CHAPTER

WHEN HE HAD SWUM OUT OF THE SYCAMORE holt, Tarka had turned to deeper water and gone under the railway bridge twenty yards below—the line with its embankment and three bridges cut the S from south to north. He kept close to the left bank, in the margin of shade. The copse ended at the bridge; below was a meadow. He rose to breathe, heard the hounds, and swam on under water. He passed a run of peal, which flashed aside when they saw him, and sped above the bridge at many times the pace of a travelling otter. Sixty yards below the bridge, by the roots of a thrown alder, Tarka rose to listen. Looking around, he saw neither hound nor man, and knew that he was not being followed. He thought of the holt under the oak tree above the next railway bridge and swam on down.

Where the river's bend began to straighten again, the right bank lay under oak trees growing on the hill-slope to the sky. Tarka dived and swam across the river to the holt he had remembered as he left the roots of the sycamore. This holt had a sunken opening, where no terrier could enter. Here Tarka's sire had been asleep when hounds had found him two years before. Tarka swung up, coming into a dark cavern lit by a small hole above, and stinking of the paraffin poured there the previous afternoon. He sniffed the oil film on the water, and turned back into the weir-pool.

Again he made a hidden crossing, to listen under

Beam cover of flag-lilies for more than a minute. The river
Weir was quiet. He heard the sound of falling water, and
swam slowly down, often touching under the bank.
He passed under the middle arch of the railway
bridge, and reached the weir slanting across the
river. The summer water tumbled down the fish-
pass, but glided thin as a snail's shell over the top
end of the concrete sill. The lower end, by the
fender at the head of the leat, was dry. Tarka
walked along the sill, nearly to the end, which
was two inches above the level of the pool. He
stretched his weary back on the warm concrete and
sprawled in the sun.

He lay basking for more than an hour, enjoying
the sound of water tumbling in the pass and sliding
down the face of the weir. Swallows dipped in the
pool, and sometimes a peal leapt in the shadow of
the bridge. Tarka's head was always raised before
the fish fell back, but he did not leave the sill. Warm
and brilliant sunflickers on the shallows below
dazed his eyes, and made him drowsy. But when a
hound, working alone down the left bank, climbed
on the sill by the pass and shook itself, he was
instantly alert. Half lying down, he remained
quite still, while the hound lifted its muzzle to sniff.
Something moved on the bridge—otter and hound
turned their heads together, seeing a man behind
the railing. At first the man saw only the hound,
but when it walked along the sill and ran down
the face of the weir, he saw the otter it was following. The man had come along the railway to see

if many fish were in the pool; he was a poacher *Sunken*
nicknamed Shiner, and the top of one of his fingers *Tree*
was missing. He had no love for otters. Along the *Pool*
railway line he hastened, and shouted to the otter-
hunters.

Followed in silence by the hound Pitiful, Tarka
swam leisurely. He watched, from under a tree, a
single enemy working down the shallow, crossing
to deeper water to seek his scent along the banks. He
let it come within a few feet of his head, then dived
and swam away. Pitiful never saw him, or the chain
of bubbles. Often she followed the wash carried down
with the current; and when it grew weak, she would
amble along the banks until she found where the
otter had touched.

Tarka felt neither fear nor rage against the hound.
He wanted to be left alone. After several hidden
swims from bank to bank and finding no holding
where he might lie up and sleep until evening, he
walked out by a cattle-trodden groove in the right
bank, and ran away over land. He followed the otter-
path across a quarter of a mile of meadow, and came
to the river again by the third oak above Canal
Bridge.

Tarka drifted under the high lime-spiky arches of
the bridge, and the white owl, roosting on a ledge
below the parapet, beside the briars of a dog-rose growing there with hawkweeds, saw him going downstream.

Bees came to the wild roses, crammed more pollen
into their laden thigh-bags, and burred away over
the bridge. A petal dropped, a swallow played with

The it as it fell, clipping it with first one wing and then
Kelt the other, until it dropped into the water, and was
Pool carried away, past the gap in the bank where the
Owlery Oak, Tarka's birthplace, had been held by
its roots two years before.

Then Pitiful swam under Canal Bridge, and after
her the pack came down, and many men, and the
owl was driven into wavy flight down the river. It
pitched in the tree of Leaning Willow Island, as a
dull clamour broke out half a mile up the river.
Hounds had marked the otter under a hover, and
driven him out.

The water of the pool was swimming-deep from the
shallow above Canal Bridge to the shallow above
Leaning Willow Island. The surface above Tarka
mirrored the bed of the river—the dark rocks,
the weed, the sodden branches, with the legs
and bodies of hounds—until ripples broke the
mirror into shards of light. In this underwater realm,
where sounds were so distinct—the crush of nailed
boots on stones, the tip-tap of poles, the thresh of
hounds' legs, and even the flip of cyclops and water-
flea—Tarka swam until he was forced to vent,
which he did at the river verge, under the banks, or
by clumps of yellow flags. Sometimes he crept on the
stones, hiding himself under overhanging roots as he
sought refuge, until dreading the nearness of
hounds he slipped into the river again, covered with
a silver skin of air. As he swam, twin streams of
bubbles came out of his nostrils, raced over his head
and neck, and shook off his back to lie on the surface

Huntsman cheering on the pack, which is of drafted fox- and stag-hounds, and a few rough Welch otterhounds.

The in a chain, watched by many eyes. Up and down
Kelt the pool he went, swimming in midstream or near
Pool the banks, crossing from side to side and varying
his depth of swimming as he tried to get away
from his pursuers. Passing under the legs of hounds,
he saw them joined to their broken surface-
images. From under water he saw men and women,
pointing with hand and pole, as palsied and distorted shapes on the bank. However hard he swam
with his three and a half webs, always he heard the
hounds, as they spoke to his scent lying in burst
bubble, in seal on muddy scour, on leaf and twig.
Once in mid-river, while on his way to a clump of
flags, his breath gave out, and he bobbed up to
breathe a yard from Deadlock. He stared into the
eyes of his old enemy; and dived. During forty
seconds he swam a distance of seventy yards, to a
bed of reeds, where he breathed and rested. No one
saw him; but they saw the chain.

Up the river again, past the Peal Rock, and under
the middle arch of Canal Bridge to the shallow,
crossed by a line of men and women, white and blue
and green and red and grey, standing close together.

Tally Ho!

He turned and reached covering water just before
hounds.

Get on to 'm! Leu-on! leu-on! Wind him, old fellars!

The huntsman was wading up to his waist in the
water, scooping the air with his grey hat. Bellman,
a small-footed hairy black-an-tan, cross between
a drafted harrier and a Dumfries-shire rough

otter-hound, yelped his impatience, seeming to snap *The* the water as he swam. Sometimes the huntsman gave *Kelt* an encouraging spit-note on his horn. Tarka went *Pool* down river, but a blurred and brilliant colour band stretched from bank to bank above Leaning Willow Island. He tried to get through the stickle, but stocking'd leg was pressed to stocking'd leg, a fixed barrier behind plying poles. The owl flew out of the willow, miserable in the sunlight with small birds pursuing it.

Tarka turned and swam upstream again, leaving hounds behind. For five minutes he rested under a thorn bush. Deadlock found him, and on he went, to Canal Bridge once more, where he lay in the water, weary after the long chase. At the beginning of the sixth hour he tried to pass the higher stickle, but his enemies stood firm on the stones. The tongues swelled under the bridge. He was nearly picked up by Hurricane, the Irish staghound, but the blunted canine teeth could not hold him.

The chain became shorter. Tarka was too weary to seek a holding in the banks. He breathed in view of his enemies. Seven and a half couples of hounds swam in the pool, their sterns throwing behind them arc-lines of drops on the surface. Others splashed in the shallows under the banks. The huntsman let them work by themselves.

During the sixth hour the otter disappeared. The river grew quiet. People not in uniform sat down on the grass. The huntsman was wading slowly up-stream, feeling foothold with his pole and keeping an

The eye on Deadlock. Stickles stood slack, but ready to
Kelt bar the way with pole-strokes. Look-outs gazed at
Pool the water before them. It was known that the otter
might leave the river at any moment. The boy with
the warped pole, on whose cheeks were two patches
of dried otter-blood, was already opening his knife,
ready to cut another notch on the handle, in the
form of a cross.

But more than an hour the sun-thongs flickered
across the placid water; and in softening light the
owl returned, flying high over the bridge, to the
mouse runs in the quiet meadow beyond.

A fallen bough of willow lay in the pool near one
bank, and Tarka lay beside it. His rudder held a
sunken branch. Only his wide upper nostrils were
above water. He never moved. Every yard of the
banks between the stickles was searched again. Poles
were thrust into branches, roots, and clumps of
flag-lilies. The wading huntsman prodded Peal Rock
and the rock above it. Hounds sat on the banks,
shivering, and watching Deadlock, Render, and
Harper working the banks. The crack of a whip,
a harsh voice rating—Rufus had turned a rabbit
out of a bramble and was chasing it across the
meadow. He returned to the river in a wide circle,
eyeing the whip.

At the beginning of the eighth hour a scarlet
dragonfly whirred and darted over the willow snag,
watched by a girl sitting on the bank. Her father, an
old man lank and humped as a heron, was looking

out near her. She watched the dragonfly settle on *Grassy*
what looked like a piece of bark beside the snag; she *Islet*
heard a sneeze, and saw the otter's whiskers scratch
the water. Glancing round, she realized that she
alone had seen the otter. She flushed, and hid her
grey eyes with her lashes. Since childhood she had
walked the Devon rivers with her father looking for
flowers and the nests of birds, passing some rocks
and trees as old friends, seeing a Spirit everywhere,
gentle in thought to all her eyes beheld.

For two minutes the maid sat silent, hardly daring
to look at the river. The dragonfly flew over the pool,
seizing flies and tearing them apart in its horny jaws.
Her father watched it as it settled on the snag, rose
up, circled, and lit on the water, it seemed. Tarka
sneezed again, and the dragonfly flew away. A grunt
of satisfaction from the old man, a brown hand and
wrist holding aloft a hat, a slow intaken breath, and,
Tally Ho!

Tarka dived when the hounds came down, and the
chain showed where he had swum. Many saw his
dark sleek form as he walked by the edge of a grassy
islet by the twelve trees. The hounds ran to him, and
Tarka turned and faced them, squatting on his short
hindlegs, his paws close against his round and
sturdy chest. He bit Render in the nose, making his
teeth meet. In an instant he drew back, tissing, and
bit Deadlock in the flews. The narrow lower jaw
snapped again and again, until the press of hounds
hid him from sight.

He squirmed away through legs and under bellies,

T

The biting and writhing a way to the water; and the *Island* chain drew out on the surface of the pool while *Run* hounds were still seeking him on the stones where he had sat and faced them.

Leu-on, then! Leu-on! Ov-ov-ov-ov-over!

Tarka's pace was slow and his dives were short. In the water by the Peal Rock he lay, glancing at the faces along the banks, across the river, and in the river. His small dark eyes showed no feeling. He turned away from the human faces, to watch the coming of the hounds. He was calm and fearless and fatigued. When they were his length away, he swung under, showing the middle of his smooth back level with the surface, and swimming past their legs. He saw the huntsman's legs before him joined to the image of legs, and above the inverted image a flattened and uncertain head and shoulders. Up and down he swam, slower and slower.

At the beginning of the ninth hour an immense fatigue came over him, greater than his fatigue when in the long hard winter he had lived for over a month on seaweed and shellfish in the estuary. He was swimming up from the lower stickle when the water seemed to thicken at each thrust of his webs. He ceased to swim and drifted backwards. Barbrook touched his neck as he dived. He reappeared two poles' length away, and lay still, looking at the huntsman wading nearer.

For ten minutes he rested, between dives of a few yards only, and then he rolled from Deadlock's bite and went downstream. He swam with his last strength, for upon him had come the penultimate *Weare* desire of the hunted otter, the desire that comes when *Giffard* water ceases to be a refuge, the desire to tread again *Water* the land-tracks of his ancestors. He crawled half up the bank, but turned back at the thudding of many feet, and swam down to the stickle. The sideway ply of a pole in a turmoil of water struck him on the head. He pushed past the iron point, but it was brought down on his shoulder, to hold him against the shillets. Hounds were fifteen yards away, urged on by hat and horn and the yarring cheers of the whippers-in. Thrice Tarka's teeth clicked on the iron pressing his shoulder as he strove against the weight of the sportsman trying to lift him back. A second pole was brought down from the other flank, crossing with the first. The wooden pincers held him; he twisted like an eel and bit into a leg. With furious strength he writhed from the crossed poles, and through the stickle, as Deadlock bore down upon him and pulled him back by the rudder. Amidst the harsh cries of men and women and the heavy tongues of hounds Tarka was overborne by the pack. The Master looked at his watch— eight hours and fortyfive minutes from the find in the Dark Pool. Then the screeching, yarring yell of one of the honorary whips:

Yaa-aa-ee-io! Leu-in on 'im! Yaa-ee-oo!

for again Tarka had escaped from the worry, and had merged into the narrow stream of water that hurried to Leaning Willow Island.

Below the island the river widened, smooth with the sky. Tarka swam down slowly, bleeding from

The many wounds. Sometimes he paddled with three *ebb-tide* legs, sometimes with one, in the water darkening so strangely before his eyes. Not always did he hear the hounds baying around him. At the beginning of the tenth hour he passed the banks faced with stone to keep the sea from the village, and drifted into deeper water, whereon sticks and froth were floating. Hounds were called off by the horn for the tide was at flood.

But as they were about to leave, Tarka was seen again, moving with the tide, his mouth open. The flow took him near the bank; he kicked feebly, and rolled over.

Tally-Ho!

Deadlock saw the small brown head, and threw his tongue in triumph as he jumped down the bank. He seized it, and lifted the otter high, flung him about and fell into the water with him. They saw the broken head look up beside Deadlock, heard the cry of *Ic-yang!* as Tarka bit into his throat, and then the hound was sinking with the otter into the deep water. Oak-leaves, black and rotting in the mud of the unseen bed, arose and swirled and sank again. And the tide slowed still, and began to move back, and they waited and watched, until the body of Deadlock arose, drowned and heavy, and floated away amidst the froth on the waters.

They pulled the body out of the river and carried it to the bank, laying it on the grass, and looking down at the dead hound in sad wonder. And while

they stood there silently, a great bubble rose out of *The*
the depths, and broke, and as they watched, another *ebb-tide*
bubble shook to the surface, and broke;
and there was a third bubble
in the sea-going waters,
and nothing more.

HERE ENDS TARKA THE OTTER BY HENRY
WILLIAMSON, BEGUN IN JUNE 1923 AND
FINISHED IN FEBRUARY 1927 IN THE
VILLAGE OF HAM IN DEVON, AND ILLUS-
TRATED BY C. F. TUNNICLIFFE BY THE
TAW AND TORRIDGE RIVERS IN 1932